The AZTECS

RICHARD F. TOWNSEND

The AZTECS

Third Edition

With 163 illustrations, 22 in color

Ancient Peoples and Places
FOUNDING EDITOR: GLYN DANIEL

For Pala

AUTHOR'S NOTE
Our understanding of the Aztecs and other Indian civilizations continues to expand with archaeological excavations, ethnohistoric researches, art historical inquiries, and linguistics, as well as public museum exhibitions and university courses. The achievements of ancient societies, and the contemporary cultural and political renaissance of indigenous communities take ever greater hold throughout the Americas. Aztec studies have always occupied a pivotal place, for their society, economy, religion, and history were the most carefully and extensively documented of all the peoples encountered by the Spanish in the early 16th century. The present thoroughly revised third edition of *The Aztecs* traces essential lines of inquiry from the remote archaeological past to colonial sources and to recent and ongoing investigations. Fresh attention is given to aspects of earlier Mesoamerican cultural history adapted by the Aztecs, in their ambition to rise from tribal beginnings and surpass the ancients. The evolution of their 15th- and early 16th-century empire and their dynamically changing society and institutions are amply described. Breakthroughs in Nahuatl hieroglyphic decipherment are outlined. Special attention is given to a form of religious thought and behavior that, for all its fearsome excesses, still held at its core a cosmological tradition of great antiquity in which rulers had an obligation assure the regularity of the seasons, the abundance of crops, and the prosperity of society from year to year.

Frontispiece: Colossal basalt sculpture of the earth goddess Coatlicue.

First published in 1992 in the United States of America by
Thames & Hudson Inc., 500 Fifth Avenue, New York, New York 10110

thamesandhudsonusa.com

Third edition 2009

Library of Congress Catalog Card Number 2008908216

ISBN 978-0-500-28791-0

Printed and bound in China by SNP Leefung Printers Ltd

Contents

Introduction

Anyone traveling in the Valley of Mexico can drive the winding mountain road from Amecameca to the pass between the two snowcapped volcanoes, to experience the siting of the highland basin where people have been living for perhaps 20,000 years. Here, as in the Valley of the Nile and between the Tigris and Euphrates, or along the Huang-Ho River and in coastal valleys of Peru, early tribes and chiefdoms developed city-states and empires whose trade, technologies, conquests and alliances, and exchanges of ideas with foreign peoples, made this once-fertile basin one of the places in the world where ancient civilization was created (pl. 1; ill. 1).

Varied topography, the annual cycle of rain and drought, and diverse and abundant natural resources formed an underpinning for this complex process of development. From our viewpoint on the pass, it is possible to see three sides of the Valley contained by mountain ranges. The long escarpment to the east has the two majestic peaks: Popocatepetl ("Smoking Mountain") stands at 5,452 m (17,887 ft), and Iztaccíhuatl ("White Woman") reaches 5,286 m (17,342 ft). Both rise as gleaming icons seen throughout the highland region. A lesser height, Mt Tlaloc, lies northward on this range. To the south the broken skyline of the dark Ajusco Sierra is marked by old volcanic cindercones standing above lava flows and grassy fields of ash. The rugged Sierra de las Cruces forms the western barrier, but the northern end of the Valley opens out in fields and low-lying hills reaching toward the arid lands of the Great Plateau of Mexico. All the heights are covered by forests of fir, pine, oak, and alder. At this latitude the long dry season lasts from late September into June, and in that sunstruck time of year the fields lie somnolent and fallow. Tall dust devils begin to form by January with slender columns slowly spiraling across the land. Dry winds sweep up from the south between late February and March, leaching out the last remaining moisture. The rains arrive in summer between June and September, when warm moist air flows inland from the Gulf and the Pacific. This time of change is everywhere awaited with the same anticipation as the first warm day of spring in northern countries.

As the heat of day advances the air begins to rise and cool around the great volcanoes and other major mountains. Mists cloak the upper elevations, and by mid-afternoon huge cumulo-nimbus clouds condense and billow miles above the peaks. A black storm-wall extends over the east horizon with forks of lightning and resounding thunder. Winds arise, and dark rain curtains sweep west along the Ajuscos and across the basin toward the west. Within days the land turns green, planted seeds begin to sprout, and the time for cultivation begins. The Valley forms a vast container for waters draining to the interior, and until little more than 100 years ago large tracts of the basin floor were covered by interconnected lakes and marshes: lakes Chalco and Xochimilco to the south, Zumpango and Xaltocan to the north, and the broad sheet of Lake Tetzcoco spreading in the center. These linked waters and wetlands covered an area of *c*. 400 sq. miles (1,000 sq. km). Abundant aquifers from the Ajusco Sierra supplied the southern lakes, while the northern wetlands were replenished by lesser springs and summer rainfall. All waters flowed into Lake Tetzcoco, which was saline from evaporation. For millennia in this Valley and adjacent basins of the Central Highlands, the predictable, recurring cycle of birth, fruition, death, and renewal governed the order of societies and their annual rhythms of endeavor.

The threat of rainy-season floods had always been a source of worry for people living at the lakeshore level. But it was not until the late 19th century, when Mexico City began to grow beyond all earlier measure, that hydraulic engineers were commissioned to design and build a system to permanently drain the shallow lakes and marshes. From that time to the present the original appearance of the inner basin has changed radically. The great aquatic landscape with its teeming wildlife and resources from the mountains can barely be imagined now, with only a few fragments remaining of the ancient wetland setting. From our standpoint on the pass today the vast metropolis of Mexico City can be seen spreading across the flat dry lakebeds and nearby mountainsides. As in Los Angeles, São Paulo, Tokyo, or Shanghai, burgeoning populations have produced one of the largest urban concentrations on the planet. At the beginning of the 21st century Mexico City is perhaps the world's second most populous city, inhabited by upward of 23 million souls. The immense man-made landscape is a place where time converges, where layers of collective memory are contained by ancient ruins, the downtown Spanish colonial capital, rows of glittering highrise towers, and miles of residential districts. New and ageing industrial zones are linked by sprawling traffic systems, and townships extending from the urban core continue to grow and coalesce, enveloping millennia-old villages and cities around the basin.

For thousands of years the Valley of Mexico, with its great diversity of natural resources, was a destination for migrating peoples. A succession of settlements, towns, city-states and empires left one of the most complex and richest archaeological zones in the world. Archaeologists have revealed that there was a gradual shift from a remote hunting and gathering way of life to sedentary villages and eventually large urban centers. In the 1940s, near the towns of Tepexpan and Santa María Ixtapan, mammoth skeletons and extinct late Pleistocene fauna were unearthed in association with stone implements, testifying to the presence of early hunting bands. During the 1970s at Tlapa-coya, stone artifacts, hearths, and animal bones were tentatively dated to 19,000 BC. Maize may have been domesticated in Mesoamerica as early as 7000 BC, followed by beans, squash, chile peppers, and other cultigens. Again at Tlapa-coya in 1976, archaeological evidence was found of early settlements dating to 5500 BC, long after the late Pleistocene big-game hunters but not yet the time when pottery was made. In the late 1920s and early 1930s, explorations on the northwestern side of the basin at the villages of Zacatenco, Ticoman, and

1 The volcanoes of Iztaccíhuatl and Popocatepetl overlooking the eastern Valley of Mexico, seen from the summit of Mt Huixachtlan (ancient site of the New Fire ceremony). Cortés' expedition crossed the pass between these volcanic peaks.

El Arbolillo, yielded critical evidence of an economy based on fishing, aquatic bird-hunting, and maize cultivation, dating to the middle 1st millennium BC. To the south in the Lake Chalco basin, a pyramid of superimposed platforms surmounted by a temple with a high two-sided roof was excavated at Cerro del Tepalcate. At Tlatilco on the western shore, where clays were dug for local brickyards, an ancient burial ground with large offerings of ceramic vessels and figurines was discovered during the 1940s. Archaeological excavations at this important site revealed that Tlatilco was related to nearby Ticoman and Zaca-tenco; foreign influences were also evident, with figurines and vessels reflecting cultural extensions from powerful political, economic, and ceremonial centers in the Valley of Morelos, ultimately related to the great Olmec centers in the forested riverine lands of southern Veracruz and Tabasco.

Excavations at Cuicuilco in the late 1920s uncovered a circular pyramid con-structed in superimposed levels, with east–west ramps leading upward to a dual temple aligned with the path of the equinoctial sun. An altar was excavated,

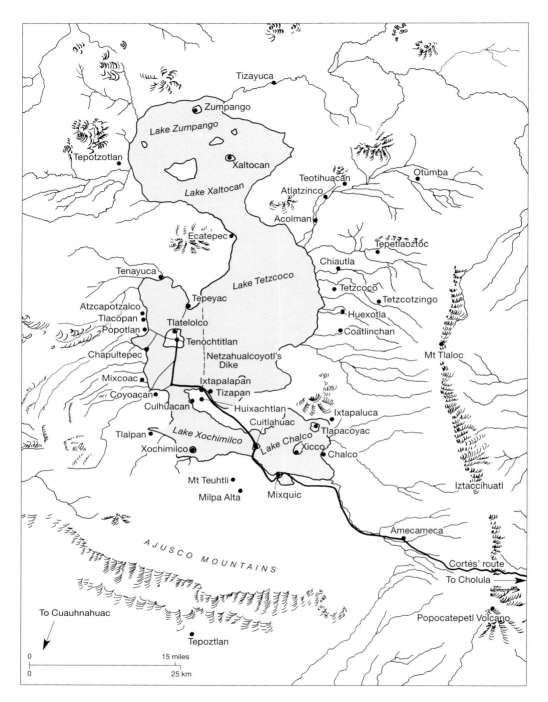

2 The Valley of Mexico. The island city of Tenochtitlan-Tlatelolco was linked to the mainland by causeways, and protected from the brackish water of Lake Tetzcoco by Netzahualcoyotl's dike. Lakes Chalco and Xochimilco, fed by springs, were the site of major *chinampa* plantations.

yielding the ceramic figurine of an old man bearing a brazier on his back – an image suggesting the ancient worship of fire. The town of Cuicuilco surrounding the pyramid may have been inhabited by as many as 20,000 people. All of Cuicuilco was buried by lava when the nearby volcano Xitle erupted around 200 BC, a natural catastrophe that propelled a shift of population into the northeastern section of the Valley, where the city of Teotihuacan was already beginning. For some 800 years this first true metropolis, with its colossal pyramids, processional way, ceremonial precinct and market plaza, and spreading grid of residential compounds, set a lasting urban model for Central Highland Mexico. The cosmological layout of Teotihuacan reflected the ancient practice of ritually coordinating the activities and organization of human society to the earth and sky and the annual cycle of the seasons.

As Teotihuacan declined and collapsed (by AD 750), other seats of power arose in neighboring highland valleys: Cacaxtla and Cholula in the Valley of Puebla, Xochicalco in the Valley of Morelos, and Toltec Tula toward the northern deserts. In these places the cultural inheritance of Mesoamerica was transmitted and reshaped. Although the Valley of Mexico was bypassed by this series of capitals, substantial towns continued to flourish around the southern lakes and on the western side; even at its lowest ebb the Valley never wholly lost its metropolitan character. Ancient ways were kept at Chalco, Xochimilco, Atzcapotzalco, Culhuacan and other towns, and it was from these older communities that the culture transmitted from earlier civilizations was readapted by migrating tribes arriving in search of land to claim and settle.

Our present history is about these incoming peoples, from their remote tribal origins in northern deserts and a life bound by the stark necessity of survival, to their arrival in the bountiful Valley where long-established agricultural towns engaged in the worship of the sun, the rain, and the earth's cycle of fertility. Beginning in the early 13th century a long process of acculturation began, as Tepanec, Acolhua, Chichimec, and Mexica peoples grafted themselves upon the land and the cultural traditions of communities settled long before. In this process they began to find, within a certain shared experience, subtly divergent and distinct patterns of existence. Three hundred years later, the brilliant capital Tenochtitlan, of some 200,000 people, stood where reedbeds and an island lay on the western side of Lake Tetzcoco; the independent allied capital, Tetzcoco, of approximately 45,000, commanded a string of smaller cities along the eastern piedmont, where few settlements existed before. The Chalco-Xochimilco basin was almost wholly covered by horticultural *chinampa* (raised-bed) gardens spreading from the shoreline towns. And to the west and toward the north, Atzcapotzalco, Tlacopan, and a score of other established communities continued to flourish. Trade thrived with the ease of water transportation from rural parts of the Valley to urban centers. During the first half of the 15th century a turning point was reached. The Valley of Mexico again became a dynamic and powerful center as the allied cities of Tenochtitlan, Tetzcoco, and Tlacopan engaged in conquering what rapidly became the most extensive empire in Mesoamerican history. Today these diverse people are collectively called Aztecs, a term derived from the mythical land from which the Mexica tribe had migrated. By extension, the denomination Aztecs has also

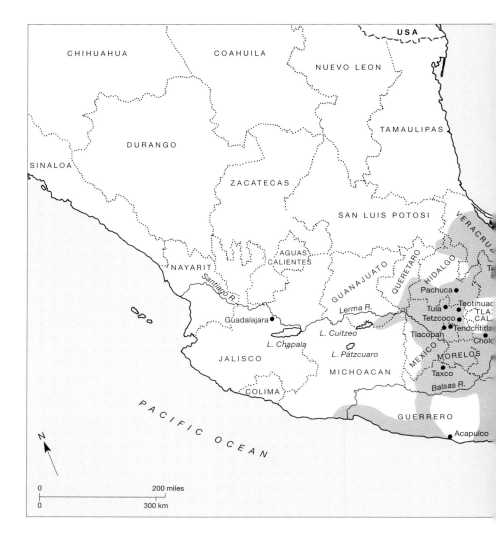

3 The extent of the Aztec empire in 1519. The larger cultural region of Mesoamerica extended from the north of Veracruz across to Nayarit and Sinaloa, and southeastwards into Honduras and El Salvador.

come to embrace the older towns of diverse ethnic origin in the Valley of Mexico at the time of the Triple Alliance in the 15th and early 16th centuries. By the time the Spanish arrived in 1519 the population of the basin numbered approximately a million and a half.

In the following chapters we shall see how the imperial endeavor was the outcome of a process of cultural and social transformation, set in motion when the migrating tribes arrived in the Valley of Mexico. Yet the acceleration of this complex process of change was not only due to policies and wars directed by

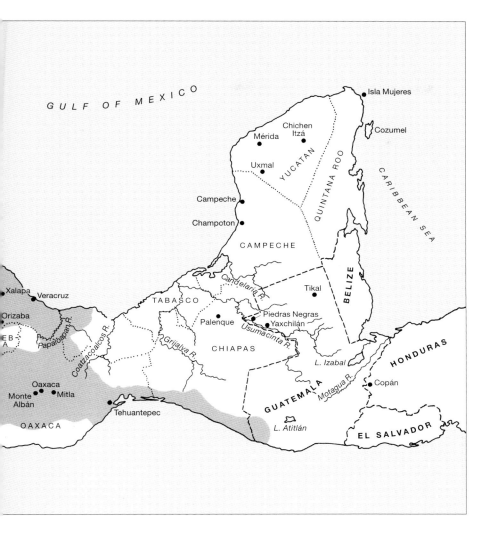

ambitious warrior leaders, and the vast amounts of tribute regularly sent by subject peoples under the threat of violent retribution. The Aztec achievement must also be understood in terms of a collective enterprise, a communal venture by vital peoples who instinctively recognized the potential of many new resources, who saw the opportunity of trade, the security of more developed farming methods and the technical skills required for manufacturing a wider range of products. As the original tribes grew in numbers, ethnic diversity, and increasing social stratification, imaginative leaders also grasped the practical benefits of a legal system that favored the rule of the state. Their intellectual communities inherited and absorbed a greater knowledge of the cosmos, mythology, and legendary history; and artists created expressive forms in art, architecture, and ritual performance to achieve a greater degree of social coherence, to instruct the populace and promote a warlike sensibility, and to affirm an active role in maintaining, through religious means, the productivity of the land and the regularity of the seasons. The Valley of Mexico had not been the setting of such events since the apogee of Teotihuacan 1,000 years before. An aspiration rose in the Aztec imagination, to renew and surpass the hallowed world of Mesoamerican antiquity.

There was no loss of energy and the enterprise was still aggressively expanding in the year 1518, when the presence of outlandish strangers in sailing ships along the Gulf Coast of Tabasco and Veracruz began to be reported in the palaces and marketplaces of Tenochtitlan. When in November 1519 the Spanish expedition of Hernán Cortés and his new Tlaxcalan Indian allies crossed the pass between Iztaccíhuatl and Popocatepetl and descended the mountain roadway toward Amecameca, they saw the Valley spreading below with shining lakes, towns and gardens, and causeways built across the waters leading to their destination, the metropolis of Tenochtitlan (ill. 4). At that time the *huey tlatoani*, "great speaker, commander," Motecuhzoma II had been reigning for 16 years. As the most powerful leader of the Triple Alliance he had continued the program of conquests ongoing for almost a century. But the way the people and rulers of Tenochtitlan perceived themselves was different from the outlook held by neighboring communities and other still unconquered peoples, among whom Tenochtitlan and its allies were seen to be implacable enemies, rapacious and feared. These attitudes are also part of our present history, for many among these resentful and fractious nations would eventually rise in response to the prospect of liberation and revenge offered by the strangers' arrival.

In barely two years all would end in defeat and catastrophe. The siege and surrender of the great city Tenochtitlan was a major turning point in the history of the Americas, not simply because it marked victory by the Spaniards and their Indian allies, but because violent encounter set in motion a new process which profoundly and permanently changed a whole cultural frame of existence. Of all the Spanish American territories, Mexico was the first and most thoroughly colonized. With surprising rapidity new forms of economy, religion, and government were imposed on Mexico in the image and ideals of Spain. The idea of conquest was charged with a medieval crusading spirit, and the construction of a new social edifice on the ruins of the old was tied to the prospect of bringing the new dominion into the sphere of Christendom. Even as the remains of Tenochtitlan were being razed to build colonial Mexico City, a group of Franciscan friars arrived at Cortés' request. These and other men who followed were highly trained and motivated religious radicals, determined to realize the utopian social visions of Erasmus in Rotterdam, Thomas More in London, and Juan Luis Vives in Salamanca. In Mexico their complex mission was to extirpate native forms of religious life and to implant the precepts of Christianity.

In the process of spiritual conquest, friars such as Bernardino de Sahagún, Toribio de Benavente (Motolinía), Diego Dúran, and others, as well as descendants of the old Indian nobility such as Fernando de Alva Ixtlilxóchitl, Hernando Alvarado Tezozomoc, and Domingo Cuautlehuanitzin Chimalpahín, compiled extensive records of the old indigenous life. This knowledge

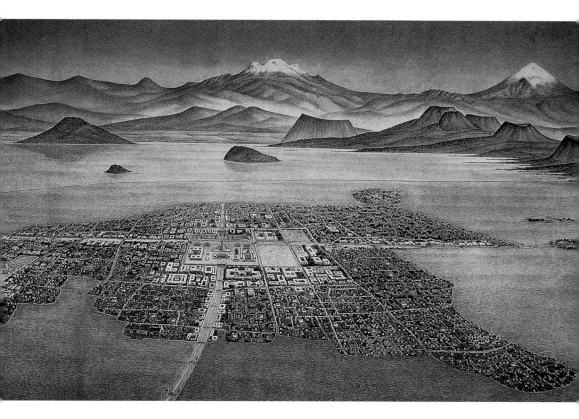

4 Reconstruction view of Tenochtitlan in Lake Tetzcoco. The city is depicted skewed slightly to the right (southeast). The east-west avenue and the Great Pyramid were originally aligned toward the equinoctial sunrise over Mt Tlaloc on the eastern skyline. Painting by Luis Covarrubias.

would aid conversion and record a whole way of life before its memory vanished. These records reflect a probing intellectual effort and concern for accurate and comprehensive description. Who were the Tepanecs, Chichimecs, Acolhua, and Mexica and their neighbors who today have come to be called the Aztecs? Where did they come from? What was their history? What could be said of their laws, government, and social organization? What principles ruled their beliefs, rites, and religious symbolism? And what might be recorded about their daily life and the land on which they lived? Such questions lay behind the compilation of encyclopedic illustrated texts, prepared by friars who learned the Nahuatl language and interviewed members of the native intelligentsia, and by historians of Indian descent. These written sources plus eyewitness accounts by Spanish soldiers and administrators form a priceless record, the largest and most detailed body of information on any New World peoples encountered by Europeans in the 16th century.

Their information has since been expanded by archaeological explorations. Since Mexico's independence from Spain was declared in 1810 and continuing to the present, the nation has developed a view of its past that acknowledges the heritage of its diverse peoples. The Aztecs occupy a place of particular interest and symbolic importance in this national project. Serious archaeological exploration of Tenochtitlan, buried under downtown Mexico City, began at the start of the 20th century. Major excavations have continued intermittently, as well as at other places around the Valley of Mexico and in the neighboring highland region. The interpretation of material remains brought to light by these is immeasurably aided by the abundance and detail of the 16th-century ethnohistoric texts. Conversely, excavated sites and objects have revealed aspects of Aztec life and thought that the 16th-century scholars had not perceived or only partly understood, or had deliberately withheld from the record. Today, ongoing archaeological excavations, historical studies, linguistics, and the interpretation of works of art, architecture, and ritual performance continue to broaden our perspective. All of these sources will be used in this book to examine what made the Aztec achievement distinctive, what threads of tradition provided continuity between them and the Mesoamerican past, and how it was that this powerful empire fell so abruptly, its internal defects and fissures unable to withstand the determined assault by a small Spanish force and its thousands of Indian allies.

PART ONE

....

Coronation at Tenochtitlan

1 · Motecuhzoma II Takes Power

Quiet reigned in Tenochtitlan as a royal procession walked silently from the palace into the walled ritual precinct in the middle of the city (pl. II; ills. 5–7). In the first light of a day in late 1502, the newly elected *huey tlatoani*, Motecuhzoma II, was being escorted away from daily duties and activities for four days and nights of retreat and seclusion in the sacred enclosure. He had been formally stripped of all finery. Now, dressed in a simple loincloth and accompanied by high state officials and priests, he was led through the gate and up the wide stairs of the Great Pyramid in the middle of the city. Feigning weakness as a sign of humility, he was supported on the arms of the allied rulers of Tetzcoco and Tacuba. The looming monument rose in four stepped-back levels, with the broad upper platform extending in front of the blue-striped temple of Tlaloc, god of rain and fertility, and the red-painted temple of Huitzilopochtli, the mythical Mexica warrior-hero. Standing some 60 m (*c.* 180 ft) above the stone pavement of the enclosure, the wide platform commanded a sweeping view of the city and the surrounding lake rimmed by mountains in the distance. A rite of passage was beginning to unfold, by which Motecuhzoma II would be invested in office.

From the high pyramid platform the assembled royalty, nobles, warriors, and priests looked onto the panorama of the city (ills. 8–9). Four straight pedestrian avenues led from the gates of the ritual enclosure toward the cardinal directions dividing the city into quarters. Two large palaces stood immediately outside, the old Palace of Motecuhzoma I and the newer Palace of Axayacatl, constructed with wide courtyards, apartments, reception halls, and lodging for guests, as well as judicial chambers, council halls, and kitchens, storerooms, and treasure-chambers; their broad flat roofs and parapets overlooked the white-plastered and painted masonry houses of nobles and magnates. A regular grid of narrow walkways and canals extended into dense residential districts, each divided into smaller wards occupied by specialized crafts people, and smaller wards and neighborhoods of less specialized occupations. Thatched house-compounds and local ward temples were built on plots of land reclaimed from the shallow lakebed. Dwellings were arranged around open patios, and lines of tall thin willow trees defined the edges of the earthen platforms, many of which also served as household horticultural *chinampa* (raised bed) gardens. To the north the once-independent city of Tlatelolco could be seen within the urban area, distinguished by its own tall pyramid and the famous marketplace. Waving reedbeds and marshes rimmed the periphery of the island city, extending here and there into the expanse of the lake. The four principal avenues quartering Tenochtitlan led to causeways connecting the island with mainland shores on the north, west, and south, and a landing-place opened on the lake toward the east. There were no wheeled vehicles nor beasts of burden, and all goods were transported by lines of human porters or in canoes and wide-bottomed scows. Fresh water was brought to the urban center by an aqueduct leading from copious springs at the base of Chapultepec Hill, across the marshes to the southwest. Perhaps inhabited by as many as 200,000 people at the beginning of the 16th century, Tenochtitlan was the most populous city in the Americas.

A light haze from early breakfast fires drifted above the city. But in contrast to everyday teeming activity, few people were walking the causeways or narrow pathways and pedestrian streets, and no canoes laden with produce were seen on the canals to the marketplace. In keeping with ritual decree, silence was kept throughout the city. The rites now in progress had been set in motion following the death of the *tlatoani* Ahuitzotl in late 1502. He had been the most ruthless warrior, mercilessly suppressing rebellious tributary towns and extending the empire with conquests in the Toluca Valley and beyond toward the north, to the Gulf Coast and the Valley of Puebla to the east, and in Guerrero toward the Pacific; his latest expedition had ventured beyond mountainous Oaxaca to the Tehuantepec Isthmus and Xoconusco far to the south. Ahuitzotl had been everywhere feared. In Tenochtitlan itself he developed the spectacle of human sacrifice beyond all previous custom, as a means of intimidation to foreign ambassadors and to inure the population to bloodshed and war as a way of life. Within the ceremonial precinct, a tall skull rack was strung with the heads of thousands of sacrificed victims. Ahuitzotl's funerary bundle was cremated in a pyre set up before the temple of Huitzilopochtli on the platform of the Great Pyramid, and his ashes together with many offerings and the remains of sacrificed attendants were interred beneath the precinct pavement below. It was now for Motecuhzoma II to carry the imperial project. The new *tlatoani* had been elected by a supreme military council including Cihuacoatl, "Serpent Woman," the internal affairs chief of Tenochtitlan. He was also an accomplished commander in the field, having led in strategy and in the forefront of battlefields during Ahuitzotl's last campaign in Tehuantepec and Xoconochco. Motecuhzoma II was described 18 years later in Tenochtitlan by Bernal Diaz del Castillo, who saw him in the company of Hernán Cortés in 1519 when the Spanish expedition first entered the city:

> [He was] about 40 years old, of good height and well-proportioned, slender and spare of flesh, not very swarthy, but of the natural color and shade of an Indian. He did not wear his hair long, but so as just to cover his ears, his scanty black beard was well shaped and thin. His face was somewhat long, but cheerful, and he had good eyes and showed in his appearance and manner both tenderness and, when necessary, gravity.[1]

As in other societies of the ancient world, the idea of rulership was understood by the Aztecs not only in political, military, and economic terms, but also in terms of religious activities by which the prosperity and continuity of society were ensured. By the reign of Motecuhzoma II the office of *tlatoani* had steadily grown in power, now standing at the summit of the social structure,

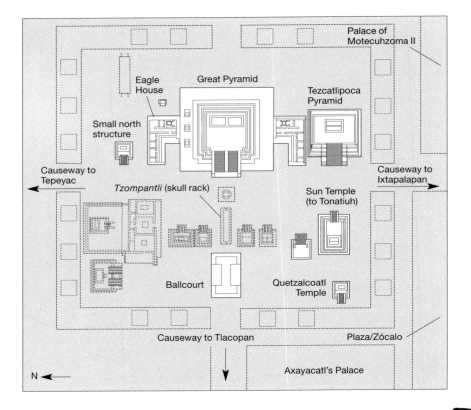

Palace of
Motecuhzoma II

Eagle
House

Great Pyramid

Tezcatlipoca
Pyramid

Small north
structure

Causeway to
Tepeyac

Causeway to
Ixtapalapan

Tzompantli (skull rack)

Sun Temple
(to Tonatiuh)

Ballcourt

Quetzalcoatl
Temple

Causeway to Tlacopan

Plaza/Zócalo

N

Axayacatl's Palace

The ritual precinct

5, 6 ABOVE A plan of the ritual precinct at Tenochtitlan. The Great
Pyramid, Eagle House, and buildings in the southwest quadrant are
known archaeologically. Other features are hypothetically depicted.
RIGHT A reconstruction of the precinct, representing an older
interpretation but suggesting the spatial dimensions of the site,
c. 1519–21. (See also pl. II.)

7 RIGHT Bernardino de Sahagún's plan of the ritual precinct at Tenochtitlan from the Codex Matritense. The temples of Tlaloc and Huitzilopochtli rise in the middle. Other monuments include the gladiatorial stone, the skull rack, the ballcourt, the Yopico Temple (lower right), and other temples (lower left).

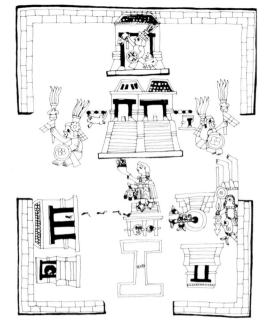

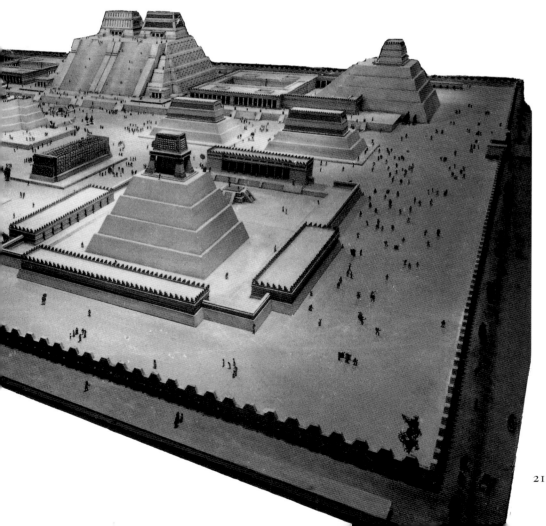

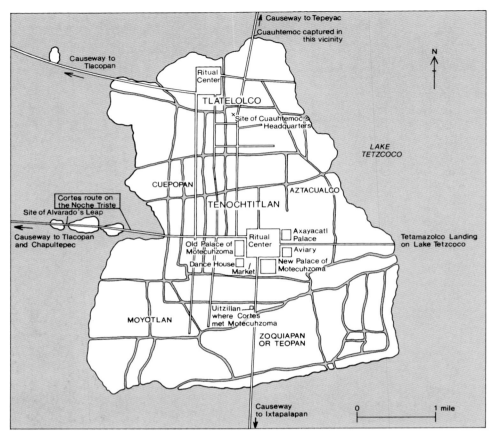

Causeway to Tepeyac

Cuauhtemoc captured in
this vicinity

N

Causeway to
Tlacopan

Ritual
Center

TLATELOLCO

× Site of Cuauhtemoc's
Headquarters

LAKE
TETZCOCO

CUEPOPAN

AZTACUALCO

TENOCHTITLAN

Cortes route on
the Noche Triste

Site of Alvarado's Leap

Ritual
Center

Axayacatl
Palace

Causeway to Tlacopan
and Chapultepec

Old Palace of
Motecuhzoma

Aviary

Tetamazolco Landing
on Lake Tetzcoco

Dance House

New Palace of
Motecuhzoma

Market

MOYOTLAN

Uitzillan
where Cortes
met Motecuhzoma

ZOQUIAPAN
OR TEOPAN

Causeway
to Ixtapalapan

0   1 mile

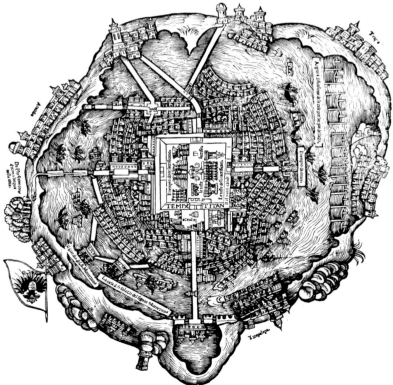

fulfilling indispensable religious functions as well as commanding the warriors and politically directing all important matters of state. These themes were vividly expressed in the pageantry of royal funerals and coronations. At these special times of transition, the most telling symbolic imagery and activities were displayed to demonstrate the deepest values of the Aztecs. At Tenochtit- lan the coronation rites were organized in distinct episodes, featuring elaborate processions, speeches, prayers and performances for dramatic effect. The Great Pyramid formed the central stage and point of reference. Consecrated by thousands of offerings and artifacts deposited in successive layers as the pyramid was enlarged in previous reigns, the building was at once a cosmic symbol and a sign of the ancestral and mythical past. The royal rites of passage unfolded in four phases: Separation and Retreat; Investiture and Coronation; The Coronation War; and Confirmation. Each segment of the process would be connected to the Great Pyramid, to other temples and monuments in the sacred precinct, and to the royal palace outside. The covenants of kingship and the symbolic places where they were to be made, were designed to affirm spiritual bonds between the ruler, the community, the ancestral mythical hero, and the deified forces and phenomena of nature upon which life depended.

Separation and retreat

Motecuhzoma was now beginning his transition into office. On the upper plat- form of the Great Pyramid he was stained black by a principal priest. Others dressed him in a dark green sleeveless jacket, veiled his face, and covered his head with a green fasting cape designed with bones; he was given a green cotton bag with incense, also decorated with bones, and carried a copal incense ladle painted with the skulls of the dead. These garments and objects signified his withdrawal from everyday life to a "primordial" state, a contemplative time of beginning. The new ruler offered copal smoke incense before the sculptural effigy of Huitzilopochtli. The haunting sound of shell trumpets was heard. Accompanying lords were likewise dressed, and the dark procession with veiled faces descended the pyramid and made their way among silent attendants to the nearby Tlacochcalco, a house of military command within the sacred precinct. Here began the retreat, marked by fasting, penance, and restricted movement between the Tlacochcalco and the pyramid at regular intervals of day and night. During this time, the ruler contemplated the meaning and burdens of office and the responsibilities of command. The Aztec coronation texts, recorded soon after the Spanish Conquest, give examples of many elo- quent speeches by the ruler during the retreat, with traditional metaphors

8, 9 OPPOSITE ABOVE A schematic plan of Tenochtitlan–Tlatelolco, showing the location of the principal features, including the internal canal system, and main roads to the causeways. By 1519 the two cities had become a single urban zone, inhabited by some 200,000 to perhaps 250,000 people. Today the area is covered by downtown Mexico City. OPPOSITE BELOW Plan of Tenochtitlan, first published in 1524. Following contemporary cartographic conventions, the ritual precinct dominates the center of the map, with the buildings and natural features surrounding it diminishing in size and importance.

portraying himself in terms of humility and abasement. One of the most significant speeches was addressed to the deity Tezcatlipoca, whose titles "wind," "night," "lord of the near and the nigh," suggested the breath of life, invisibility, and pervasiveness.

> O our master, O our lord, I leave myself, I place myself completely in thy hands, for I cannot govern myself; for I am blind, I am darkness; I am the corner, I am the wall. May thou incline thy heart; require that I deserve, that I merit a little, a firefly-flash of thy torch, thy light, thy mirror, in order that, as if in dreams, as if seeing in dreams, [I endure] for a while, a day. I shall bring about for thee the ruination of government, the laughable, the folly on thy reed mat, on thy reed seat, on thy place of honor.[2]

The Tezcatlipoca cult was of ancient origin, was especially identified with royalty, and the deity was considered a "brother" to the Mexica tribal warrior hero, Huitzilopochtli. As the period of seclusion drew to a close, Motecuhzoma and his entourage again walked in procession, returning by the gate of the ceremonial enclosure to the palace.

Investiture and coronation

The next episode vividly contrasts with the somber mood of the foregoing retreat. Brilliant spectacles were now to be staged, demonstrating the ruler's return to society and the assumption of his new social role. Before the retreat, notice had been sent to the allied city-states of Tetzcoco and Tlacopan as well as the many tributary cities within and beyond the Valley of Mexico, to send contributions of foodstuffs and many other provisions and sumptuary goods required for the celebrations. Strings of porters had been crossing the mountains, carrying loads by tumpline on their backs. Invitations and summons were issued, and official guests and foreign emissaries were arriving in Tenochtitlan as the time of the ceremonial events drew close. Before dawn on the appointed day, parties of high-ranking chiefs began walking the causeways from cities nearby on the mainland. Others came swiftly in long canoes from cities around lakes Chalco, Xochimilco, and Tetzcoco, and from northern towns around Xaltocan and Zumpango. As these groups passed, bedecked in their finery, common people stood in the dawn light, watching from maguey-lined fields and shoreline *chinampa* plots; fishermen and bird-hunters looked up from their nets; and other travelers and bearers moved aside on the causeways to let the high delegations walk by. Thousands began crowding in Tenochtitlan to see the parties on their way to the palace.

On top of the Great Pyramid and across the pavement of the sacred precinct, attendants and priests were carefully sweeping every straw and trace of refuse. Inside the palace apartments, royal families and guests, nobles, commanders, and provincial officials were preparing. All were freshly bathed and their hair arranged according to rank and custom. Personal attendants busily unpacked the finest maguey-fiber and cotton capes woven with elegant geometric and figurative designs. Embroidered breechcloths, obsidian earplugs and labrets, jade and shell necklaces, gold bracelets, armbands and legbands, and head-dresses wrought with colorful feathers of tropical birds were all laid out and readied. Warriors of the eagle, jaguar, and wolf orders donned their close-fitting body suits and adjusted the grimacing helmets. Special shields woven with feathers were brought out from the armory, displaying emblems, figures, and abstract signs. Ambassadors from allied nations and tribute-paying towns, and some also from enemy nations, likewise made ready their distinctive regalia.

Preparations were also unfolding in the palace kitchens, where stacks of fine pottery awaited the feasts to be later served, while in the immense open court-yard, musicians set up the tall *huehuetl* and two-tongued *teponaztli* drums, carved or painted with animals and hieroglyphic inscriptions. Shrill whistles, flutes, rattles, and rasps were heard above the tumult of orders and exclama-tions. Everyone, from the high city council to allied rulers, veteran warriors, and representatives of local and distant communities including enemy ambas-sadors, saw themselves joining in a rare and powerful event. As the morning advanced all finally stood ready.

On this day Motecuhzoma II was to be officially installed in office. Donning the prescribed regalia of state signaled a first step in reconstituting the empire, following the symbolic dissolution of the retreat. Only royalty could crown royalty, and Netzahualpilli, the allied *tlatoani* of Tetzcoco, assisted by Toto-quilhuaztli, the allied *tlatoani* of Tlacopan, were to conduct the ceremony. In the grand patio of the palace, surrounded by glittering nobility, warriors, ambassadors and guests,

> The king of Tetzcoco took the crown of green stones, all worked in gold, and placed it upon his [the new ruler's] head, and piercing the septum of his nose he inserted a green emerald as thick as a quill pen, and in his ears two round emerald earplugs in gold settings, and on his arms from elbow to shoulder two very resplendent gold bracelets, and on his ankles, anklets with dangling gold belts, and he [the Tetzcocan] shod him with jaguar-skin sandals all elegantly gilded and clad him with a precious mantle of henequen-like fiber, very thin and shining, all gilded and painted with elegant pictures, and he put a waistband around him of the same, and taking him by the hand he led him a throne they called *cuauhicpalli*, meaning eagle-seat, also named ocelot-seat, for it was decorated with eagle feathers and ocelot-hides.[3]

Many eloquent speeches were made by the nobles, praising, admonishing and instructing the new ruler, who responded to each in turn.

Once dressed, crowned, and seated, Motecuhzoma II was carried by litter seated on the eagle and ocelot throne, out of the palace to the ritual precinct and again up to the Great Pyramid platform. Before the fierce image within Huitzilopochtli's temple, the ruler was given a jaguar's claw to draw blood from his ears and legs as an offering. More admonishments, speeches, and prayers were made and quail were also offered. Through these blood sacrifices the ruler affirmed a covenant with the ancestral Mexica tribal hero and the pyramid-mountain he was obliged to defend. The procession descended to another location, described as the place of a *cuauhxicalli*, "eagle vessel" (ill. 10), while other accounts mention a "sun-stone." The monuments may have been one and the same, for the eagle was at once a sign of the ruler as warrior, and was also a solar symbol. The *tlatoani* again offered royal blood taken from his arms and legs and again sacrificed quail. Another covenant was thereby made, confirming his office in Tenochtitlan at the center of the world, in the present "sun" or era of world-creation. From this site the ruler was carried in his litter to a building known as the *coateocalli*, the "house of (foreign) gods." Within a darkened chamber, captured sacred fetishes and religious paraphernalia of foreign nations were kept as hostages of the spiritual identity of tributary peoples. In the *coateocalli* the ruler again offered blood sacrifice, and affirmed his obligation to attend to seasonal cycle of festivals.

The final station was the earth-temple known as Yopico, a symbolic architectural cave. The inner chamber had a sunken receptacle in the floor for offerings during spring planting festivals. It was through sacrifice to the earth at this place that the transfer of power to the new *tlatoani* was ultimately consecrated and made legal. The action at Yopico expressed in a highly ceremonial way, the custom of touching one's lips and then touching the earth to witness the truth of an event. Emerging from Yopico, the *tlatoani* was symbolically reborn into his new social role. Springtime rites to the deity Xipe Totec housed in Yopico were primarily agricultural, yet also assumed a military nature in the initiation rites of young warriors who captured prisoners for the spring sacrifice. The connection between war and agriculture was vividly demonstrated when the *tlatoani* formally addressed a representative of the common people, who in turn acknowledged the ruler's discourse to show that his commands were understood.

Motecuhzoma's itinerary within the ceremonial precinct now ended, and he was brought back to the palace for the concluding Ceremony of Speeches. In each form of speech made by the elders, nobles, and chiefs, the *tlatoani* was admonished and encouraged to perform as expected of a person in his supreme office. In response the *tlatoani* exhorted the population to war and to cultivate the land. The Ceremony of Speeches ended and at last the long day concluded with feasts offered by the new *tlatoani* to all the attending guests. In many respects the spectacular ceremonies and all their conspicuous consumption and ostentatious gift-giving resembled the potlatch system of feasts of Northwest Coast Indian tribes. Feasting and the sponsoring of feasts formed a social

10 A *cuauhxicalli*, "eagle vessel", a massive receptacle for sacrificial offerings excavated at the Great Pyramid site. Late 15th or early 16th century.

compact by which rulers and nobles competed to establish personal and social ascendancy within their domains and in competition with leaders from allied or rival communities. This aspect of rulership by which wealth was regularly accumulated and distributed through festivals – especially in the great rites of passage – was widespread throughout Mesoamerica and was practiced by the Aztecs on an imperial scale.

The Coronation War

Before the *tlatoani* could be considered fully confirmed, he was required to prove his leadership in battle, to win tribute, and to capture prisoners for sacrifice in the final confirmation ceremony. Motecuhzoma had the challenge of Ahuitzotl's achievements to match. He led the army some 400 miles (640 km) over the mountains to the south, to the region of Nopallan near the coast of Oaxaca. As was customary, the campaign took place in the dry season months when trails were passable and warriors and porters from around the valley were not otherwise occupied for cultivation and harvest. The towns of Nopallan proved to be well defended, and the principal center was finally assaulted by constructing scaling ladders to overwhelm the fortified enemy. Motecuhzoma personally led the action, splendidly attired for battle as was the custom. The defeated local chieftains rendered their submission and were admonished by Motecuhzoma that rebellion and failure to send regular tribute would result in annihilation. The victorious expedition began the long return march to Tenochtitlan, winding along the trails laden with booty and a line of dejected prisoners destined for sacrifice.

Confirmation

This was the final step in the kingship rites. As the month of June drew near with impending rain and the renewal of life, proclamations were made and invitations sent again to allies, administrative officials, and important rulers, including those of enemy nations. As the time drew close, all chieftains, traders, and treasurers were expected to send gifts – failure to do so might well lead to exile or loss of rank. In due time the presents began to arrive. Bundles of cloth and clothing, containers of gold and jade jewelry, bundles of feathers, cargos of maize, of cacao, and perishables in the form of baskets of fruit and vegetables, flocks of turkeys, deer, and quail fresh from the hunt, as well as fish of many kinds were brought in astonishing abundance. Within the city, lapidary artists, jewelers, featherworkers, and many other craftspeople had also been making preparations. Masons and plasterers had set to work months before, repairing old buildings and constructing new ones.

As had been experienced during the investiture and coronation, the feasts that followed were offered by the *tlatoani* in a striking expression of his personal control of wealth. But the distinguishing act of this final confirmation episode was his personal distribution of insignia of rank to every official. This procedure began on the first day, when the allied rulers of Tetzcoco and Tlacopan were formally presented with regalia of office by the new *tlatoani* –

11 LEFT The Lordly Dance, from the Tovar Manuscript.

12, 13 OPPOSITE RIGHT The Coronation Stone of Motecuhzoma II, proclaiming the ruler's title to the earth. Glyphic signs of the five cosmogonic ages appear in counter-clockwise order. The square cartouche contains the date 11-reed (1503), the year when Motecuhzoma completed the coronation process. OPPOSITE LEFT The rear, originally face down, is carved with the sign 1-rabbit, the mythical date marking the beginning of the present era.

thus making clear the supremacy of Tenochtitlan over the allied cities. The rulers then dressed and waited to attend a spectacular dance (ill. 11). Singers and musicians began the rhythm on a standing *huehuetl* drum in the grand courtyard of the palace, and a deep chorus began the songs of praise and victory. The ruler of Tetzcoco and Tlacopan led 2,000 nobles, chieftains, and high-ranking officials in a stately dance. At a prescribed moment Motecuhzoma made his triumphal entrance. Enveloped in the incense smoke of copal, the splendidly attired ruler was encircled by the vast concourse of dancing lords. Standing by the commanding drum, he appeared as a living icon, the heir to the deified ancestor-warrior Huitzilopochtli, reaffirming his virtue and warlike purpose at the center of the Aztec world. Returning to the throne, the new ruler continued his personal distribution of insignia. All high officials, including nobles, warriors, and priests, as well as elders from the wards of the city, provincial governors, tax collectors, and chieftains, received gifts and emblems of authority directly from the hand of the *tlatoani*. This event symbolically affirmed the reintegration of the whole social order after the dissolution of Ahuitzotl's funeral. The long process that had begun with the death of Ahuitzotl and the election of Motecuhzoma II concluded with the sacrifice of prisoners taken during the Coronation War.

The rites by which the ruler was installed had not only economic and social functions. They were also deeply symbolic events, theatrically designed to affirm mythology, history, and national ethos. We shall see in later discussions of the Aztec symbolic world that the dual Great Pyramid of Tenochtitlan was at once Tlaloc's symbolic Tonacatepetl, "Mountain of Sustenance," mirroring the rain-mountains rimming the valley, and also a man-made representation of Huitzilopochtli's legendary Coatepetl, "Serpent Mountain," the hero's mythic mountain of victory. In a more immediate historical sense, the monument also carried the memory of past rulers and of Tenochtitlan as a community. The iconic format of the Great Pyramid allowed the events of a present ongoing history and the obligations of rulership to be seen not as ephemeral or transitory, but as an integral part of the cosmological setting and the annual alternation of the seasons. This association was as apparent to village farmers as to the rulers and priests. The pattern of rites and monuments, seen in the context of the highland landscape, portrayed the empire as part of the permanent eternal order.

To commemorate the coronation, sculptors were commissioned to design a monument for the sacred precinct. This Coronation Stone (ills. 12, 13) reflects the visual imagery being created in Tenochtitlan and Tetzcoco, grounded in past traditions yet designed to communicate the history and legitimacy of the new allied city-states. All six sides of the rectangular block are covered with hieroglyphs, dates, and figures taken from pictorial manuscripts. The images are intended to be read in relation to the shape of the stone itself. The pictorial text recounts the history of the world from the mythic time of origins to the historical present, as a progression of five ages or epochs, each ending in

violent disaster. The reading begins in the lower right-hand corner and continues in counterclockwise order. The picture of a jaguar head with four surrounding dots signifies "four jaguar," the calendrical name of the first era of creation that ended in a plague of jaguars. Next is "four wind," represented by the beaked mask of Ehecatl, a wind god; this was an era that ended in hurricanes. The third era appears in the upper left corner as the mask of Tlaloc the rain god, in sign of "four rain," corresponding to a fiery rain that brought this epoch to a close. Below left is the head of Chalchiuhtlicue, "Jade Skirt," the goddess of ground water, representing springs, rivers, lakes, and the circumscribing sea. This was an era that ended by flood. The present era appears in the center of the panel, as the X-shaped sign Ollin, "movement," referring to a prophecy that the end would come in earthquakes. Finally, a square cartouche below center contains the year sign 11-reed, corresponding to 1503 in the Christian calendar; above, a small figure with a dot is the day-sign "one alligator" corresponding to 4 June, the year and day when Motecuhzoma II completed the coronation process as *huey tlatoani* of Tenochtitlan.

Each side of the monument is identically carved with the squatting figure of the earth goddess Tlaltecuhtli with the hieroglyphs for water and fire, "flood and conflagration," the Nahuatl language metaphor for war. The underside of the stone, which faced the earth and was not intended to be seen, is carved with the year sign "1-rabbit," the mythic day of the world's creation. In paraphrase the text would read, "From sacred time of first creation to the successive ages and the present epoch, the earth is affirmed as a sacred patrimony conquered by war, to which on this year and day Motecuhzoma II is heir." The text thus affirms a charter of divinely sanctioned inheritance by which Motecuhzoma II claimed title to the world as determined since the time of first creation.

In terms of symbolic expression the empire was thus portrayed as an outcome of cosmological history. The following chapters aim to chart Aztec cultural history, in terms of archaeology and monuments and the abundant ethnohistoric texts that describe the early migrating tribes and their eventual achievements as imperial people. What has been outlined about the Valley of Mexico, the city of Tenochtitlan and its allies and neighbors, and Motecuhzoma II's coronation in 1502, not only reflects the project of conquest and the theatrical rituals of power; it also reflects an endeavor in progress for 200 years. This process was no mere imitation of Mesoamerican antiquity, but an imaginative cultural synthesis whereby the Aztec communities adapted and made their own creative adjustments within the traditional framework of older civilization. Unfolding events led the Aztecs to a growing perception of themselves as successors to the sequence of ancient societies whose ruined capitals were seen dotting the highland landscape. The following chapter will begin by exploring the archaeological sites of Teotihuacan, Xochicalco, Cacaxtla, and Tula, as places where certain features of this cultural heritage may be traced.

PART TWO

· · · · · · · · · · · · · · · ·

Urban Traditions,
Tribal Peoples

2 · An Ancient Heritage

City states, cultural themes

Aztec society and culture were bound in innumerable ways to the ancient fabric of Mesoamerican civilization. Centuries before the migrating tribes arrived in the Valley of Mexico, a widely shared body of knowledge had evolved in the Central Highlands as a succession of states arose and collapsed. The way the structure of the world was imagined, how the forces of nature were perceived, and how the cycle of the seasons followed in regular progression, formed a cosmic template and an integrating model for social organization and activities. It is essential to consider certain earlier archaeological sites and monuments for what they reveal about this enduring framework.

Older capitals display plans, orientations, architectural features, and sculptural images recording structures of cultural memory that the Aztecs sought to assimilate in their quest for the authority and prestige of the legendary past. First in their imagination was the metropolis of Teotihuacan, constructed between the 1st and 6th centuries AD. Its ruins were destined to become especially significant in Aztec mythology, and its monuments portray a relationship of rulership and cosmological order that would eventually inform the functions of Aztec leaders and the dominant urban pattern of Tenochtitlan. The hilltop ruin of Xochicalco, overlooking the Valley of Morelos, displays a synthesis of Teotihuacan and Classic Maya traditions during the 8th and 9th centuries, especially in hieroglyphic inscriptions and figures and architectural features. Certain inscriptions are clearly related to later Aztec writing. The ruins of Tula, dating from the 10th to the mid–12th centuries, are located about 65 miles (100 km) northwest of the Valley of Mexico. Tula, the seat of the warlike Toltec people, was the setting of a legendary history concerning the ruler Quetzalcoatl, ("Quetzal (feather) Serpent"), whose rise and tragic fall was to figure prominently in Aztec chronicles. Certain communities in the Valley of Mexico claimed prestigious Toltec descent, and it was from one of their lineages that Tenochtitlan would eventually receive its first royal ruler.

Teotihuacan

The pyramids of Teotihuacan rise in dun-colored masses, framed by the looming mountain Cerro Gordo. Built on an almost geological scale, the ceremonial architecture echoes the shapes of the surrounding landscape. The largest unifying feature is the Processional Way, running on a 2-mile (3.2-km) long north–south axis traversing the city. Lined by platforms and residential compounds, this ceremonial avenue leads past the immense Sun Pyramid

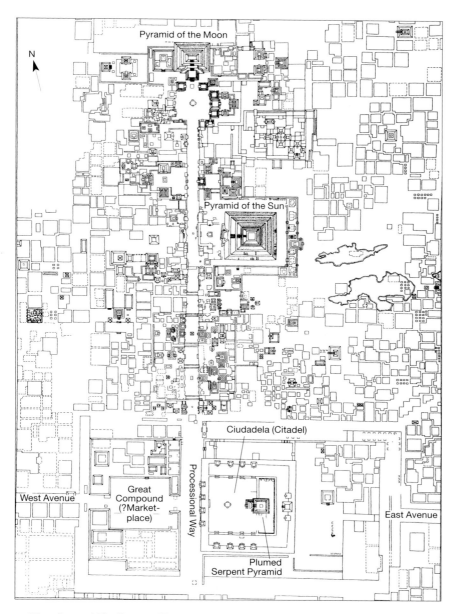

N

Pyramid of the Moon

Pyramid of the Sun

Ciudadela (Citadel)

Great Compound (?Market-place)

West Avenue

Processional Way

East Avenue

Plumed Serpent Pyramid

14 Plan of central Teotihuacan. The avenues and surrounding residential zones were laid out according to the alignment of the Pyramid of the Sun toward the equinoctial path of the sun. The Processional Way points northward to the Moon Pyramid and to the sacred mountain beyond, a source of underground water. To the south, the avenue leads to springs and fields.

before ending in a broad plaza below the Pyramid of the Moon, with the line of sight extending beyond to the summit of Cerro Gordo. This mountain, named Tenan, "Stone Mother" in the Nahuatl language, is the source of an underground aquifer and was the sacred mountain of Teotihuacan. The southern end of the Processional Way lacks monumental definition, leading into open land with springs and cultivated fields where fossil *chinampa* gardens have been found. Immediately south of the Sun Pyramid lie the courtyards and foundations of what is assumed to have been a palace and administrative center. Two vast quadrangles stand beyond, symmetrically placed on opposite sides of the Processional Way. Roads lead east and west from these central architectural features. The west quadrangle has no monumental definition, and is thought to have served as the marketplace of the city. On the eastern side, the Ciudadela ("Citadel") forms a ceremonial plaza, surrounded by a continuous elevated platform set with temple platforms and stairways at regular intervals. The entire ensemble is commanded from the eastern side by the Plumed Serpent Pyramid (ill. 16) which functioned as the seat of government.

15 The Ciudadela, Processional Way, Sun Pyramid, and Moon Pyramid, with the sacred mountain Tenan framing the city in the distance.

The original sculptured façade of the Plumed Serpent Pyramid was covered by the later "Piramide Adosado." This earlier pyramid presents the imagery of rulership. Rising tiers display panels of repeating units, combining low relief and three-dimensional forms. Originally brilliantly polychromed, the basic sculptural units portray a dragon-like figure with a rattlesnake tail and the body covered by long plumes of the quetzal bird. The composite animal has a feline head with fangs, and a serpent's forked tongue projecting from a ruff of petals and feathers. Toward the tail of the creature, a headdress composed of rectangular and trapezoidal shapes is set with roundels and surmounted by an elaborate knot with waving plumes. The snout displays rows of teeth and staring eyes to either side. The Plumed Serpent is a complex ideogram of the metaphor Quetzalcoatl, "quetzal serpent," alluding to one of the most dramatic and powerful forces of nature experienced in the natural environment. A thousand years later in Aztec Tenochtitlan, this figure of speech was recorded in the Nahuatl language:

Quetzalcoatl: he was the wind; he was the guide, the roadsweeper of the rain gods, of the masters of the water, of those who brought rain. And when the wind increased, it was said, the dust swirled up, it roared, howled, became dark, blew in all directions; there was lightning; it grew wrathful.[1]

The metaphor Quetzalcoatl described a powerful seasonal phenomenon, and by extension it was also a title of rulership or priestly office. The elaborate headdress-mask carried on the tail of the serpent may be an abstract representation of an alligator, associated with the earth and ground water, and it may have been worn as the crown of office at Teotihuacan.

The Sun Pyramid is aligned to the place on the east horizon where the sun rises on the equinox. Traditionally in Mesoamerica, the spring and fall equinoxes divided the year into the "summer" rainy season and the "winter" dry season. The rainy season was the "female" time for planting, cultivation, and harvest, when people stayed close by the city and worked the surrounding fields. The dry season was the "male" time for long-distance trade, travel, hunting, and war. Such corresponding cosmological and social categories surely regulated life at Teotihuacan, just as they were also to obtain among the Aztecs.

The north–south Processional Way and the east–west path of the sun over the Sun Pyramid provided the lines for a grid plan of residential and manufacturing compounds covering an 8 sq. mile (20 sq. km) area. At its height Teotihuacan was inhabited by some 100,000 to 150,000 people. It was the

16 OPPOSITE Façade of the Plumed Serpent Pyramid. Composite dragon-like heads with undulating feathered bodies and rattlesnake tails carry headdresses with quadrangular snouts, staring eyes and twin forehead roundels; the surface represents jade mosaics. Seashells fill the interstices. This Pyramid commanding the Ciudadela was the seat of Teotihuacan rulership.

17, 18 The Aztec custom of using stone masks in rituals derives from a tradition established over 1,000 years before, during the ascendancy of Teotihuacan. BELOW LEFT This stone mask, inset with shell and obsidian, was made in Teotihuacan but recovered from the foundations of Tenochtitlan's Great Pyramid. BELOW RIGHT An Aztec stone mask found at the Great Pyramid, made from green alabaster.

largest city in Mesoamerica and commanded resources as far south as Maya capitals in Guatemala, and north to mines in Zacatecas and Durango. A vast obsidian deposit near Pachuca, Hidalgo, was exploited as a prized commodity, widely traded for the manufacture of blades and points. Within Teotihuacan colonies of foreigners engaged in trade and manufacturing a range of products. The central civic and religious buildings were wrecked around AD 750, bringing the long-lasting hegemony of the city to an end. Nevertheless, the urban zone continued to be substantially populated and in time assumed new shape, forming the cluster of small separate towns that have continued to the present.

The abandoned pyramids and plazas of Teotihuacan were viewed with awe by the Aztecs, and in the middle of the 15th century the ruler Motecuhzoma I commissioned a ritual platform to be built opposite the Sun Pyramid in the middle of the Processional Way. This monument became a place where ceremonies commemorating mythic world-creation were celebrated. Teotihuacan was invested with mythological significance in Aztec creation stories as the place where the present era of the world began. The narrative describes a primordial setting of silence and darkness; a council of gods was convened and a great bonfire was lit; two of the deities cast themselves into the fire, to be reborn as the sun and the moon. Hence the names "Sun Pyramid" and "Moon Pyramid," for the Aztecs saw the buildings as memorials to this auto-sacrifice of the gods in the time of beginnings (see Chapter 7). The term Teotihuacan, "place of the gods," was an Aztec name for the city, whose original name remains to be identified in its hieroglyphic system.

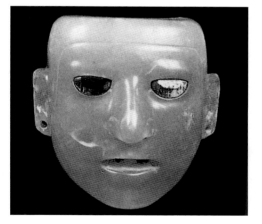

19 ABOVE The Xochicalco ballcourt, of Maya design, aligned to the western Processional Way and the Temple of Agriculture.

20 OPPOSITE The Plumed Serpent Platform, like its predecessor at Teotihuacan, was the seat of rulership at Xochicalco. Seated Maya-like lords utter speech-glyphs alluding to royal commands and admonitions in the Nahuatl language. Above, rectangular panels display seated figures with place-glyphs, suggesting a state-like assembly of local rulers.

Xochicalco

The ruins of Xochicalco are dramatically sited on a mountaintop about 15 miles (25 km) southwest of the city of Cuernavaca in the Valley of Morelos (ill. 19). The pyramids, ballcourt, palace, and the Plumed Serpent Platform were built between AD 600 and 900. The site was coeval with late Teotihuacan and Classic Maya capitals, but survived their disintegration and collapse. The elegant sculptural reliefs of the Plumed Serpent Platform display kingship imagery salvaged from Teotihuacan and Classic Maya traditions, adapted to express new political and historical circumstances during a time of intensive change. At Xochicalco it is possible to trace key themes in the cultural inheritance that would be retransmitted and adapted centuries later in the Valley of Mexico. Xochicalco was abandoned by c. 1100; some 300 years later, when the Aztecs conquered towns in the Valley of Morelos, visitors to Xochicalco would have had no difficulty in recognizing the significance of its ruined principal buildings.

Xochicalco's architects modified the irregular mountain with four imposing concentric terraces rising to the summit. A long straight walkway leads upward into the ruins from the floor of the valley to the south. Short flights of stairs bring the visitor to an open plaza faced by a three-temple complex, with low temple platforms flanking the rising levels and steep stairway of the central pyramid framed by the mountain immediately behind. The composition stems from Teotihuacan, where the long north–south Processional Way carries the eye to the Pyramid of the Moon and the framing mountain Tenan.

To the west a low promontory was leveled to create one of the most beautiful architectural passages in archaeological Central Highland Mexico. A ballcourt with sloping sides recalls those of Classic Maya centers at Piedras Negras and Copán. A cluster of sweat-bath rooms lie beyond this major feature, and the sequence is contained at the end by a large rectangular platform that supported the temple of an agricultural deity. The steep chasm of the River Tembembe lies behind and below the promontory, and the view leads westward toward fertile valley bottomlands and the distant Sierra Madre. The summit of Xochicalco is covered by the ruins of a palace and an esplanade with the Plumed Serpent Platform (ill. 20). The latter monument is aligned on an east–west axis to the equinoctial sun. A panel-and-slope profile displays the sculptural program, with six undulating plumed serpents disposed around the rear and flanks of the build-ing, and two additional abbreviated serpents flanking the front stairway. This format is reminiscent of the design of Mixtec screenfold pictorial manuscripts in later centuries, but the undulating serpents derive from Teotihuacan mural art.

Seated chieftains within the plumed serpent undulations stem from Classic Maya sources: similar seated rulers are painted in courtly scenes on Maya ceramic vases, and the profiled headdresses worn at Xochicalco also show unmistakable similarities with headdresses depicted on three stelae at

Maya Piedras Negras. Only on these stelae do such headdresses appear in Maya country, suggesting a dynastic connection between the two 7th-century sites. However, contrary to Maya custom, the Xochicalco figures do not portray individuals, nor do they seem to commemorate specific rulers. Instead, the seated lords conform to an abstract mode of imagery as standardized icons within plumed serpent units – a convention that must be attributed to the legacy of Teotihuacan. Another crucial factor at Xochicalco is that the figures are not accompanied by an independent hieroglyphic text as in Maya tradition; instead, glyphic elements are subordinated in the larger design program – another trait of Teotihuacan mural art. Unmistakably the Xochicalco Plumed Serpent Platform was made for a literate highland audience, because glyphic elements (smoke-volutes, speech-scrolls, and cloud symbols) can be read in terms of Nahuatl language metaphors. These metaphors were specifically associated with rulership, and we will find them expressed again in formal speech and glyphic signs used by the Aztecs four centuries later.

Each seated figure utters a speech-scroll with several components: (1) a long downward curving volute with two quetzal feathers; and (2) an upward-turning scroll with a trilobed element and two small volutes springing from the top. These components can also be identified on Aztec monuments and interpreted by consulting the 16th-century encyclopedic ethnography and history, The Florentine Codex by Fray Bernardino de Sahagún:

> His Breath, his Word. Precisely this saying was said of the words of rulers. It was said: "The breath, the word of the ruler; not [just] anyone's word; precisely the word, the breath of our lord."
> This letter means: His Breath or spirit or his word. And it is said metaphorically of the reasoned speech that the lord makes to his principals or the preacher to his listeners.[2]

Two long feathers attached to the speech-scroll may be read as follows:

> The very broad, the very deep green precious feather. This saying was said of that with which the ruler, or nobleman, or magistrate admonished one well. He who was admonished was told: "Grasp the discourse, the very broad, the deep green, like a precious feather. The lord, the ruler, hath shown thee mercy. This letter means, rich plumage of perfect color. And metaphorically it means an elegant, sensible, and well composed speech.[3]

Other elements qualifying this complex speech-scroll are curling volutes alluding to the metaphor "smoke" and a trilobed variant of a "fire" sign, both corresponding to well-known figures of speech in the Nahuatl language later spoken by the Aztecs.

Above these sculptured serpents and seated lords on the sloping sides of the Plumed Serpent Platform, a narrow panel band is divided into compartments, each containing a small seated figure wearing a "trapeze and ray" headdress, possibly identified with military status; below, an open jaw and quartered circle

21 Tlamacazapa place-glyphs from the Plumed Serpent Platform at Xochicalco, *c.* 800–900 AD (left), and the Codex Mendoza, *c.* 1525 (right).

may indicate location, and a different hieroglyph in every unit may correspond to the names of towns.

Above the slope and panel, the remaining panels of the original superstructure are also carved with hieroglyphs and figures. On the southeast corner, Janet Berlo has identified the name of the town Tlamacazapa, not far from Taxco, Guerrero, about 25 miles (40 km) south of Xochicalco (ill. 21). In the 16th-century Aztec *Matrícula de Tributos* (Tribute List), this town is represented by the sign of a water channel surmounted by a human head with an earring, as seen at Xochicalco many centuries earlier. No other place names have been identified with this degree of assurance, but the Tlamacazapa sign demonstrates the continuity of hieroglyphic writing conventions in Central Mexico and supports the evidence from smoke-volutes, speech-scrolls, and cloud symbols for centuries of Nahuatl being spoken and recorded in hieroglyphic writings of this region.

Cacaxtla

Among all the deep-seated cultural themes inherited by the Aztecs, none is more fundamental than the ancient idea of rulers as pivotal participants in the network of religious and economic connections binding society and city to the forms of the land and the annual cycle of world renewal. The archaeological site of Cacaxtla, on a commanding hilltop in the Valley of Puebla, was built in the time of change following the collapse of Teotihuacan and many regional Maya capitals. As at Xochicalco, Maya-connected rulers of Cacaxtla commissioned works of art and architecture as settings representing their authority and obligations in terms understandable to the native populations of this highland region. The murals of Cacaxtla were surely painted by a master trained in the Maya school of Usumacinta River centers. A scene of battle covers a wall facing an open courtyard, while ritual events are depicted on the outer walls and around the doorjambs of an upper chamber. The latter images encode the religious obligations of Cacaxtla's rulers. The composition features two confronted human figures emblematically attired as a jaguar (left) and an eagle (right); the jaguar holds a ceremonial bar and stands upon a jaguar-serpent, while the eagle holds a similar bar and stands upon a green-feathered serpent. Date-glyphs and place or name-glyphs are displayed around the figures. None are Maya; the places or names suggest Teotihuacan affinities, while the numbers follow a Mixtec-like system. The doorway is framed by a curvilinear design. At one point in the history of Cacaxtla the painted frame was covered by terracotta plaques, one of which is still attached to the left. The original design also featured stalks of maize painted within the curving frame. Twin streams of water are represented emerging below from the doorways, and these streams in turn form the frames around the eagle- and jaguar-clad figures. Aquatic plants and animals swim in this watery setting. Finally, two other standing figures are depicted in the doorway jambs. To the left, another jaguar-clad man holds a waterpot painted with the mask of Tlaloc, associated with rainstorms that form upon the summit of mountains. This theme is borne out by depicting the pot in the act of watering a maize plant. The theme of plant growth is also expressed by a vine springing from the jaguar-man's umbilicus, while the aquatic theme is echoed by a dancing black-painted figure carrying a large conch shell, depicted on the right-side jamb.

Eagles and jaguars are widely associated with the sky and earth in Mesoamerica, and representations of maize plants, Tlaloc vessels, umbilical vines and flowing water affirm that these murals commemorate rites of regeneration and agricultural abundance. The painted doorway unifies the entire iconographic program. The frame is more than decorative, for its inward-curving lower "arms" and small curling motifs on the sides are the same as those that continue to appear on representations of mountains in late Post-

22 Cacaxtla, upper chamber entryway panels, *c.* 900. The right side curvilinear frame encloses a maize plant; the originally matching left side was covered by a ceramic panel at a later date. The curvilinear framing motif symbolized the entrance into a mountain from which water issues

Classic pictorial manuscripts such as the Codex Nuttall, and the early colonial Codex Borbonicus. The Cacaxtla doorway stands as the entrance to a symbolic mountain, prefacing the Aztec architectural and pictorial imagery of mountains as places where rain clouds form and springs issue forth. The Nahuatl terms *tonacatepetl*, "mountain of sustenance," and *altepetl*, literally "water mountain," meaning "city," convey the sense of the human community and its dependence on the land that gave them life. The doorway at Cacaxtla commemorates obligations to participate in rites of renewal that transformed the long season of death and drought into the season of rain and rebirth (ill. 22).

Toltec Tula

Much of the information concerning the Toltecs stems from 16th-century annals of highland peoples who linked their histories to the powerful city of *Tollán*, or Tula. These annals, written in Spanish and/or Nahuatl and illustrated during the early colonial period, record older native accounts transmitted through oral tradition or portrayed in original pictorial manuscripts now lost. Communities scattered across the Central Highlands narrated their histories, combining actual events with imaginary happenings and conventionalized legends, often connecting local ruling lineages to the prestigious Toltecs. For the Aztecs and their neighbors, the term "Toltec" denoted a

below. Rulers attired as a jaguar and an eagle correspond to social divisions (moieties) and alternating ritual and economic activities of the annual seasonal cycle. A Maya artist painted the panels, but dates and place-signs or name-glyphs belong to a highland Mexican writing tradition.

people admirable, noble, and accomplished; *Toltecayotl*, "to have a Toltec heart," was to excel, to be worthy, to possess extraordinary qualities in the manner of the ancients.

The problem of identifying the mysterious Toltecs emerged during the 1930s and 1940s as archaeologists and ethnohistorians sought to reconstruct the sequence of major societies that once flourished in central Mexico. Some believed that many of the "idealized" ethnohistoric accounts pointed to the existence of an actual place – Tollán – that might be found and archaeologically explored, just as Homer's *Iliad* led the German archaeologist Heinrich Schliemann to the site of ancient Troy. However, the place-name Tula or Tollán proved to be inconclusive, for it occurs in several locations, signifying "place of reeds" in Nahuatl, figuratively alluding to towns where people were "as thick as reeds." Could Tollán perhaps refer to the vast city of Teotihuacan, whose ruins suggest the grandeur attributed to the Toltec capital in the ethnohistoric sources? American archaeologist George Vaillant supposed this to be the case, and he developed a chronology linking events described in the annals to archaeological phases in the evolution of Teotihuacan. But a different story emerged as Mexican historian Wigberto Jimenez Moreno sifted through the documents. Tracing the old tribal migration routes, noting geographical references, and correlating dynastic genealogies with calendrical information and stories concerning the legendary ruler Quetzalcoatl, Jimenez Moreno established that a large archaeological site near the Spanish colonial city of Tula was the original Toltec capital, Tollán. His outline suggested that Toltec Tula flourished between the 10th and mid-12th centuries, long after the collapse of Teotihuacan and before the emergence of Aztec city-states in the Valley of Mexico.

According to Jimenez Moreno's widely accepted view, Toltec history began with a semi-civilized people, the Tolteca-Chichimeca, who migrated from northern deserts into the Valley of Mexico during the late 9th century. The Tolteca-Chichimeca first settled at Culhuacan in the Valley of Mexico under the leadership of the chieftain Mixcoatl. Mixcoatl fathered a son, Topiltzin, born on the day 1 reed (AD 935 or 947). Upon coming of age, Topiltzin assumed the name Quetzalcoatl as his traditional title of office. Descriptions of Quetzalcoatl's youth and early manhood are filled with accounts of wars and conquests. At last he settled at Tula and became a renowned priestly ruler. In Fray Bernardino de Sahagún's version of the story, and also according to the Codex Chimalpopoca, Quetzalcoatl's Tula had pyramids and artisans' workshops or houses where luxury goods from long-distance trade and tribute were kept: "and there stood his greenstone house, and his golden house, and his seashell house, and his snail shell house, and his house of beams, his turquoise house, and his house of precious feathers."[4] Other passages describe the city as a place of skilled craftsmen, and accomplished farmers who raised ears of maize, squashes, and amaranth plants of exceptional size and abundance. Cotton was said to grow in colors of red, yellow, violet, green, white, gray, and brown. The Codex Chimalpopoca relates how Quetzalcoatl assumed priestly functions at Tula, describing austere religious penances: "and he punctured himself with thorns ... and he made his thorns of jade and his needles of Quetzal plumes. And for incense he burned turquoise, jade, and red shell.

He only sacrificed serpents, birds, and butterflies."[5] Quetzalcoatl's example was widely influential as a model for priestly rulers. But factional disputes inevitably arose, for as Tula became a city of diverse peoples, a power struggle ensued, personified by Quetzalcoatl's rivalry with Tezcatlipoca, described as a shamanic wizard or trickster whose warlike faction demanded human sacrifice, setting the stage for the tragic drama of Quetzalcoatl's fall.

At one point Quetzalcoatl became ill; Tezcatlipoca saw an opportunity and, remembering a strict prohibition against drunkenness in Tula, changed himself into an old man and slipped by the guards to offer Quetzalcoatl a curing potion. In reality this was a bowl of fermented maguey juice, *pulque*. One draft was followed by more, and soon all the royal attendants were drinking. Quetzalcoatl called for his sister, Quetzalpetlatl, who also partook of the *pulque*. Their drunkenness led to incest. Overcome by remorse and scandal, Quetzalcoatl resigned from power, destroyed or buried his property, and departed from Tula with a band of followers. One version of Quetzalcoatl's journey into exile describes his route over the snowy pass between Popocatepetl and Iztaccíhuatl, where many followers froze to death. The sorrowing hero traveled on toward the Gulf of Mexico. In another account Quetzalcoatl arrived on the Gulf Coast where he dressed in precious feather garments and a turquoise mask before setting himself on fire, rising from the pyre as the morning star. Yet another story says that he and his followers set out on the waters towards the east, traveling on a raft of woven serpents. Curiously, this colorful account of the journey is echoed by Maya stories from the Yucatan Peninsula, telling of the arrival of a Mexican warrior named Kukulcán (the Maya equivalent to Quetzalcoatl) who conquered the country. In Yucatan, the archaeological ruins of Chichén Itzá have murals depicting Toltec warriors arriving by sea. Many sculptural forms at Chichén depict military themes in a style that borrows from native Maya prototypes, yet also remains closely identified with the monuments of Toltec Tula.

The archaeological zone of Tula is located on a bluff overlooking the Spanish colonial and modern town, with river bottomlands below. The first archaeological explorations were conducted in 1888 by the Frenchman Desirée Charnay, who noted similarities between Tula's sculpture and those of Chichén Itzá. It was not until the 1940s that the archaeologist Jorge Acosta, following Jimenez Moreno's ethnohistoric investigations, began excavations and restorations at the ceremonial center. Beginning in the 1970s a series of projects directed respectively by Eduardo Matos Moctezuma of INAH, Richard Diehl of the University of Missouri, and Robert Cobean and Guadalupe Mastache of INAH, have disclosed a chronology beginning with villages in the late 1st millennium BC to a larger settlement during the apogee of Teotihuacan, followed by abandonment between AD 700 and 800 before reoccupation by a new group – perhaps the Tolteca-Chichimeca described in the annals. Major developments took place between AD 950 and 1150, when Tula grew to cover 5.4 sq. miles (14 sq. km), with a heterogeneous population estimated between 30,000 and 40,000. An imposing ceremonial center was built and streets were laid out on a grid-like plan, following principles of orientation established at Teotihuacan. The main plaza is flanked by two impressive pyramids with a colonnaded

Tula and Chichén Itzá

23, 24, 25 The Aztecs drew
on ancient artistic themes to
associate themselves with the
great traditions of Mesoamerican
antiquary. Recumbent figures of
ritual attendants (chacmools)
from Chichén Itzá (TOP), the
Toltec capital of Tula (CENTER)
and an Aztec sculpture from
Tenochtitlan (BELOW).

26, 27 OPPOSITE TOP Made in
drum-like segments fitted
together, the colossal warrior
columns feature carefully
sculptured emblems and
accoutrements. OPPOSITE BELOW
Pyramid B at Tula was the seat
of supreme authority at the city,
with grim warrior columns
supporting the roof of the
upper chamber.

walkway linking these monuments to a palace-like building with three contiguous patios. Two ball-courts and the base of a skull rack complete the monumental ensemble. The most fully restored building, Pyramid B, rises in five tiers (ills. 28, 29). Four columnar warriors stand above; other square columns are also carved with warriors, and the remains of circular columns are covered with long feather designs. The sculptured forms were discovered deeply buried inside the pyramid, where they were placed when Tula was violently destroyed. Originally they had supported the roof of a throne-room or place of command akin to the Plumed Serpent Platforms at Teotihuacan, Xochicalco, and the Temple of the Warriors at Chichén Itzá. At Tula the surface of the pyramid was sheathed with painted sculptural reliefs depicting prowling felines, eagles, and coyotes or wolves, all emblems of military societies. Sacrificial themes are repeated on a wall enclosing the northern side of the pyramid precinct, where rows of skeletons intertwine with rattlesnakes, alternating with bands of stepped geometric designs; a crenellation of cloud motifs crowns the wall.

Agricultural themes are not entirely lacking in Tula's sculptural vocabulary, but they are certainly not numerous or varied as in Teotihuacan or Classic Maya art, nor are they as critically important as would be seen in the Aztec sculptural repertoire.

Toltec images affirm the harsh ethos of a warrior aristocracy that sought wealth and power through the conquest of tribute-paying domains. Too little is archaeologically known to be able to speak confidently about the extent of the Toltec "empire." The heartland would have embraced the region around Tula itself, perhaps extending into the nearby Toluca and Tulancingo valleys and parts of the Valley of Mexico. This empire would not have been held as contiguous territory with permanent garrisons and defined borders. Judging from Aztec custom, towns conquered by the Toltecs would have been obliged to pay tribute on a regular basis while keeping their own government and religious cults. The threat of punitive action kept the system operative. The intimidating imagery of Tula does not portray a deep-seated flexible state religion incorporating the cults of diverse communities, and archaeological evidence has not yet pointed to other significant mechanisms for integrating far-flung social groups in a cohesive system of government. It is speculated that a sustained drought may well have precipitated the disintegration of ill-knit polities, opening the way to incoming migrations and political realignments, resulting in internal fissures and the eventual destruction of Tula.

According to the ethnohistoric sources, internal factional disputes of the kind suggested by the story of Quetzalcoatl fractured Tula around the middle of the 12th century. The last Toltec ruler, Huemac, led a large Tolteca-Chichimeca group into the Valley of Mexico, where they established a new settlement near the springs of Chapultepec. Other groups hung on before finally abandoning Tula and moving south to the Valley of Mexico and the Valley of Puebla. The end of Tula came violently. Major buildings were burnt, monuments were overturned, and archaeologists have found skeletal remains of people killed in action. It is not known who wreaked this destruction. Silence descended on the ruins where Toltec chieftains had surveyed their captives, booty, and warriors parading to the sound of war drums, whistles, and fierce songs of triumph.

We shall see that the need to develop adequate mechanisms for integrating a complex empire was likewise to prove a central problem for the Aztecs, whose ancestors at this stage were still tribal nomads in the semi-arid lands far north of the Valley of Mexico.

28 OPPOSITE ABOVE Coatlepantli wall, Tula. Enclosing the north side of Pyramid B, the wall features alternating bands of linked stepped motifs (possibly representing mountains) and repeated rattlesnakes intertwined with skeletal figures. A line of carved stones representing sections of conch shells crowns the wall. A sectional conch was one of Quetzalcoatl's emblems in later Aztec times.

29 OPPOSITE BELOW Frieze of relief panels from Pyramid B at Tula featuring lines of prowling felines and coyotes alternating with lines of eagles devouring blood-offerings. Recessed panels portray frontal views of open-jawed creatures from which a human mask-like face emerges; plumes indicate high status. The form may be an emblem of rulership. The animals of prey were emblems of military societies in Aztec Tenochtitlan.

Migrating tribes: Tepanecs, Chichimecs, Acolhua, and Mexica

In the 13th century, the place that eventually became Tenochtitlan was an unimpressive cluster of marshy islands in Lake Tetzcoco, with willow groves, waving reeds, and nopal cacti growing among upturned rocks. Eagles, herons, ducks, cranes, and many other waterfowl shared this wetland setting with teeming aquatic life. The eastern side of the Valley was sparsely inhabited, as it had been since the collapse of Teotihuacan. To the north, the small towns of Xaltocan and Zumpango stood amid marshes. The western shore of Lake Tetzcoco was by contrast more populated. Atzcapotzalco was the principal town, initially established in the time of Teotihuacan. Subsequently, perhaps during Tula's hegemony, the district was occupied by Tepanec people originally from the Toluca Valley who were to make Atzcapotzalco a powerful city. Near Chapultepec and in southern communities around lakes Chalco and Xochimilco, refugee groups arrived and settled at the time of the Toltec dispersal. This district was economically stable, for it had copious summer rains, abundant freshwater springs, and a tradition of *chinampa* agriculture and hillside farming terraces. The arrival of Toltec groups meant that towns such as Culhuacan, Xico, and Chapultepec would eventually be ruled by lineages tracing an aristocratic descent from that ruined but still prestigious city.

Archaeological excavations have yet to explore this period thoroughly and due to the ongoing growth of Mexico City this may never really be possible. Nevertheless, the lack of major monuments, plus the accounts of pictorial codices and early colonial written histories, indicate that the slow pace of provincial life was not substantially altered after the fall of Tula. The rhythm of these communities was predominantly set by the eternal round of the agricultural cycle, enlivened by the drama of local ritual festivities and the seasonal excitement of small-scale hostilities. This somewhat uneventful pace began to shift, almost imperceptibly at first and then with rising momentum, as new tribal groups began arriving from the north.

Among many groups ranging into the Valley of Mexico during the 13th century, four were destined to play a critical role in the rise of the Aztec empire. Traditional histories of these peoples reflect "official" versions prepared long after the actual events. The migration accounts show how the Aztecs and their neighbors elaborated their own histories by interweaving actual events with legends borrowed from earlier peoples, by inventing mythological episodes and superhuman heroes, in great measure reflecting the longing of primitive incoming peoples for an acceptable "Toltec" ancestry. Despite the elaborations, it is possible to sketch a pattern of migration and the ongoing process of acculturation, as tribal peoples began to settle and assimilate the ways of the older urban populations.

The first major group were the Tepanecs, who have already been mentioned as possibly originating in the Valley of Toluca. The Tepanecs intermarried with peoples of the western Valley of Mexico and eventually settled in Atzcapotzalco, Tlacopan, and nearby towns. The Chichimecs (a name also generically applied to all the immigrant groups) are said to have been led by the chieftain Xolotl, who may be a semi-legendary personification of various tribal leaders whose names appear in different histories. The Acolhua were the third

30 Chichimec migrants arrive in Acolhuacan. A founding couple settle in a cave while other personages hunt in the surrounding landscape. From the Mapa Quinatzin.

migrant contingent, affiliated with the Chichimecs, who moved into the eastern side of the basin. By the time the fourth and last major group arrived toward the middle of the 13th century, few lands remained unclaimed. This group, the Mexica, was itself a mixture of various others. They also intermarried with established communities before settling on the islands that became Tenochtitlan. The interactions of all these incoming peoples with the older, settled communities began to alter the character of life in the Valley – slowly at first during the 14th century, but then with an increasing momentum that set the stage for the dynamic changes that were to follow in the 15th century.

The arrival of the Chichimecs and Acolhua is chronicled in pictorial manuscripts such as the Codex Xolotl, the Mapa Quinatzin, and the Codex Aubin, as well as in written histories by Fernando de Alva Ixtlilxóchitl, Fray Diego Durán, the Codex Chimalpopoca, and others (ill. 30). The pictorial manuscripts – called codices – and the written texts are closely related, for they draw on older, lost codices and oral histories. They portray a simplified, dramatic version of what was actually a complex process of adjustment by semi-civilized tribes to the urbanized culture of the Valley. The initial page of the Codex Xolotl shows the Chichimecs approaching the Valley, scouting for land to settle (ill. 31).[6]

31 The Codex Xolotl narrates Acolhuacan history. The lake system is schematically represented below, with the chieftain Xolotl in a cave at Tenayuca. Nopaltzin is seated upon the hill Tetzcotzingo (above center), overlooking the hills of the Acolhuacan Crescent.

They dressed in hides, carried bows and arrows, and other implements for survival in the desert. The chieftain Xolotl is depicted establishing a base at the site of Tenayuca in the northwest of the Valley, where a large dual pyramid would later be built. The codex continues with an account of colonization on the eastern side, as Xolotl's son Nopaltzin set out from Tenayuca on a reconnaissance. He viewed the unclaimed landscape from the foothills of Mt Tlaloc, and climbed the summit to survey the entire region. The Hill of Tetzcotzingo, later to become an important ritual place, is well drawn as a significant landmark. Following Nopaltzin's favorable report, incoming bands of Acolhua, linked to the Chichimecs, were directed to this district. The Mapa Quinatzin and Codex Aubin depict them as they settled in rock shelters and other places along the foothills and piedmont. These first settlements would become the important towns Oxtoticpac, Tzinacanoztoc, Coatlinchan, and Huexotla. Tetzcoco, later the Acolhua capital, may have existed as a primitive lakeshore settlement prior to these arrivals. Nopaltzin's son Tlohtzin was eventually made ruler of this eastern district and established his seat at the Hill of Tetzcotzingo. By the 1420s Tlohtzin's son Quinatzin moved the center of government to Tetzcoco, the better to have access to the lake and easier transportation by water.

However rudimentary their economy, the early settlers must not be imagined in terms of simple hunting and gathering bands. The actions of Xolotl and Nopaltzin suggest the existence of a social order of at least a tribal level. Xolotl played a part of considerable authority in "assigning" different groups to specific areas of settlement. He also extended his influence to the north and formed alliances by arranging marriages between leading Chichimec families and those of neighboring towns. It is likely that the urban peoples quickly appraised the newcomers' warrior skills and enlisted their support in the small-scale feuds and raids endemic in the Valley. Economic power was also increasingly vested in the Chichimec and Acolhua chieftains, a significant step away from the economic egalitarianism of bands or even tribal societies. A manifestation of this tendency was the construction of special hunting enclosures in the foothills of Mt Tlaloc. The Codex Xolotl depicts these enclosures with Xolotl and Nopaltzin, showing how these areas were supplied with rabbits and other game obtained as tribute from communities to the north and east. Knowledge of agriculture and the acquisition of farming lands were another step to economic privilege and security. The Chichimecs and Acolhua had basic knowledge of farming when they arrived in the Valley, but this was far from the specialized practices of *chinampa* and terrace farming. The Codex Xolotl depicts the agricultural zones of the southern district where Chalco, Atenco, and other towns are shown with canals and canoes representing *chinampa* plantations. When Nopaltzin married a lady from Chalco, his son Tlohtzin was largely brought up in that town, where he learned about intensive horticultural cultivation. Upon inheriting the authority vested in his father, Tlohtzin proclaimed his intention of converting the still semi–civilized Chichimecs and Acolhua into a settled farming people:

> Once sworn in, and having received the empire, Tlohtzin placed special care in the cultivation of the land. And since he had lived for the most part in the province of Chalco since the time of his grandfather Xolotl, and what with the communication that he had there with the Toltecs and Chalcoans (his mother was a lady native to these peoples), he saw how it was that corn and the other seeds and vegetables were necessary for human sustenance. And he had especially learned from Texpoyo Achicauhtli, who had his house and family on the hill of Xico; Texpoyo had been his guide and teacher, and among the things that he had taught him was the way to cultivate the land. And, as a person habituated to this, he now gave order that everywhere the land should be cultivated and worked. And even though many Chichimecs thought that this was a convenient thing and they put it into effect, others who were still in the backwardness of their ancestors left for the hills of Metztitlán and Tototepec ... and from that time on the land began to be cultivated everywhere, and the corn was sown and harvested, and other seeds and vegetables, and cotton in the warm country for their clothing.[7]

The claiming of a large and unsettled territory with varied natural resources; the pattern of alliances and intermarriage with townspeople; the adoption of agriculture and its ancient religious cults; the tendency to consolidate authority and economic power in the hands of a governing elite; and the tendency of that elite to adopt the language and culture of the city populations, all formed part of a conscious movement during the 13th and 14th centuries that established the base of a new social order from which the future state of Acolhuacan with its principal city Tetzcoco began to evolve.

The Mexica

Of all the migrant groups, the early history of the Mexica is known in greatest detail. The legends about them before they founded Tenochtitlan are recounted in Mexican schoolbooks today. The orthodox version of their migration was composed from older written and pictorial sources, and is often expressed in metaphoric terms. Several scholars regard the Mexica migration as a composite of stories assembled by a small tribe after arriving and intermarrying in the Valley of Mexico, since many motifs appear to have had a long earlier history among the urban peoples.[8] Yet there can be no doubt that the legend was thought of as historical fact by the inhabitants of Tenochtitlan, just as the epic of Troy, the legendary travels of Aeneas, and the story of the founding of Rome were true historic events to the Roman population. The following outline will show how this legendary history took root in the Mexica collective imagination, coloring their beliefs, religious rites, and eventually affecting the fabric of their empire.

According to oral histories recorded by Fray Diego Durán late in the 16th century, the ancestors of the tribe had originally emerged from caves or springs in the time of genesis.[9] This is a version of a virtually universal motif in Mesoamerican mythology, alluding to the birth of people from the earth, the primordial mother of things. Perhaps during the early 12th century the tribe departed from its ancestral homeland, described as an island within a lagoon somewhere to the north. The name of this place was Aztlán, "place of cranes," from which the archaic name *Aztec* was taken. It was not until later during the migration that these peoples assumed the name Mexica by which they were known by the Spaniards. The original term "Aztec" reappeared again in scholarly studies of the 18th and 19th centuries, and has become accepted as a generic if somewhat unsatisfactory name for the peoples of the Valley of Mexico at the time of the Spanish Conquest.

The geographical location of Aztlán was much debated among modern scholars, as it was among the Mexica themselves by the middle of the 15th century. Some researchers thought that Aztlán night correspond with one of several lakes in Michoacán, Jalisco, or Guanajuato states. Others suggested the coastal lagoon named Mexcaltitlan on the distant Pacific coast of Nayarit, where an island-town preserves its aboriginal four-quarter layout.

The quest to find the original Aztlán was actually begun by Motecuhzoma I who ruled Tenochtitlan from 1440 to 1469. By that time, the location of the original Mexica homeland was a mythic memory, but as the empire began to

32 The Aztec migration begins from the
legendary island of Aztlan (left), led by a
priest carrying an effigy of the deified hero
Huitzilopochtli (right). From the Codex Boturini.

expand and its rulers became actively engaged in strengthening a collective
sense of identity, the notion of finding a place of origin appears to have assumed
a special significance. Motecuhzoma I despatched an unusual expedition, said to
consist of some 60 priests and shamanistic mediums. They traveled north
beyond the ruins of Tula. Diego Durán describes this odd journey to a location
said to be the birthplace of their deified ancestral hero, Huitzilopochtli. The
delegation was met by a supernatural being who magically transformed everyone into birds and other winged beasts. In this guise they flew to Aztlán where
they resumed human form, and were greeted in Nahuatl by kinsmen paddling in
canoes. The adventure continues as a "perilous journey" describing how having
arrived in Aztlán, the Mexica emissaries were taken to an aged man, said to be
related to Huitzilopochtli. After a series of questions, this guide took them on
yet another journey full of dangerous trials. During the travels he revealed his
magical powers, and scolded the Mexica for their luxurious life in Tenochtitlan.
At last they were brought into the presence of Huitzilopochtli's ancient mother,
to whom they offered rich presents and recounted the history of their successful
and powerful city-state in the Valley of Mexico. But she replied with a dire
prophesy, to the effect that they would be conquered one day just as they had
conquered others. With this oracular pronouncement the visitors returned with
a report to Motecuhzoma I. In this magical adventure, Aztlán emerges as a
mythic location, not an actual geographical place.

According to the migration legend it was not until after leaving their homeland
that the original tribe was joined by a second group calling themselves "Mexica."
The legend says that it was Huitzilopochtli – appearing at this time as living
chieftain who later became the deified hero – who ordered the two groups to
share the name Mexica and to carry the equipment of nomadic peoples: bows,
arrows, and gathering-nets. The consolidated tribe continued wandering across
the tablelands and mountain ranges, settling in favorable places for as long as 20
years before moving on to newer locations. They knew basic farming skills and
raised maize, beans, amaranth, chia, chiles, squash, and tomatoes. It is noted that

they even built rudimentary temples and ballcourts at longer stopping-places, yet they always moved on, urged it was said, by a vision of destiny conveyed post-humously by Huitzilopochtli through priestly mediums:

> We shall proceed to establish ourselves and settle down, and we shall conquer all peoples of the universe; and I tell you in all truth that I will make you lords and kings of all that is in the world; and when you become rulers, you shall have countless and infinite numbers of vassals, who will pay tribute to you and shall give you innumerable and most fine precious stones, gold, quetzal feathers, emeralds, coral, and amethysts, and you shall dress most finely in these; you shall also have many kinds of feathers, the blue cotinga, the red flamingo, the *tzinitzian* and all the beautiful feathers, and multicolored cacao and cotton; and all this you shall see, since this is in truth my task, and for this have I been sent here.[10]

Such curiously "imperial" prophesies, supposedly from the deified hero, were certainly added to official Mexica history by chroniclers from Tenochtitlan during the 15th century. The migrating Mexica also knew of the Mesoamerican ritual calendar, for they marked the passage of every 52 years (a "century" in this system of time-counting) with ceremonies of renewal. The migration legend describes a route of travel leading to two important places: Culhuacan, "Curved Mountain," and Chicomoztoc, "Seven Caves." The exact location of these places remains unclear, although some scholars agree that they lie to the north-east of the Valley of Mexico (the mountain Culhuacan is not to be confused with the town Culhuacan in the Valley of Mexico). Mount Culhuacan of the migration story may perhaps be a height near the present town of San Isidro Culhuacan, and the location of Chicomoztoc may be nearby to the east. The scholar Paul Kirchhoff argued effectively that the seven caves were actually a feature of the curved mountain Culhuacan.[11] The early Spanish colonial pictorial manuscript Historia Tolteca-Chichimeca records that earlier migratory groups had named Chicomoztoc-Culhuacan, before journeying to settle in the Valley of Puebla. A famous page from the Historia depicts Culhuacan-Chicomoztoc as a mountain with its curved top and interior womb-like caves, representing the widespread notion of the sacred mountain as a source of life (pl. III).

The next episode in the narrative opens with tribal quarrels. A dissident faction split from the main body, followed by a more serious division when Huitzilopochtli's "sister" Malinalxóchitl also abandoned the tribe with her people. This faction continued into the forested sierra some 50 miles (80 km) southwest of the Valley of Mexico where they founded the town Malinalco – a place that appears again in the 15th-century history of Mexica imperial expansion, and which we will later encounter as an important archaeological site. The third internal challenge to the main group developed at Coatepetl, "Serpent Mountain." The dramatic events at Coatepetl are described in mythic terms. The summit was crowned by an earth-shrine kept by a priestess, Coatlicue, "Serpent Skirt" (see frontispiece), also a metaphoric name for the earth itself. Coatlicue is described as an aged woman, alluding to the antiquity of the religious worship of the earth. She is described as the mother of a powerful

33 Mt Coatepetl (Serpent Mountain) is regarded by Mexica-Aztec chieftains. Tenoch, chieftain of the Mexica, is named by his glyph *tetl* (rock) and *nochtli* (prickly-pear cactus). His name was also given to Tenochtitlan.

woman, Coyolxauhqui, "Painted with Bells," and of a host of others known as the Centzon Huiztnaua, the "Four Hundred Huiztnaua." One day while Coatlicue was sweeping the shrine at the mountaintop, she was magically impregnated by a ball of feathers that fell from the sky. This was the supernatural conception of Huitzilopochtli. We must remember that although Huitzilopochtli had already appeared in the migration legend as an ancestral leader, this episode is not intended to follow chronological logic. Its purpose is to describe Huitzilopochtli as a supernatural warrior. Upon learning of Coatlicue's impregnation, the outraged daughter Coyolxauhqui and her Four Hundred siblings gathered on the plain below in order to attack the mountain and kill their dishonored mother. However, one of them ran ahead to inform Huitzilopochtli, still within Coatlicue's womb, of the impending assault. As the enemy charged up the mountain, Huitzilopochtli was suddenly born as a fully armed and invincible warrior. Wielding a *xiuhcoatl*, "Fire Serpent" (a ray of the sun), he dispatched Coyolxauhqui, whose dismembered body rolled down the slope, and then scattered the Four Hundred in all directions.

At Tenochtitlan, the Great Pyramid with Huitzilopochtli's shrine would be named Coatepetl, in commemoration of this mythic battle. An imposing sculpture of Coyolxauhqui was placed at the foot of the pyramid stairs on the Huitzilopochtli side of the building (ills. 96–98). The most sacred monument of Tenochtitlan thus replicated the mythical scene of Huitzilopochtli's triumph. All in all, this episode stands independently in the quasi-historical migration legend, and appears have been adapted by the Mexica from the formula of older legend. We have seen at Xochicalco and Teotihuacan how serpent imagery is displayed on pyramid platforms that were seats of authority, a custom also traceable at Tula, Chichén Itzá, and at Tenayuca in the Valley of Mexico, suggesting a long prior history of Coatepetl in Mesoamerica.

The migration story continues as the Mexica made their way to Tula, where they camped in the ruins before continuing to the Valley of Mexico. Traveling down the west side of Lake Tetzcoco, they stopped briefly at Tenayuca and passed Atzcapotzalco to arrive at Chapultepec, where they settled near the springs at the base of the hill. The following period of about 25 years (45 years by some accounts) was critical for the newcomers. Unlike the Chichimec-Acolhua who had settled on unclaimed land, and unlike the earlier Tepanecs who inter-married and became integrated in the town of Atzcapotzalco, the Mexica faced a hostile reception. The first threat came from a distant relative, Copil, "son" (a descendant) of Huitzilopochtli's dissident "sister" Malinalxóchitl described in the migration story as the founder of Malinalco. Based at Malinalco, the chief-tain Copil conspired with the lakeshore towns to throw out the newcomers. In a battle that followed, the Mexica were driven from Chapultepec, although Copil was killed. Legend says that his heart was cut out and thrown across the water to land on the island where Tenochtitlan would later be founded.

At this point the migration myth enters the realm of actual history. Returning to Chapultepec, the Mexica faced another threat, this time from a coalition led by the Tepanecs of Atzcapotzalco and supported by neighboring Culhuacan. The coalition aimed to regain control of the Chapultepec springs, a coveted resource located between the territories of the two communities. The Mexica were decisively defeated and the refugees dispersed into the countryside and nearby marshes while their leader was taken to Culhuacan to be sacrificed. Eventually a principal group of Mexica refugees made their way to Culhuacan to beg protection of its rulers. The council of Culhuacan decided to grant the supplicants some land at Tizaapan, an inhospitable lava-flow near today's University City. Displaying courage and endurance, and drawing on their long experience in hunting and gathering, the Mexica proceeded to make the best of the unlikely environment. Small plots for cultivation were also built among the crags, and gradually the people were allowed to trade in nearby Culhuacan.

As a degree of acceptance grew, courtship and intermarriage followed. The Mexica soon began styling themselves "Culhua-Mexica" and by virtue of newly established bonds of kinship, they also began to regard themselves in some measure as "Toltec" descendants. After all, Culhuacan was a town where Toltec refugees had settled after the fall of Tula. The Mexica position in Cul-huacan was strengthened when they took part as allies in a small-scale war against neighboring Xochimilco. In an ensuing battle along the lakeshore the Mexica warriors saved the day, and as proof of their triumph they presented the Culhua ruler with a pile of ears cut from Xochimilco warriors. The Mexica boasted of their triumph in the marketplace. Their insolence failed to impress the Culhua aristocrats, who viewed their neighbors as barbarous inferiors and remained uneasy of their warlike disposition.

As discontent arose, the Mexica precipitated their own violent departure. Obeying the promptings of Huitzilopochtli's priests, they approached Achito-metl, one of the Culhua magnates, asking for his beautiful daughter as their "sovereign" and "wife of Huitzilopochtli." Not understanding the implica-tions of this request, Achitometl acceded to the honor; his daughter went to Tizaapan, where she was splendidly arrayed and sacrificed. The body was flayed and a priest donned her skin in an ancient agricultural rite symbolizing the renewal of life. The unsuspecting chieftain Achitometl, invited to the con-cluding festivities, recognized the remains of his daughter worn by the priest.

The outraged Culhua took arms immediately and were joined by others; in a wild melee of javelins and arrows, the Mexica were driven into the brackish swamps of Lake Tetzcoco. Next day they made their way in canoes and makeshift rafts across the water to the uninhabited islands.

Although this episode reads as an historical event in the Mexica migration, it may also be a way of expressing the tribe's intention to become an agricultural people through ceremonial marriage with a woman who figured as a symbolic personification of an "earth mother" deity. A similar motif is expressed by the stories of Xolotl's Chichimec and Acolhua warriors marrying noble women who brought knowledge of cultivation from the old *chinampa* towns. Anthropologist Susan Gillespie has noted that the women in these stories are all connected to agricultural fertility – and in the case of Achitometl's daughter, to a female deity representing the earth's regenerative powers.[12]

The founding of Tenochtitlan

When the Mexica refugees arrived on the island in Lake Tetzcoco, one of Huitzilopochtli's priests is said to have had a supernatural vision of the ancestral hero, reminding him that Copil's heart had been thrown onto the island, and that this sacred spot would be marked by a nopal cactus upon which an eagle would be perching. This would be Huitzilopochtli's sacred sign for the wandering tribe to found their city. The migration story concludes by telling how the Mexica spread out into the reeds the following morning and saw the eagle on the cactus. They built a rude earthen platform with a reed hut as the shrine of Huitzilopochtli. This humble structure was the precursor of the Great Pyramid of Tenochtitlan, which continued to mark the foundation-place. Other sacred signs were said to have been witnessed, such as springs of

34 Rear of the Teocalli Stone (Pyramid of Sacred War) depicting the founding vision of Tenochtitlan. The water-goddess lies below, representing Lake Tetzcoco, with a rock *tetl* in her middle; the cactus *nochtli* rises with an eagle screaming the war-cry *atl-tlachinolli*, "water" (deluge), "fire" (conflagration).

59

blue and red water. In fact, all of these signs were prefigured in foundation myths of earlier peoples. The Mexica thus claimed the island as their permanent home. The name Tenochtitlan refers to *tetl*, "rock," *nochtli*, "prickly-pear cactus," and *tlan*, the locative suffix. These happenings took place in the year 2 House (1325 by some reckonings, 1345 by others). Following prescribed custom, the new settlement was laid out in four districts as the community began to organize.

The founding of Tenochtitlan and the sister-community Tlatelolco on the northern side of the marshy island brings the long migration story to a close. The Mexica were now in their place of permanent residence. Unlike the Tepanecs, they had not become assimilated in an older city. Unlike the Chichimec-Acolhua, they had not found a large tract of unclaimed land upon which to settle. The arrival of the Mexica in the Valley had been marked by battles and displacements. Through adverse fortune they came to rest on the islands of a brackish lagoon, where agricultural prospects were meagre, building materials were lacking, and where they were surrounded by indifferent or hostile neighbors. Remarkably, they had the determination to begin anew. These hard circumstances were to have a profound effect on subsequent attitudes and actions of the Mexica.

There were some positive features of the island. Birds, fish, and many edible forms of aquatic life were abundant. Communication and transport by canoe to other lakeshore cities could be achieved with minimal effort – an advantage in a land without wheeled vehicles or beasts of burden. And the islands were strategically placed between three important communities – Culhuacan to the south, Atzcapotzalco to the west, and several towns along the eastern side of Lake Tetzcoco. Tentatively at first, and then with increasing assurance, the Mexica strengthened their position. A council was held among elders who debated the possibility of offering the tribe as tributaries to one of their powerful neighbors in exchange for wood, stone, and other supplies to build a permanent city. This notion was dropped in view of their neighbors' scorn and their own concern to avoid ill-treatment. As it turned out, it was enterprising Mexica women who strengthened the economy by carrying fresh fish, frogs, birds, and various greens gathered from the lake, to trade at weekly markets around the lakeshore towns. Markets were also established in Tenochtitlan and Tlatelolco, as described by the 16th-century historian Fray Diego Durán:

> They began to fill their city with people from neighboring towns and to take them in marriage. In this way they won over the people of Tetzcoco and others. They treated travelers and strangers well, they invited merchants to come to the markets of Mexico with their goods, for such commerce always enriches a city (and this same Aztec nation today has this quality; for to towns where a man is well received and flattered and given to eat and drink he will go willingly, especially if he sees inviting faces, which is what most appeals to him).[13]

These modest beginnings laid the foundation of what eventually became a far-reaching trading network. Efforts were also made to construct a *chinampa* system. This was a long-term, laborious task and was only of high agricultural value on the freshwater (western) side of the island. The problem of acquiring agricultural land became all too apparent, and was to remain a critical concern. Even at the time of the Spanish Conquest the *chinampas* of Tenochtitlan and Tlatelolco were far from meeting the needs of the populous cities. Military conquest was to be the final means of acquiring productive land, but it was not until later that such action could be taken.

Transformation of social organization

Changes in social organization began to take place as the Mexica community settled. At the time of Tenochtitlan's foundation the Mexica were led in part by the chieftain Tenoch. He is depicted with others on the opening page of the Codex Mendoza (pl. IV), with his name-glyph *tetl*, "rock," and *nochtli*, "nopal cactus." Derived from the chieftain's name, the place-sign of Tenochtitlan is painted in the center of the page with the eagle perched on the cactus. The status of Tenoch as *tlatoani*, "speaker" or "commander," is indicated by the speech-scroll in front of his mouth.

The foundation depicted in the Codex Mendoza also alludes to the well-known four-part division of Tenochtitlan. Yet some ethnohistoric sources also offer indications of an old dual system of social organization. Rudolph Van Zantwijk noted that the eagle, cactus, and rock emblem on the Mendoza foundation-page implies a dual division. The eagle is symbolically associated with the sky, the ascending sun, and the direction east; the eagle was also an emblem of Huitzilopochtli and his earthly representative, the *tlatoani* who commanded the warriors in offensive actions and who conducted the external relations of the community. Below, the stone and cactus and the lake waters from which they arise carry connotations of the earth and regeneration; correspondingly, this cosmological stratum was associated with a leader in the sphere of agriculture, defensive activities, and the internal affairs of the community. In addition, Van Zantwijk noted the existence of two tribal *calpullis*, "clans," respectively associated with the *tlacochcalco*, "spear house," the (male) seat of military command, and *cihuatecpan*, "female place of command"; and he speculated that the principal founding chief Tenoch and another chieftain, Aatlmexitin, respectively belonged to these *calpullis*. The possibility of an old dual system of social organization, ceremonialism, and political and economic life at Tenochtitlan has been further explored by Marshall Becker.

Becker explains that such dual arrangements are widespread in the Americas and are known as moiety systems (from the French *moitié*, half). As societies grow in complexity, moieties are obliged to assume broader functions. Becker points out that among the 14th-century lakeshore towns of the Valley of Mexico, with growing ethnic diversity, increasing specialization of military, religious, and economic activities, increasingly marked social stratifications, and the need to negotiate a variety of inter-city relationships, "political" moieties were in the process of evolving. As we shall see in the following pages, relationships between the *tlatoani*, "commander" as chief of external affairs, and the *cihuacoatl*, "woman-serpent," the internal affairs chief, would undergo important changes as the Aztec empire developed between the early 15th and early 16th centuries. The *tlatoani* Tenoch had been elected to office by a council of *calpulli* elders, and he governed as external affairs chief in continual consultation with this group. An internal affairs chief, holding the title *cihuacoatl*, was elected in similar fashion. But by the time Tenoch died some 25 years after the foundation, the office of the external affairs chief was gaining in prestige and power in response to the need to manage the growing degree of interaction between the residents of the city and external populations and resources. Decision-making began to be streamlined from an old tribal council of elders to a dominant individual leader, the elders becoming his counselors. At this point, the internal affairs chief still retained important autonomous functions.

After the funeral of Tenoch, a Mexica delegation was sent to their former enemies, the Culhua. During the brief time when the Mexica had been allowed by the lords of Culhuacan to reside in the lava-beds of Tizaapan, a degree of intermarriage had taken place between the two communities. Now the Mexica hoped that despite tensions incurred when they were expelled, the blood-ties that bound some of their people with the Culhua would affirm closer ties with this important town of the Valley. The Culhua aristocracy, it will be remembered, held a prestigious lineage claiming Toltec descent. A Mexica delegation approached the Culhua lords with a petition to ask for Acamapichtli to become *tlatoani* of Tenochtitlan, as a noble descended from Mexica and Culhua families. The choice of Acamapichtli was astute, for his family also had connections with leading Acolhua families in Coatlinchan on the eastern side of the Valley. Soon thereafter Acamapichtli was ritually invested as *tlatoani* of Tenochtitlan, assuming the duties of a dominant external affairs chief.

By this time the old tribal clans, or *calpullis*, were increasing in size and number, and were becoming closely identified with specific locations. When Tenochtitlan was founded, according to ancient custom each *calpulli* was assigned its own place with its temple and local cult within a four-quarter division of the city. These *calpulli* territories were owned communally; and as horticultural *chinampas* were developed, individual families were assigned hereditary farming rights to particular tracts. The users paid a form of tax or tribute for their farming privileges, and the land could be reassigned if it was neglected or if the user died without heirs. These farmers – *macehualtin* – were the free commonfolk of the nation.

As Mexica leaders began to intermarry with the nobility of neighboring towns, the community became increasingly stratified in terms of socio-economic classes, as was also happening among the Acolhua-Chichimecs east of the lake. The *tlatoani* and the *pipiltin* ("nobles") possessed lands or the income from lands, owned outright or captured in war. This gave them a basis of economic power independent from the old tribal *calpullis*. In the early years of Tenochtitlan, exclusive private control of land was hardly established; but as the practice of war began to increase, the acquisition of land beyond the island was to become a principal reward for the rising warrior class, and a dominant factor in the changing economy. Thus, during the latter half of the 14th century new forms of social organization and sources of wealth were evolving.

3 · Birth of an Empire

The Tepanec expansion

In the years after Acamapichtli became *tlatoani*, Tenochtitlan was subordinated to the old Tepanec capital Atzcapotzalco, where an extraordinary man rose to power in 1371. Tezozomoc was a ruthless genius of political intrigue and skill as a warrior commander, who established the first state-like society in the Valley of Mexico since the collapse of Teotihuacan 700 years before. Tezozomoc was destined to rule 55 years. When he died in 1426, the towns paying tribute to Atzcapotzalco included many beyond the Valley to the north, south, and west. Tezozomoc's shifting alliances, dynastic relationships, military campaigns, and ceaseless intrigues are chronicled by Diego Durán, Fernando de Alva Ixtlilxóchitl, Alvarado Tezozomoc, and Domingo Chimalpahín, each writing from his own perspective. Their narratives, based on native oral histories and pictorial manuscripts, portray Tezozomoc as a shrewd military strategist who also made effective use of flattery, bribery, assassination, and treachery in a career worthy of a Renaissance tyrant. Here, no less than in Renaissance Italy, the pragmatic aims of politics were never confused with idealism, much less with morality. But the ruler's accomplishments and fortunes were also interwoven with the changing life of a civilization. From the perspective of the Mexica and the Acolhua, the expansion of the Tepanec empire was a critical stage in an experience that was to propel them from subservient status into conquering states, with concomitant developments in the systems of law, administration, economy, religion, and military organization.

The political events described retrospectively by the early Spanish colonial historians provide a framework from which to outline this process of cultural transformation. During Acamapichtli's rule the Mexica were obliged to pay tribute to Tezozomoc in Atzcapotzalco. One form of tribute was to send levies for his army. The Mexica thus participated in a series of campaigns under Tepanec command. Eventually they were allowed by the Tepanecs to wage war on their own. In this way the Mexica subordinated several *chinampa* towns in the Xochimilco area and demanded tribute on a regular basis, thus partially solving their own lack of cultivated land. Other expeditions were carried out in conjunction with the Tepanecs as far south as Cuauhnahuac (Cuernavaca), west into the Toluca Valley, and also into old Toltec lands to the northwest. A war was begun with Chalco that was to persist intermittently for two generations. This state of affairs continued when Acamapichtli's son Huitzilihuitl became *tlatoani* of Tenochtitlan in 1396. Following tradition this ruler was elected by the council of elders, for authority was never automatically passed from father to son. Huitzilihuitl married one of Tezozomoc's granddaughters, thereby ensuring a privileged place for the Mexica among the Tepanec subordinates. Continuing to participate in Tepanec conquests, they fought in a major campaign against Xaltocan, for which they were awarded significant tracts of land. Another expeditionary force was sent to Cuauhtinchan in the Valley of Puebla, and yet another war pitted them against the Acolhua of Tetzcoco.

Tezozomoc's ambition to conquer Tetzcoco was partly provoked by injudicious claims made by the new Tetzcocan ruler, Ixtlilxóchitl, a descendant of the Chichimec chieftains Xolotl and Nopaltzin. Ixtlilxóchitl had married a princess of Tenochtitlan, a daughter of the future Mexica *tlatoani* Chimalpopoca. Ixtlilxóchitl rashly proclaimed himself "Lord of the Chichimecs," and urged the Mexica to join him against the despotic Tezozomoc. But when Chimalpopoca became *tlatoani* of Tenochtitlan in 1417, he wisely chose to remain subordinated to Atzcapotzalco. Political intrigues and sharp military actions took place, in which Ixtlilxóchitl at first almost succeeded in besieging Atzcapotzalco; but the Mexica-Tepanec relationship stood firm and in 1418 Ixtlilxóchitl's warriors were compelled to retreat and abandon Tetzcoco itself. Ixtlilxóchitl fled, and was trapped in a ravine in the foothills of Mt Tlaloc and killed. His violent end was watched by his young son Netzahualcoyotl from a hiding-place in a tree. Netzahualcoyotl escaped into the mountains, destined to become one of the most famous men in all of ancient Mexico (pl. XI). In the debacle Tetzcoco was captured and awarded to the Mexica as a tributary city. By 1426 the Mexica had thus risen from tributary status to the *de facto* allies of Atzcapotzalco, for they were now tribute-gatherers in their own right and serious contenders for power.

The turning point

A decisive turning point in the relationship between Tenochtitlan and Atzcapotzalco was reached that same year, 1426. The aged Tezozomoc died and his son Maxtla assumed authority after murdering a rival brother. The outcome of this intrigue and power struggle in Atzcapotzalco soon reached Tenochtitlan. Maxtla dispatched a force of warriors to assassinate the Mexica *tlatoani* Chimalpopoca. Guards rushed in with the alarm of their approach. The royal Mexica party ran to the lakeside landing to make a desperate escape by canoe. They were pursued, overtaken, and killed on the open water. In the fearful shock of Chimalpopoca's death and the instability that followed, a new ruler, Itzcoatl, was quickly elected in Tenochtitlan. This able warrior was supported by Motecuhzoma Ihuilcamina, a seasoned commander who himself would be *tlatoani* one day, and by his younger brother Tlacaelel, an audacious warrior and strategist whose statecraft would match Tezozomoc's model. These three hard-thinking men of action saw the opportunity to throw off their vassalage to Tepanec Atzcapotzalco and establish Tenochtitlan as an unrivalled power.

Public speeches were made and tensions grew as cautious representatives of the Mexica population voiced fears about the dangerous Tepanecs. Tenochtitlan was blockaded by Tepanec warriors at the causeways into the city, and Atzcapotzalco was placed on a warlike footing. Lacking the diplomatic subtlety and intelligence of his father Tezozomoc, and hampered by a volatile temper,

I José María Velasco, *The Valley of Mexico*, 1877, detail. In the late 19th century the Valley still appeared much as it was when Aztec Tenochtitlan flourished where downtown Mexico City is today. The long line of the causeway that linked Tenochtitlan to the hill Tepeyac is clearly seen. In early Spanish colonial times, Tepeyac became the site of the Virgin of Guadalupe shrine. The Ajusco mountains are on the horizon with the snowcapped cone of Popocatepetl to the extreme left. Most of this section of the Valley is now covered by the metropolis of some 20,000,000 people.

II Reconstruction of the central ritual precinct in Tenochtitlan, by Stuart and Scott Gentling. The tzompantli skull rack rises in front of the dual Great Pyramid. The temple of Tlaloc, devoted to rain and fertility, stands on the (north) side of the pyramid symbolizing the mountain of sustenance. The temple of Huitzilopochtli, devoted to the Mexica deified warrior-hero, stands on the (south) side representing Coatepetl "Serpent-Mountain", the mythical mountain of victory. Controversy continues to surround the exact placement and appearance of most of the buildings within the spreading enclosure. Only the Great Pyramid foundations and those of adjacent structures in the immediate vicinity have been excavated in downtown Mexico City. This view admirably captures the character of the spacious, sunlit precinct and the scale of its fearsome monuments.

III OVERLEAF LEFT The Historia Tolteca-
Chichimeca depicts the curved peak of the
cactus-covered hill, Culhuacan, and the
seven caves of Chicomoztoc as the symbolic
womb of the mountain. Seven tribes are
shown within. A priest strikes the entrance
with his magical staff to summon them into
the outer world.

IV OVERLEAF RIGHT The opening page of the Codex Mendoza
illustrating the legendary founding of Tenochtitlan. The eagle and
cactus rise from a rock in the center, above a shield with arrows or
darts signifying war. The crossed bands and enclosing square
frame represent Lake Tetzcoco. Early Aztec tribal chieftains are
depicted with their name-hieroglyphs. Below, victories over
Colhuacan (left) and Tenayuca (right) are shown with the sign of
burning temples and their respective place-hieroglyphs. Year-signs
surround the composition, and Spanish glosses also identify the
names of people and places.

tenochtitlan

colhuacan. pueblo.   tenayucan. pueblo.

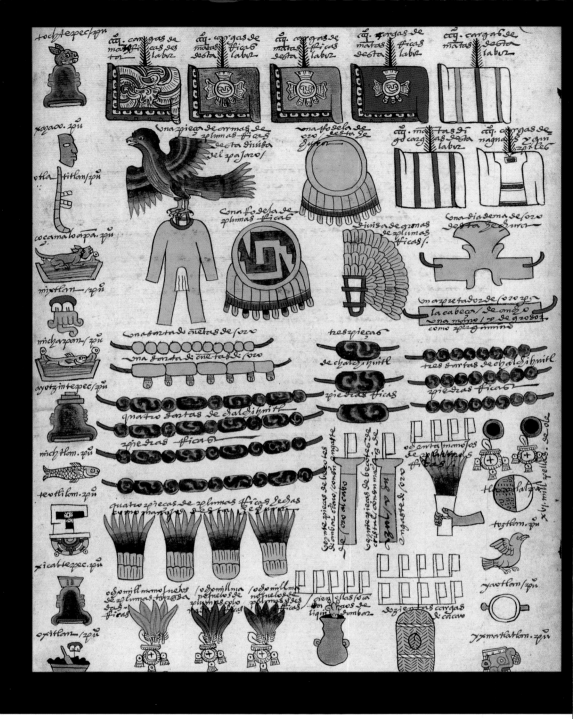

V A page from the Codex Mendoza tribute-list, depicting the place-hieroglyphs of towns – with Spanish glosses – in the column to the left, and the lists of required items of tribute including finely-woven mantles; a military body-suit with a quetzal emblem; shields; gold bead necklaces and other jewelry; jade or greenstone bead necklaces; bunches of colorful feathers; and loads of chocolate beans (cacao).

VI OPPOSITE ABOVE A procession of high-ranking military officers depicted in the Codex Mendoza. Their elaborate attire features back racks holding insignia, shields with heraldic devices, gold, shell, and stone jewelry, and protective body-suits, in addition to obsidian-bladed spears.

VII BELOW LEFT A fan made of feathers, with a butterfly sign in the center. Featherworking was a highly developed art in ancient Mexico, and the rare and colorful feathers were items of luxury trade and tribute. Objects incorporating featherwork included garments, blankets, shields, and emblematic devices displayed on ceremonial occasions. This art rapidly declined after the Spanish Conquest.

VIII BELOW RIGHT Gold casting of a warrior holding emblems of rank and office. Bells dangle from the waist and staff, and the hollow body once held a piece of jade or another valuable stone. Such emblems of authority were personally distributed by the ruler to state officials during coronation rites.

IX RIGHT An effigy of Tlaloc in regal attire, holding a symbolic lighting-bolt and feathered shield. The figure is depicted with a suggestion of Renaissance contrapposto stance, but the symbolic items of dress and jewelry are carefully rendered reflecting Aztec tradition. Such attire is mentioned in Fray Diego Durán's account of seasonal rites calling for rain performed by Aztec rulers at the Mt Tlaloc temple. The figure is depicted in an enclosure surrounded by a crenellated parapet. From the Codex Ixtlilxóchitl, late 16th century.

X ABOVE Tlaloc vessel from an offering in the Great Pyramid of Tenochtitlan, late 15th century. Ritual waterpots with Tlaloc imagery have a long history in Mesoamerica, notably seen in the mural art of Teotihuacan (*c.* 500 AD).

XI RIGHT Netzahualcoyotl, ruler of Tetzcoco, from the late 16th century Codex Ixtlilxóchitl. The figure is depicted with Europeanized features and three-dimensional shading, but the swastika-like "action" pose and meticulous rendering of symbolic attire reflect Prehispanic religious and artistic conventions.

Maxtla targeted the Mexica. In angry outbursts he insisted they renew paying tribute in sign of submission. The crisis spiralled and signs of wavering were seen in Tenochtitlan as the commoners sought compromise, some spokesmen suggesting that the image of Huitzilopochtli should be sent captive to Atzcapotzalco as a symbol of subordination. Deputations crossed between the island and the mainland. The last of these parties was led by Tlacaelel, who succeeded in delivering a warrior's headdress to Maxtla, a traditional declaration of war. Returning after this perilous mission, he encouraged the hesitant Mexica population. A heated discussion ensued. According to the official account, the leading warriors struck a bargain with the commoners: "If we are unsuccessful in our undertaking, we will place ourselves in your hands that our bodies may sustain you, and you may thus take your vengeance and devour us in dirty and broken pots." The people then replied: "And thus we pledge ourselves, if you should succeed in your undertaking, to serve you and pay tribute, and be your laborers and build your houses, and to serve you as our true lords."[1]

At this time a surprising new player entered the scene. Netzahualcoyotl, son of the murdered ruler of Tetzcoco, had fled southeast across the mountains to Huexotzingo in the Valley of Puebla, and returned in 1422 to live with relatives in Tenochtitlan. While in the city he came of age as a warrior and is said to have presented war captives to Tezozomoc himself. For a brief period after Maxtla's accession in Atzcapotzalco, Netzahualcoyotl returned to his ancestral seat in Tetzcoco. Soon enough a delegation from Atzcapotzalco arrived, posing as an embassy but in fact charged by Maxtla to murder Netzahualcoyotl. Their plot was discovered by Netzahualcoyotl's attendants, and for the second time the young prince fled his homeland across the mountains to stay among friends in Huexotzingo. Word soon came to him of Maxtla's assassination of Chimalpopoca and difficulties with the new Mexica *tlatoani* Itzcoatl (Netzahualcoyotl's uncle). When a delegation from Tenochtitlan arrived in Huexotzingo seeking alliance, Netzahualcoyotl immediately seized the opportunity to present his own petition.

Itzcoatl's request for support was successful, and Netzahualcoyotl returned to Tetzcoco at the head of an allied force. A base of operations was established there for the campaign against Atzcapotzalco. Netzahualcoyotl and his Huexotzingo and Tetzcoco formations crossed the lake in a fleet of canoes, to land and march south toward the enemy city. Simultaneously the Mexica from Tenochtitlan, joined by allies from the rebellious Tepanec town of Tlacopan, invested Maxtla's capital from the opposite direction. Other formations joined the force, from Xaltocan and from Tlaxcala in the Valley of Puebla. After 114 days the Atzcapotzalco defenses were breached. According to Fernando de Alva Ixtlilxóchitl, who wrote from the Tetzcocan point of view, Netzahualcoyotl himself led the final assault.[2] Maxtla was dragged from hiding in a sweatbath by his own embittered countrymen and delivered to Netzahualcoyotl.

Then followed a rite that dramatically shows how inseparable rulership, war, and human sacrifice were in ancient Mexican culture. A primary objective of warriors was to capture an enemy in battle and take him for sacrifice. Netzahualcoyotl had a platform built in Atzcapotzalco to perform this ritual of triumph. Victorious warriors were called to assemble in all their panoply. Jaguar warriors wore black-spotted suits and snarling helmets, while eagle warriors wore beaked helmets and feathered suits with talons. Standard-bearers stood among the assembled formations, with wicker racks tied with emblems on their backs – rectangular banners with geometric patterns, great birds with spreading wings, tree-like forms with open flowers set with butter-flies, and other devices designed with colorful feathers. Many held painted shields with heraldic signs – step-frets, concentric circles, stripes, bars, and animal and floral emblems. Commanders were distinguished by ear-plugs, nose-plugs, and lip-plugs of obsidian, jade or crystal. Tetzcocan contingents stood apart from this brilliant array, wearing simple white loincloths and mantles devoid of ornament. Maxtla was brought, stripped of all signs of rank and authority, and held down across a sacrificial block by four attendants. With a blow from an obsidian knife, Netzahualcoyotl struck open Maxtla's chest and tore out the heart, scattering blood to the four directions. The body was then disposed of with the funerary honors accorded a *tlatoani*. On one level, the performance by Netzahualcoyotl may be seen as an expression of personal vengeance and an assertion of his entitlement as the ruler of Tetzcoco, although he did not officially become *tlatoani* until 1431.

The Triple Alliance

The dramatic overthrow of Atzcapotzalco made land and tribute available in quantities hitherto beyond the experience of the victors, and consolidated changes in social and political organization that were already in progress. After the warriors from Huexotzingo and other distant places went home, presumably pleased with plunder, the three cities entered into a formal alliance and divided the Tepanec domains. Tlacopan, the junior associate, assumed control over the western side of the Valley with its old Tepanec towns. Tetzcoco was allotted the eastern basin with its various independent Acolhua and Chichimec communities. Tenochtitlan (together with Tlatelolco) was assigned control of regions to the south and to the north. This distribution in some measure determined the geographical pattern of future expansion. Although detailed information is lacking about the way land was divided within the allied communities, the historian Fernando de Alva Ixtlilxóchitl noted that in Tenochtitlan, Tlacaelel and Motecuhzoma each received ten parcels (units of land), while military commanders of lesser rank each received two, and the *calpullis* each received one parcel for the upkeep of their temples. This information points to a significant change in the economic structure, favoring the rulers and the rising class of warriors, who now found a personal source of prestige, rank, and wealth. As Nigel Davies has pointed out, "Private holdings of land had probably existed previously, apart from those controlled by the ruler himself – but on a relatively modest scale. Now, however, the conquest of Tepanec and other territories radically altered the balance. The proportion that was individually occupied increased out of all proportion."[3]

A course of economic exploitation was set which lasted until the Spanish arrived a hundred years later. By that time, private land tenure was of two basic kinds. First came the largest holdings controlled by the *tlatoani* and a small class of nobles, *pipiltin*, many of whom were directly related to the ruling lineage. These lands were tended by serfs who were legally bound to the soil. The second form of tenure consisted of lands theoretically owned by the rulers, but awarded to leading warriors who held them in a manner similar to the way *calpulli* lands were held by individual families; thus, distinguished warriors were rewarded for their service and in actual practice a warrior's tenure tended to become hereditary. Communal lands were held by royal palaces (*tecpantlalli*) and the temples (*teopantlalli*). The *calpullis* continued to be landholders at the base of the social order. These changes were in progress by the time of the Tepanec war, undoubtedly reflecting economic changes within Atzcapotzalco itself. The success of the allies ensured the growth of a socio-economic organization with war as a principal means of acquiring land and tribute and for exerting social control.

Important transformations were also happening to the functions of leaders in Tenochtitlan. By 1427–28 the external affairs chief attained preeminence as war leader. This responsibility also carried important religious duties in regard to the worship of the nature gods and ancestral heroes. Itzcoatl and Netzahual-coyotl were external affairs leaders in their respective cities. Nevertheless, there is ample evidence pointing to the continuing importance of an internal affairs chief, the *cihuacoatl*. In Tenochtitlan this post was occupied by Tlacaelel, brother of the future *tlatoani* Motecuhzoma I. Marshall Becker describes this office, noting that as internal affairs chief the *cihuacoatl* rarely left the city. He served primarily as a domestic counselor, governing the city especially when the *tlatoani* was away at war; he attended to visiting dignitaries, organized the complex ritual cycle, and acted as judge in matters of crimes by high-ranking people. Dual leadership between external and internal chiefs was not simply a sharing of power, because the roles were distinct in function and reciprocal in operation. In reality, the divisions of leadership were not always so strictly defined, for the *cihuacoatl* could also act as a chief counselor in political strat-egy and in matters of war. This ambiguity is also manifested in the religious sphere by the identity and attributes of the complex female deity also named Cihuacoatl. Historian of religions Kay Read notes that her attributes were linked primarily to the earth, agriculture, and parturition, and yet also to war-riors and conquest. Read comments that the political office of *cihuacoatl* remained strongly represented during the long tenure of Tlacaelel; but the power of the internal affairs chief appears to have diminished after the death of this highly influential and forceful personality. When Motecuhzoma II assumed power in 1502, the office of *tlatoani* was expanded and elevated, while the *cihuacoatl's* position was reduced from that of a respected strategist and co-ruler to that of a subordinate to whom tasks were delegated. By the time of Cortés' arrival, Motecuhzoma II had all but assumed the functions of a tyrant wielding both inside and outside powers. This is why the Spanish regarded him as an absolute king.

Without the checks exerted by traditional forms of communal government, the warrior rulers began to conduct ever more far-reaching campaigns. The pursuit of war, with its emphasis on discipline and the display of force, discouraged internal dissension and potential rebellion, ensuring greater social cohesion and a shared sense of purpose. The custom of human sacrifice was also to play an increasingly important role as an instrument of power, for terrifying spectacles at the temples of Tenochtitlan, Tetzcoco, and Tlacopan hardened new generations of leaders and the population to increasing levels of violence.

The war against Atzcapotzalco thus led directly to the rise of the Aztec empire during the 15th and early 16th centuries. This was a confederation of independent city-states – Tenochtitlan, Tetzcoco, and Tlacopan – each with its own tributary domain. They were never to form a single politically unified or centrally managed state. The Mexica formed the largest society, and Tenochtitlan was by far the dominant city. Tetzcoco, the Acolhua capital, was second in importance. Under Netzahualcoyotl it would also become a center of learning and culture. Tlacopan was the decidedly junior partner: while retaining hold on the old Tepanec heartland on the western side of the Valley, it was often assigned a primarily logistical role in campaigns of conquest.

The course of empire-building now began to evolve in the way of warrior-nations. Was this a repeat of Toltec history, a renascence of all that was meant by the heritage of Tula? Although the allies revered the memory of the Toltecs, their endeavor began to assume a different character from that of Tula in important respects. There were also critical lessons to learn from the sudden and violent Tepanec collapse. The social and political make-up of the Valley of Mexico in particular, and the Central Highlands in general, required a more imaginative and inclusive approach to the problem of achieving a lasting success. In this core region there were many different societies, ranging from city-states and chiefdoms to small farming communities, and even semi-civilized hunting and gathering tribal groups. Many towns had long histories, while others had formed more recently. Some were powerful, with networks of allies, while others were isolated settlements in remote mountain districts. None was strong enough to form a major unifying force except those in the Valley of Mexico. During the second quarter of the 15th century the Aztec confederation consolidated its hold in the Valley and began reaching beyond the surrounding mountains. As their conquests unfolded, it became apparent that coercion alone might not ensure a lasting imperial authority. The fate of the Tepanec city-state was valuable to consider, for its rulers had failed to build a broad base for political and social cohesion. Their empire proved too fragile, quickly succumbing to internal fissures, opportunistic associates, and rebellious vassals. The leaders of Tenochtitlan, Tetzcoco, and Tlacopan could very well see that their expanding program of conquest and intimidation might prove similarly vulnerable. More diverse and effective means for maintaining control and cohesion were required. It now became urgent to build a more complex social, economic, and religious infrastructure to support and maintain the imperial project.

PART THREE

The Imperial Project

4 · New Strategies

The brief life of the Tepanec empire was a subject of reflection among the Aztec victors, inviting comparisons with memories of Toltec Tula. Conquests and threats of reprisals would not be enough to secure an enduring imperial order. There can be no doubt that this matter was considered in the Aztec councils of state. A broader approach began to be developed by building alliances, forming networks of family connections, creating a new legal system, and organizing the tribute system and encouraging agricultural production and trade. A major program of religious rites and festivals also became a central part of this endeavor, as a means of strengthening the all-important spiritual bonds between society and nature, managing a multi-ethnic population, and redistributing goods. By the mid-15th century impressive ritual centers were being constructed with new buildings, sculptures, and associated objects, as symbolic settings for state ceremonies and the annual cycle of agricultural festivals. These works present a striking contrast to the limited vocabulary of art and architecture seen at Toltec Tula. Such ambitious projects had not been seen in the Valley of Mexico since the centuries of Teotihuacan. The efforts begun in the 1430s would lead by 1519 to remarkable transformations in the urban and agricultural landscape of the Valley. By 1519 Tenochtitlan-Tlatelolco had grown to cover approximately 12 sq. km (4.6 sq. miles), inhabited by an estimated 200,000 people. With little cultivable *chinampa* land available within the territory of the metropolis, the Aztec rulers sought control of the adjoining Chalco-Xochimilco basin where some 9,500 hectares (23,000 acres) of *chinampas* were eventually constructed. Additional lands were brought under cultivation by extending old hillside terrace systems and aqueducts in various locations around the Valley.

Claiming the *chinampa* district

Itzcoatl's first concern following the fall of the Tepanec empire in 1428 was to secure the economic base of Tenochtitlan by re-conquering and reaffirming control of agriculturally productive *chinampa* towns around the southern lake district. Enlisting the help of Netzahualcoyotl (the future *tlatoani* of Tetzcoco still resided in Tenochtitlan) and Totoquilhuaztli, *tlatoani* of Tlacopan, the Mexica leader conducted successful campaigns against Culhuacan, Xochimilco, Cuitlahuac, Mixquic, and several smaller dependencies. Today, visitors may hire a flat-bottomed scow and pole through quiet narrow canals between "floating gardens" in the vicinity of Xochimilco, but few will be aware that this setting is only a fragment of the *chinampa* system that once covered virtually all

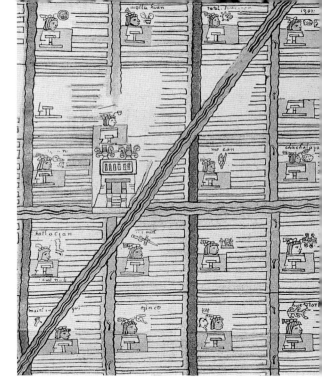

Chinampa plantations

35–37 ABOVE LEFT Aerial view of the Xochimilco basin, showing long, narrow agricultural plots which correspond to the old *chinampa* plantations. ABOVE RIGHT A detail from the *Plano en Papel de Maguey*, dating to *c.* 1523–25, showing a *chinampa* district probably located in the outskirts of northwestern Tenochtitlan. Ownership is shown by houses crowned with heads and name-glyphs. BELOW Children poling a flat-bottomed scow in the *chinampa* district of modern Xochimilco.

of the Chalco–Xochimilco lakebed. Cultivation continues on the ancient garden platforms which do not float at all, for they are securely built up from the shallow lakebed in fertile layers, and anchored by rows of slender willows. Vegetable and flower plantations still supply fresh produce and ornamental plants to the markets of Mexico City. Aerial photographs reveal the pattern of long, thin fossil fields in the former cultivated area. The regular plan of the fields, plus abundant 15th-century potsherds recovered from the surface, have indicated to archaeologists that the final conversion of the great marshland-lake into intensive agricultural lands was closely associated with the development of Tenochtitlan into a densely populated city (ills. 35–37). The chronology of this land reclamation has not yet been archaeologically charted in detail, but it has been estimated that between the time of Itzcoatl's conquest in 1428 and the arrival of the Spanish in 1519, the *chinampa* zone was made to produce half if not more of the foodstuffs entering the capital.[1]

On the eastern side of the basin, the saline waters of Lake Tetzcoco were not amenable to *chinampa* cultivation. We shall also see that as Netzahualcoyotl consolidated his rule over the towns on the piedmont and in the foothills in this district, more hillside farming terraces were built, and ambitious aqueducts and irrigated hillside terraces were constructed with extensions leading to towns on the plain. Copious springs in the Mt Tlaloc range continue to supply several of these important aqueducts to this day. Yet we are not speaking here of the rise of a "hydraulic civilization" in a manner similar to a once widely held theory about the beginnings of Mesopotamia or Chinese city-states. In the Valley of Mexico, complex societies already existed by the time of the *chinampa* and terracing expansions, and it is now seen that these endeavors were accomplished by local communities in response to population growth, tribute demands, and changing patterns of land tenure, in addition to some coercion by a *tlatoani's* authority.

Early conquests

Itzcoatl assumed the title *Culhua tecuhtli*, "Culhua commander," a name that carried certain Toltec associations. Totoquilhuaztli, the ruler of Tlacopan, became *Tepaneca tecuhtli*, undoubtedly the title once held by the great Tezozomoc. The rank of Netzahualcoyotl remained to be established, for he did not immediately return to Tetzcoco after Atzcapotzalco's defeat. Strongly independent communities along the eastern piedmont had first to be defeated and incorporated in the larger Acolhua domain he was planning. With Itzcoatl's help he began by moving in force against Huexotla, and this successful campaign was followed by strong measures to secure nearby Coatlinchan. Relentlessly, other towns along the northwestern lakeshore were defeated one by one. Netzahualcoyotl was crowned *Acolhua tecuhtli* and *Chichimeca tecuhtli* in Tenochtitlan in 1431, but he did not officially remove to Tetzcoco until 1433. Soon thereafter he led an army to capture Tollantzinco, beyond the traditional heartland, in a move that presaged a new phase of military expansion.

The allies now began to plan an ambitious joint expedition across the rim of the Ajusco mountains into the rich Valley of Morelos to the south.

The Tepanecs had once extended their reach into this warm and productive basin, of which the town of Cuauhnahuac (modern Cuernavaca) was the principal center. Crossing the Ajusco range was in many respects the crossing of a psychological as well as a political barrier, for the Aztecs were now determined to surpass the achievement of the Tepanecs. Thousands of warriors were summoned and assembled in squadrons, each identified by tall feathered emblems borne aloft by their captains. The men wore only loincloths and sandals on the outward journey, carrying tumpline bundles with their weapons, battle-dress, and jewelry, while porters bore tumpline baskets with heavier loads of provisions.

The trail led up from the Xochimilco littoral past the extinct volcano Teuhtli, winding over terraced slopes with scattered towns and hamlets. The Ajusco escarpment is still covered by cool forests, and at high elevations fields of grass grow on dark volcanic ash. Old overgrown lava flows wind among the trees, from extinct cindercones along the spine of the sierra. The route descends from the divide through wooded canyons. Small streams cascade from pool to pool towards the valley, and a vista opens from the line of cliffs to the plain below. The surface of this spreading land is scored by deep ravines, and Cuauhnahuac itself was strategically perched between two canyons. Archaeological foundations of some of its buildings may be seen today in the plaza before the Palace of Cortés in downtown Cuernavaca. Low hills traverse the valley in the middle distance where the ruins of Xochicalco are located. Green agricultural bottomlands are covered by sugarcane plantations today. The horizon to the west and south is defined by the Sierra Madre, and access to that mountain hinterland was another Aztec objective, for it was known since Olmec times 1,500 years earlier as a source of rare stones and minerals.

Historical accounts of this successful campaign and others to follow were written by Fernando de Alva Ixtlilxóchitl and Diego Durán. Other records also portray the development of conquests and lists of tribute. The Aztecs had access to old tribute-lists kept by the Tepanecs, as well as their own from previous campaigns, and new records began to be made as their expansion progressed. By the early 16th century the lists had grown long and after the Spanish Conquest compilations were made, known as the Matrícula de Tributos and the Codex Mendoza. The extraordinary pictorial record of the latter was commissioned in about 1525 by the first Spanish viceroy, Don Antonio de Mendoza. The viceroy's purpose was to learn about the history, extent, and resources of the former Aztec dominions as well as other matters concerning their life and culture. The Codex, painted by an anonymous Indian artist and annotated by a Spanish scribe, incorporated material from older native pictorial records, but it was designed in European book format instead of the traditional native screenfold. Using the Codex Mendoza and the closely related *Matrícula de Tributos* as well as other ethnohistorical texts, the scholar Robert Barlow published in 1949 a classic study of Aztec networks of tribute.[2] This was the first comprehensive effort to map the towns named on the Aztec conquest- and tribute-lists. Barlow's study has since been expanded by the work of many scholars notably Ross Hassig, who has painstakingly mapped the routes of specific campaigns.

Networks of tribute

The first section of the Codex Mendoza opens by depicting the founding of Tenochtitlan with the eagle on the cactus, and continues by listing the rulers of Tenochtitlan, the years of their reigns, and the names of the towns they conquered. Each ruler is identified by his name hieroglyph and has a speech-scroll in front of his mouth in sign of *tlatoa*, "speech" or "command," and a shield with darts representing "conquest" (ill. 38). The towns are identified by place-name hieroglyphs (annotated by the Spanish scribe), with a picture of a burning temple by each to show they had been captured. The second section of the Codex concentrates on the tribute required from these towns, listed in different groupings according to the tribute-districts developed by the Aztecs by the time of the Spanish arrival. The places are again named by hieroglyphs, followed by a list of the goods they were obliged to send to Tenochtitlan on a

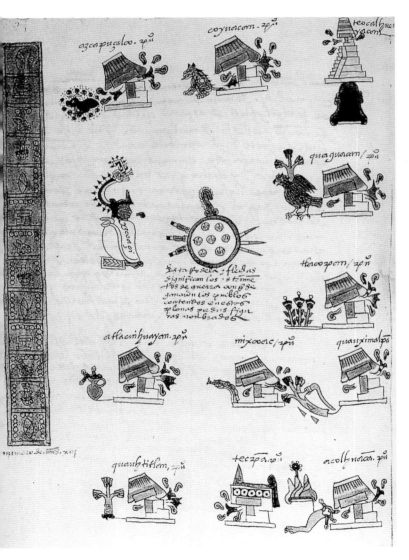

38 LEFT The conquests of Itzcoatl, depicted in the Codex Mendoza. The ruler is shown seated on a mat, with his name-glyph Obsidian Serpent. The shield with darts and spear-thrower is the sign for conquest; tributary towns are rendered as burning temples with place-glyphs, also noted in Spanish script.

39 OPPOSITE A page from the Codex Mendoza tribute list, showing Cuauhnahuac heading the place-names in its province, shown in the left-hand column. Tribute included mantles, war-dresses, shields, gold jewelry, jade beads, lip-plugs, bags of cacao, and bunches of feathers.

regular basis. For example, Cuauhnahuac is shown at the top of a column of 16 towns that were required to send mantles, loincloths, and skirts; each "feather" above an object signifies the number 400 (ill. 39). This tribute was exacted semi-annually. In addition, colorful shields and warrior's suits were payable once a year. The conquests and tribute-lists of all the rulers are listed in this manner.

While the Codex Mendoza is devoted to Tenochtitlan's tribute, other sources account for the way the goods were divided among the three allies when they collaborated on joint expeditions. Generally speaking, Tenochtitlan and Tetzcoco each acquired 40 percent of the spoils, with Tlacopan receiving the remaining 20 percent. However, variations to this basic pattern evolved as the three cities gradually developed a complex network of tribute connections within and without their respective areas of direct influence.[3] Although the

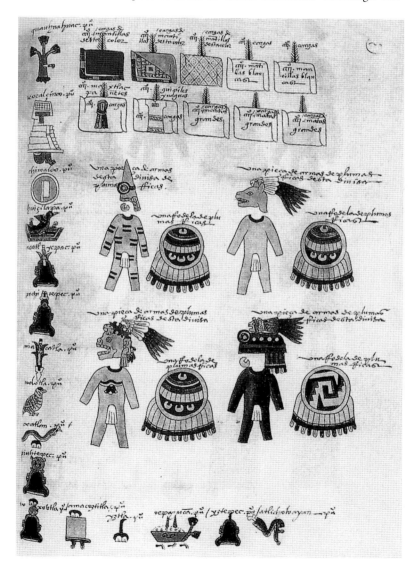

rulers of the three cities might participate in the conquest of towns in any of the three provinces, only the ruler in whose conquest-area the campaign was carried out was regarded as chief commander of that campaign. When only one ruler was involved in a particular conquest, he was entitled to retain all the booty and assign tribute. But when joint expeditions were made, a ruler could actually be assigned tribute-towns within another ruler's traditional sphere. For example, Tenochtitlan received goods from towns within the Tetzcocan region in return for Mexica support during Netzahualcoyotl's campaign of reconquest in Acolhuacan. This is illustrated in the Codex Mendoza, which shows Tepetlaoztoc as a Tenochtitlan tributary, although the town is only a few miles from Tetzcoco itself. Similarly, Netzahualcoyotl, who participated in the conquest of Cuauhnahuac, received tribute from that town and others within the region nominally in Tenochtitlan's sphere.

In addition to the tribute divided among the allied city-states, individual rulers would assign income and lands to their personal allies and friends in reward for faithful service. Many lords from the principal towns thus enjoyed income from places far from their immediate territories. In terms of tribute payment, this resulted in a system whereby some towns were obliged to pay tribute to one of the dominant Aztec cities, while a sub-section or estate within that town might also pay special tribute to a different individual.[4] It appears that in the case of joint conquests, it was customary – but not always strictly so – for the whole tribute to be sent to Tenochtitlan where it would be divided among the participants.

Jerome Offner's research has shown how aspects of the system of tribute worked at Tetzcoco.[5] Netzahualcoyotl created eight districts, and to each was assigned a tribute-collector charged with supplying the administrative palace in Tetzcoco with food and firewood. Some of these districts supplied the needs of the king's own apartments, while others were designated to provide firewood on a regular, rotating basis for the other royal residences or the temples of the city. Offner's research on the system of rotation developed in Tetzcoco has focused on a page from the early post-conquest pictorial manuscript known as the Mapa Quinatzin. This illustration depicts Netzahualcoyotl's administrative quarters within the Tetzcoco palace, whose foundations today lie beneath the downtown plaza in the colonial and modern town of Texcoco (ill. 40). The Mapa Quinatzin depicts a courtyard surrounded by porticoed rooms, in a plan similar to that of an Aztec residence excavated in 1938 at Chiconauhtla, near Texcoco. The leaders of major towns are shown seated around the courtyard, placed according to rank and age. The assembly is presided over by Netzahualcoyotl and his son Netzahualpilli, seated in a chamber above and at center.

The courtyard contains two flaming braziers, indicating the needs of the palace for firewood, which was supplied throughout the solar and ritual years by two sets of 13 towns whose chiefs were present at the meeting. As Offner points out, "this shows a type of rotational tribute that almost certainly varied in numbers and tributary towns over long periods of time, yet indicates a structure for the empire that effectively 'revolved' around Tetzcoco."[6] Among other important tribute obligations of the Tetzcocan provinces were

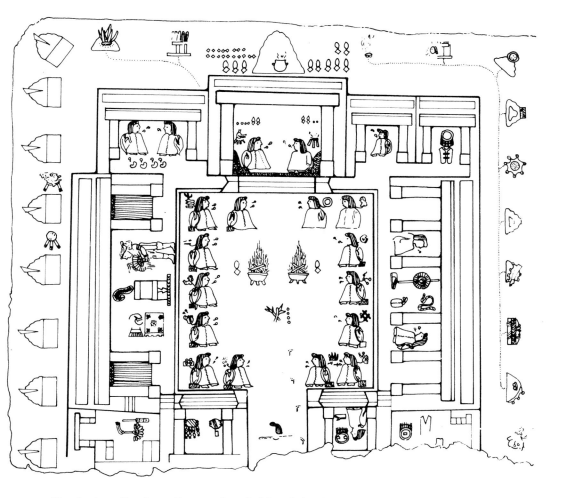

40 Netzahualcoyotl's palace at Tetzcoco, from the Mapa Quinatzin. Elders from the various Acolhuacan communities sit in council around the open patio. Netzahualcoyotl (right) and his son Netzahualpilli (left) preside from the raised porch of the main room (above center).

service in time of war and labor for the construction and maintenance of temples. Since most towns had multiple tribute obligations at different times of year, there was a constant traffic of long trains of carriers, tribute collectors, and other people belonging to the administrative system traveling in and out of Tetzcoco. This lively coming and going brought news from the provinces into the court, and also duly impressed travelers with the culture, armed might, and political power of the capital city. The network of tribute thus provided a number of administrative, economic, and social ways to achieve greater cohesion.

The income from tribute-districts allowed Aztec rulers to develop impressive courts and palaces, and provided the labor and supplies for major building projects. The letters of Cortés and the narratives of Bernal Diaz del Castillo describe the great palaces of Tenochtitlan as vast buildings with inner patios surrounded by rooms where functions of government were held, such as council chambers, audience chambers and places of adjudication. There were private apartments, kitchens supplied with foodstuffs and firewood, and extensive store-rooms for diverse goods including royal treasure. In 1519 the palace of Axayacatl was large enough to accommodate the Spanish force and their Tlaxcalan Indian allies, numbering perhaps 3,500 people, and this host was supplied by the tribute network assigned to the palace. In Tetzcoco, Netzahualcoyotl's royal enclosure was described by Fernando de Alva Ixtlilxóchitl as measuring approximately 1,032 by 817 m (3,355 by 2,680 ft), very roughly equivalent to a square mile. Surrounded by high adobe walls, the interior held diverse buildings including the ruler's apartments and quarters for the principal queen as well as servants' quarters; there was also a throne room, chambers for judges and other officials, as well as visiting ambassadors. Elsewhere, rooms were reserved for warriors and the storage of weapons. Sections were set apart for poets and historians, including an archive and a library. There were massive storehouses for tribute goods, as well as gardens and pyramid-temples. None of this city-within-a-city survives today in the downtown area of modern Texcoco.

However, excavations in the Valley of Morelos have revealed the residences of provincial lords. At Yautepec, archaeologist Hortensia de Vega Nova has directed a team in uncovering a stone-paved platform measuring about 1½ acres at the site of the local *tlatoani's* palace.[7] The sloping outer walls rose to a height of 4 m (13 ft); entrance was afforded by a single stairway on the western side. Within, excavations revealed small courtyards, rooms, and passages. Stone walls were plastered with lime and painted with polychrome murals. The ruler of Aztec Yautepec controlled four or five lesser towns in the immediate region. On a more modest scale, Michael Smith has excavated the ruins of a local magnate at the village site of Cuexcomate.[8] A series of low, connected stone platforms supported rooms around a patio; the remains of shrines were also uncovered. The trash mound nearby yielded fragments of domestic utilitarian pottery and obsidian utensils, plus shards of finer imported wares. This residence, humble by the grand standards of Tenochtitlan, Tetzcoco, or even Yautepec, was nevertheless far above the one-room thatch adobe houses of the local peasants. Smith notes that the compound was probably the residence of a low-ranking provincial noble to whom the 250 or so inhabitants of Cuexcomate paid tribute.

Creating strategic buffer provinces

Anthropologist Frances Berdan has charted another aspect of imperial economic expansion.[9] While one aspect of the Aztec economy depended on regular tribute payments exacted from conquered cities, another major source of wealth was from long-distance and local trade, and from famous markets held regularly in the provinces under Aztec control. It became important to protect the traders, markets, and resources against predatory actions from neighboring enemy states. For example, late in the 15th century the Tlaxcalans and Tarascans whom the Aztecs never succeeded in conquering were perceived to threaten Aztec-controlled territories bordering their respective domains. To achieve security the Aztecs decided to treat these outlying subject territories with leniency: instead of being obliged to meet a demanding tribute schedule, communities would simply provision Aztec warriors and commanders stationed in their region, and would only be required to send token gifts to the Aztec capitals as a sign of continuing submission. Thus the Aztecs created a system of "strategic" buffer provinces without huge expense, protecting core areas of trade, markets, and other resources. This policy developed in step with the rhythm of imperial expansion. Berdan's painstaking research of the Aztec tribute-lists and related ethnohistoric records has greatly expanded Robert Barlow's work on the Codex Mendoza, and has yielded a detailed map of the empire showing tributary and strategic provinces as well as enemy states.

In sum, from the early reigns of Itzcoatl and Netzahualcoyotl there developed a fabric of private and state-controlled land and tribute organizations, forming a criss-crossing web of economic and political relationships. The many levels of these connections enabled the *tlatoanis* to control the resources of a vast landscape, to distribute goods within their hierarchy, and to consolidate and expand their personal power as well as that of their nations.

Alliances, clients, and kinship connections

Motecuhzoma Ihuilcamina (Motecuhzoma I), succeeded Itzcoatl in 1440. This able ruler had a strong history of military accomplishment, yet he understood the need to postpone major expeditions in order to attend to pressing problems of administration within lands already subjected. Netzahualcoyotl became similarly engaged in consolidating his own web of connections between the heartland of Acolhuacan and outlying districts. This process was closely tied to the system of tribute relationships. Again, the Mapa Quinatzin provides a reference for alliances developed by Netzahualcoyotl in the region of Tetzcoco. The hieroglyphs of towns are painted around the borders of the picture, some of which were important heads of districts with many subordinate communities. Jerome Offner has shown that the seated figures around the courtyard were local rulers restored to office following the conquest of their towns by the allies, and some were men especially installed by Netzahualcoyotl himself. In Tenochtitlan, Itzcoatl had first advised the Tetzcocan ruler against the restoration of existing local rulers. But Netzahualcoyotl's personal experience at the hands of the Tepanec tyrants had made him well aware of the ambitions, resentments, and dangerous intrigues that could be presented by dispossessed leaders. He decided to minimize these threats and proceeded with his own strategy of appointments. Itzcoatl became convinced by Netzahualcoyotl's success and soon restored nine local rulers in his own domains. Totoquilhuaztli also acted on Netzahualcoyotl's advice and restored seven rulerships in the old Tepanec kingdom. At one point the Triple Alliance was governed by the three principal *tlatoanis* and 30 lesser appointee rulers who commanded the different districts.

Research has yet to disclose fully the structures of government in many lands conquered by the Aztecs. The 16th-century Spanish lawyer Alonso de Zorita, who traveled in the highlands and took a keen interest in recording previous systems of law and government, described the pattern of an administrative council in the Matlazinca capital of Malinalco before it was incorporated into the Mexica domain by the *tlatoani* Axayacatl in the 1470s:

Before Axayacatl ... waged war on the people of Maztlalcingo, they had three lords. One was the principal lord, the second somewhat below the first, and the third of lesser rank than the first two. On the death of the principal lord, who in virtue of his dignity and lordship was named Tlatuan, his place was filled by the second lord, who was named Tlacatecatle, and in his vacant place entered the third lord, who was named Tlacuxcalcatl ... Each of these lords has assigned to him certain towns and barrios that they call calpules, which rendered service to their acknowledged lord. This lord had in each town or calpul a principal, or perpetual governor ... although each of the supreme lords had his particular towns, barrios, and jurisdiction, affairs of small importance were taken to the second or third lord, and dispatched by one or both of them. They referred a grave or important question to the principal lord, and all three resolved it jointly.[10]

This type of supreme council corresponds in essential outline to the military administration system in Tenochtitlan itself. Below the *tlatoani* were two officers, the *tlaccatecatl* and *tlacochcalcatl*, and a third, the *etzhuanhuanco*, all senior commanders whose duties were largely of a military nature. A fourth office, the *tillancalqui*, is also named in some accounts. At the provincial capital of Malinalco, there is archaeological evidence that the Aztecs took advantage of this compatible local system upon installing their own military government. The famous rock-cut temple at Malinalco displays in the circular interior the stone-carved jaguar and eagle seats of the governing council (ills. 55–60). The men who sat in this chamber were military governors and adjudicators.[11] Whether they were retained local magnates or appointees of the Aztecs, these rulers were delegates of the great lord, the *huey tlatoani* of Tenochtitlan.

Netzahualcoyotl, Totoquilhuaztli, Itzcoatl, and later Motecuhzoma I, also arranged marriages and required the attendance of lesser lords or their children at the courts of their respective capitals. This was designed to prevent "thoughts of insurrection or rebellion." Lesser lords were also obliged to pay homage to their ruler on state occasions, and to assist him with men and supplies in war. It is also apparent that the leading families of the principal towns were bonded to Netzahualcoyotl through marriage to his numerous sons and daughters, and we may believe that this was also the practice in Tlacopan

41 OPPOSITE Drawing from the Mapa Quinatzin illustrating Netzahualcoyotl's rules for punishing crimes.

and Tenochtitlan. Considerable numbers of princes and princesses were born in the royal harems to ensure that the offspring of the lords would be tied by blood relationships. The Aztec rulers thus also maintained their authority through extended family connections.

Netzahualcoyotl's "legalist" system

The centralization of power in Tetzcoco and Tenochtitlan was further consolidated by the promulgation of a "legalist" code, designed to ensure government by severe but standardized laws that favored the rule of the state. Netzahualcoyotl is credited with the creation of this remarkable system. Order was created by defining behaviors and responsibilities, with punishments to be meted out with strict impartiality. Rules prescribed exclusive and concrete solutions to specific types of disputes, and these rules were mechanically applied with no regard to mitigating circumstances.

Jerome Offner, whose research brought to light the essential outlines of this system in operation in Tetzcoco, has called attention to two pages from the Mapa Quinatzin. The first of these pages depicts a series of crimes (thefts) and their corresponding punishments (strangulation) (ill. 41). The second column on the page shows punishment meted out to the son of a lord for the careless handling of property. Below, another crime against the rulers is depicted in

which a rebellious lord is dealt with: first, a Tetzcocan representative speaks to older (and presumably wiser) members of the rebellious community. Then the dissident leader himself is warned by being presented with a symbolic headdress. Finally, after conferring with warriors, the Tetzcocan representative has the dissident chieftain executed with a club. The second page from the Mapa Quinatzin shows punishments for other crimes such as adultery by jailing, burning, strangulation, or stoning. The trials of corrupt and incompetent judges are also portrayed, in which the judges are seated in buildings with the hieroglyphs of Netzahualcoyotl and his son, prince Netzahualpilli. The guilty judges appear below, strangled for having tried cases in their own houses (implying that they accepted bribes) instead of in official rooms as decreed by law. The pictures indicate that certain crimes were given prescribed punishments, but the law did not always extend to crimes committed by judges. In these instances, decisions were made on a case-by-case basis with precedents taken into account.

The Codex Mendoza shows how a similar system operated in Tenochtitlan (ill. 43). A case is illustrated in which Aztec traders are mortally wounded by the subjects of a distant chieftain. Aztec representatives arrive to reprimand the chieftain and deliver the dreaded headdress, signifying a forthcoming judgment. Finally an Aztec emissary delivers judgment (a "thorn word") and the ruler is strangled, while his wife and child are tied with slave collars around their necks.

Although there were 80 laws in the Tetzcocan legal code, not everything could actually be judged in a strictly "legalist" manner. Indeed, there was an entirely different tradition of justice which stemmed from tribal customs long before the Aztec city-states were formed. This tradition centered on the concept of "the reasonable man," under which there were no rigid prescriptions for crime and punishment but judgments were instead made according to general, culturally accepted notions of reasonable behavior. Thus the "reasonable man" element of Tetzcocan custom mitigated to a certain extent the severity of the imperial legalist system.

In considering these aspects of Aztec jurisprudence, Offner has pointed out that legalist systems have arisen rarely in the history of the world, other principal examples being in Europe and under the Ch'in Dynasty in China.[12] Legalism appears to develop in times of turmoil and change, when different ethnic groups and societies come into contact during war, migration, and urbanization. Although the harsh Aztec legalism may have had roots in an older Mesoamerican tradition, it is clear that as Netzahualcoyotl reorganized different aspects of the political and economic systems, he perceived the need for a legal code with severe sanctions and uniform applications in order to encompass all the different tribal and urban peoples. The new code standardized laws governing these diverse groups. It was also important because it controlled judges by curbing corruption and other abuses of power. It increased the efficiency of law courts, and limited the influence of dissident lords. In these respects the legalist system contributed strongly to the breakdown of old tribal society, and also helped to build greater regimentation and submission to central authority.

5 · The Great Expansion

The reign of Motecuhzoma I

The first task of Motecuhzoma I following his coronation in 1440 was to assert the supremacy of Tenochtitlan by reaffirming claims on towns already conquered by Itzcoatl in the Valley of Mexico. Having received assurances of their submission, he then used the rebuilding of the Great Pyramid as a pretext for soliciting help from additional cities. Those who acquiesced tacitly agreed to Tenochtitlan's domination, for "contributions" to the pyramid construction in the form of labor or materials were expressions of tribute. Only Chalco refused, thereby precipitating intermittent hostilities that were to last until the mid-1450s. Motecuhzoma's next step was to send an expedition to secure towns in Morelos and Guerrero which for the most part had already been tribute-payers in the old Tepanec domain.

It was not until late in his career that Motecuhzoma initiated systematic campaigns of conquest into more distant regions. During the first 18 years of his reign he effectively strengthened the cohesion of the alliance with the rulers of Tetzcoco and Tlacopan, and established firm foundations for an ambitious expansionist policy. Because of the unresolved war with Chalco and its allies, and the effects of a great famine in 1452–54, his move toward a major program of conquests had been delayed. Motecuhzoma's first step was to subdue Chalco and its allies once and for all. Chalco's defeat opened the way for a series of extraordinary campaigns that were to take the allies far from the Valley of Mexico. The sequence of Motecuhzoma's conquests are disputed today among scholars. The sequence of events outlined by Ross Hassig[1] begins in the Huaxtec region of north-central Veracruz. This was the first distant land to be visited, for the stated purpose of avenging the mistreatment and murder of Aztec merchants in Tochpan and neighboring towns. In part, the choice of this theater of operations was determined by the fact that Netzahualcoyotl of Tetzcoco had previously conquered a series of towns leading toward the Huaxtec region, thus providing the allied force with a firm logistical base. The Huaxtecs were defeated by the Aztec warriors in a well-planned feigned retreat and trap. Subjugation of the rich, tropical coastal area secured new sources of tribute, and made allies and enemies alike recognize that much larger and longer military enterprises than those previously experienced could be successfully organized and launched.

The allies' next move was into the rugged Mixtec country. The target was Coixtlahuaca, an old trading center commanding major trade routes and resources, with important connections to the principal communities of Oaxaca and south toward the Isthmus of Tehuantepec. The campaign probably took place in 1458 after the onset of the autumn dry season when the time for war was traditionally proclaimed. Although the motive was to obtain plunder and tribute, the pretext was again supplied by merchants who reported themselves attacked and pillaged at Coixtlahuaca. Following what was becoming standard procedure, emissaries were sent to demand redress and war was declared.

More is known about the Mixtecs than any other group conquered by the Aztecs at this time in their history.[2] They were – and still are – a people inhabiting ancient communities scattered in valleys separated by high mountain ranges. In the 15th century each valley was organized autonomously under the rule of a local lord, who maintained his lands by force and intrigue against neighboring rivals. The Mixtecs periodically feuded among themselves, and there are also records of short-lived confederations that mounted military raids into more distant lands. In case of foreign attack the Mixtecs could assemble considerable defensive forces on an *ad hoc* basis. But no Mixtec lord had ever been able to establish ascendancy over any large district for a long period of time.

Populous and powerful Mixtec towns such as Coixtlahuaca were organized in a class system, comprising the ruler and his extended family; a small stratum of hereditary nobles who functioned as administrators, advisors, and entrepreneurs; a broad class of farmers, tradesmen, and artisans; and at the bottom of the social order the tenant farmers, servants, and slaves who cared for the lands and households of the nobility. The region was famous for its crafts, and much of the finest gold-smithing, lapidary work, weaving, manuscript-painting, and ceramics attributed to Tenochtitlan were actually manufactured by Mixtec artisans brought to the city. Nevertheless, despite their considerable sophistication, Mixtec towns had not the cultural complexity or population density of cities in the Valley of Mexico and environs. The Mixtecs had never achieved the degree of political and social unification that might have led to a state-like society. There is little evidence of a professional warrior class like that of the officers directing the Aztec army. The Mixtecs now faced a threat greater than any yet experienced in their long history.

In Tenochtitlan, the first step in the campaign against Coixtlahuaca was to send out a call for warriors to the four wards of the city and to the allied rulers and client chieftains. Large amounts of supplies were requisitioned, and long strings of porters began to arrive with foodstuffs, arms, and equipment. Warriors assembled in their own districts and towns and moved toward areas of concentration. The maintenance of a large body of troops during the time of inactivity before marching, and the need for a regular supply of provisions, presented a major logistical task which proved again the efficiency of Aztec tribute-gathering and administration.

The Aztec order of march will be discussed in greater detail in Chapter 9, but we will note here the prescribed sequence of units. Special squads of scouts or advance raiding parties, each consisting of some four to eight warriors, held the advance position. Larger formations began departing at intervals. The entire force, totalling about 20,000 men, was supported by 10,000 porters. Their route through the Valley of Puebla probably passed by the town of Itzyocan (modern Izucar) before crossing the expanse of the plain

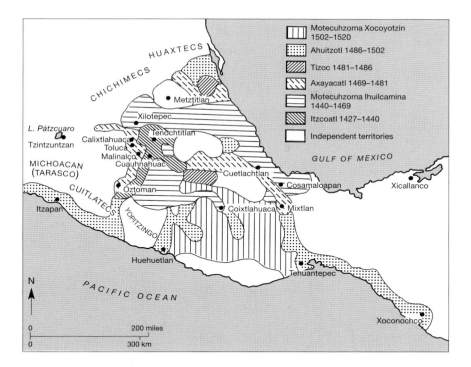

42 The expansion of the Aztec empire, showing the principal conquests from the reign of Itzcoatl.

and following the old trade route into the mountainous land to the south. Intelligence of the Aztec advance was supplied to the Mixtec ruler Atonal by his Huexotzingo and Tlaxcala allies, who arrayed themselves against their common enemy. Messengers began to arrive with descriptions of the stupefying sight of squadron after squadron of enemy warriors followed by porters, marching hour upon hour in a seemingly endless flow toward the Coixtlahuaca Valley. First came the scouts in short white cotton *xicolli* shirts and with yellow ocher on their faces, their long black hair tied in a topknot with stiff red ribbons. Their legs were bare, and every man wore a loincloth. Each warrior carried a spear, some set with blades of obsidian, but commanders were identified by feathered fans and high-backed sandals, indicating rank and authority. Conch-shell trumpets were carried to signal the army following on the trail behind. Then came the main body of warriors, still dressed lightly. The rank and file carried tumpline bundles holding their weapons and battle-dress – darts, slings, clubs, and painted shields and feathered devices – while the commanders had porters carrying their leather or feather-woven body-suits in green, red, or yellow, some spotted or striped as animals, others woven or painted with heraldic emblems. As this force spread out in the fields before Coixtlahuaca, Mixtec warriors hastened from outlying districts and towns. Even with the support of Tlaxcala and Huexotzingo, it was not easy for the

Mixtecs to improvise an effective defense against an invader who had successfully brought thousands of fighting men across the broken landscape.
Although the invading army may possibly have been smaller than the defending Mixtec host, it was led by more experienced and purposeful commanders,
accustomed to obedience and discipline.

Few details are available concerning the following battle, but enough can be
gleaned from various other campaign accounts to characterize the fighting.
The Aztecs were not practiced in the close-formation drill of Roman or
Spanish soldiers. The task of the general commander was to plan the disposition of formations according to topographic and man-made features in the
field, to maintain control personally, keeping in sight and issuing decisive
orders to surrounding subordinate officers and runners, and to be willing and
able physically to engage the enemy in the heat and stress of battle. His spirited
gestures and confident voice, and his personal display of courage and
judgment, were to be highly visible and a source of inspiration to the men. The
basic concept of battle emphasized the shock of charges, man-to-man combat,
and duels between individual champions, recalling the wild melee described by
Homer beneath the walls of Troy. The assembled ranks confronted each other
in lines across open ground. All were now dressed in their flashing plumes,
animal helmets, and body-suits, and the captains bore insignia waving in the
bright mountain sunlight. Taunts, boasts, and challenges were flung across the
field; and here and there daring youths would jump out to strike insulting or
indecent postures to belittle the enemy and show bravado to their fellow
warriors. Tension built, and the voices of thousands of men rose in a deep wave
of sound. Conch-shell trumpets were blown with full force, and suddenly the
air was filled with the piercing din of whistles, shrill war-cries, whoops, and
howls, as the lines charged towards each other in the rising dust. Volleys and
counter-volleys of stones were hurled with stunning effect, and at closer range
rattling clouds of darts were cast from *atlatl* spear-throwers. The formations
met with shocking impact as men swung heavy obsidian-bladed clubs, seeking
to cut down or capture opponents as trophies for sacrifice.

The thrust of the Aztec onslaught and the fearful sense of their discipline
and fighting spirit were something the Mixtecs had not previously encountered. The Aztec force broke through the defenders' ranks and a running battle
developed as the Mixtecs and their allies fell back through the town, fighting
between the houses. Aztec warriors were urged on by their captains toward the
principal pyramid where, sensing victory, they broke through again and ran up
the stairs to set fire to the thatch of the temple. This was the traditional signal
of victory, and as the column of smoke and flames rose up, the remaining
defenders were pursued in a rout through the dry maize fields and into the
hills. Captured, wounded, and dead warriors were stripped of their battle-
finery as the Aztec victors turned to pillage. Soon the streets and lanes of
Coixtlahuaca were strewn with broken household wreckage – pottery, boxes,
and pieces of cloth – as dogs and turkeys ran about, chased down by hungry
warriors.

That the Mixtecs and their allies had been defeated was clear to the women,
children, and elders witnessing the battle from their retreat in the mountains.

43 The attack on Aztec traders near Coixtlahuaca, and the subsequent judgment and execution of the Mixtec leader, Atonal. From the Codex Mendoza.

The Mixtecs were now obliged to buy peace. A delegation of Coixtlahuaca magnates approached the Aztec commanders and terms of submission were bargained. According to established practice the defeated chieftains were allowed to retain their positions on condition that they would provide regular tribute from their respective districts. Only the ruler Atonal's life was forfeited: he was strangled and his family were taken as slaves (ill. 43). The Codex Mendoza shows the tribute exacted from Coixtlahuaca and its environs: 2,000 finely woven blankets, 2 splendid military outfits, an unspecified number of string collars of greenstone beads, 800 bunches of green feathers, another feathered emblem such as worn by Aztec chieftains, 40 bags of prized red cochineal dye (made from the dried insects *Coccus cacti*), and 20 bowls of gold dust (ill. 44). Other accounts mention loads of cotton, chile, and salt. The Aztecs appointed a tribute-collector to ensure the arrival of these goods on a regular basis. In addition, the defeated Mixtec chieftains were obliged to present the Aztecs with a magnificent feast, and were forced to listen to their boasts and humiliating insults. The Aztec army departed with heavy loads of tribute and plunder, including important Mixtec religious paraphernalia taken from the burnt temple. The latter objects were destined to be held as spiritual

44 The tribute list of Motecuhzoma I from the Codex Mendoza. Coixtlahuaca is depicted top left.

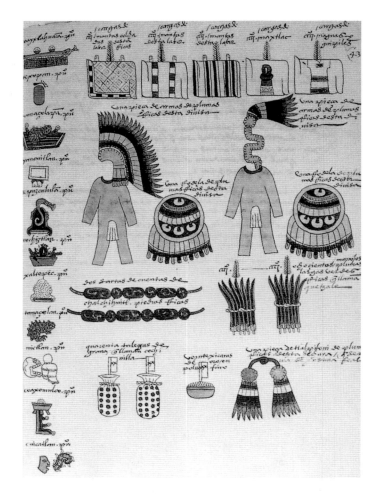

hostages in a special building, the *coateocalli*, within the main ceremonial enclosure of Tenochtitlan. The departing army was also accompanied by a line of dispirited captives, destined for ritual sacrifice.

In the cities of the Aztec homeland, the returning warriors were welcomed by jubilant crowds. Their triumph was celebrated in Tenochtitlan, where the exultant victors presented their captives at the landing of the Great Pyramid. The victims were led up the stairs through clouds of incense, to be stretched over the sacrificial block. Blood ran down the pyramid steps and the bodies of victims were flung down to be decapitated and dismembered, enacting the myth of Huitzilopochtli's defeat of Coyolxauhqui and the Four Hundred Huitznahua. The heads of the victims were strung up on the skull rack as trophies, while victorious captors were presented with a severed arm or thigh. Sahagún says that these gruesome joints were taken home amid much jubilation, to be prepared in a savory stew with chiles and tomatoes for a ritual meal. However, we must not imagine that cannibalism was a primary way of satisfying hunger among the Aztec populations. Rather, it remained an essentially sacramental act, for by ingesting the flesh of an enemy, the victor participated in the offering made to Huitzilopochtli in his temple on the Great Pyramid. These triumphs were accompanied by displays of wealth and gift-giving designed to exalt the victors' status and to impress representatives of foreign communities.

The pattern of the Coixtlahuaca campaign was repeated elsewhere. Motecuhzoma I directed his forces to Cosamaloapan in 1459, followed by a lengthy expedition to Ahuilizapan (modern Orizaba) and Cuetlaxtla in Veracruz. These were hard-fought, complex campaigns, for the native communities were assisted by considerable military units from Tlaxcala, Huexotzingo, and Cholollan,[3] all enemies of the Aztecs. Under Motecuhzoma I the Aztecs won a decisive series of conquests, setting a dynamic course of military expansion that was to dominate Aztec policy until the Spanish arrival. By the death of Motecuhzoma I in 1469 and the death of Netzahualcoyotl in 1472, lands paying tribute to the Aztecs reached into Oaxaca, east along the Gulf Coast from Totonac Cosamaloapan to Tuxpan in the Huaxtec country, and another large segment of the Central Highlands northeast of Tula to Xilotepec. Unimaginable wealth from tropical lowlands and upland plateaus poured into the imperial cities regularly, guaranteed by tribute-gatherers wielding the threat of armed retribution. Gradually the system of marriage-alliances and political clients also began to be extended into the conquered regions, but the flow of tribute was always ensured by the fear of punitive force.

Early imperial monuments

As the Aztec armies continued their advance and tribute arrived in ever larger quantities, the idea of empire was given symbolic expression through ritual performance and works of art and architecture. This aspect of the imperial program will be fully described in Chapter 6, but at this point, there are two sculptural monuments to consider for what they tell about the way the Aztecs portrayed their conquests. The first, known as the Stone of Motecuhzoma I, was discovered in 1989 buried beneath the patio of the Archbishop's Palace immediately adjoining the ruins of the Great Pyramid in downtown Mexico City. The sculpture was probably made during the reign of Motecuhzoma's successor Axayacatl (1469–81). It is similar in design to the second monument, known as the Tizoc Stone, which was discovered beneath the Plaza de la Constitución in 1790 (ills. 45–47). The latter much-studied sculpture was certainly carved during Axayacatl's reign. Both monuments represent the empire of Tenochtitlan in the form of a cosmic diagram. The flat upper surface of the cylinders are carved with a sun-disc with four main rays pointing to the cardinal directions. On Motecuhzoma I's monument, the side of the cylinder is covered with a band of compartments, each portraying a Mexica warrior grasping the deity of a foreign community by the scalp – a standard way of signifying "capture." Each deity is distinguished by its identifying costume and the hieroglyphic place-name of the community. Conquests are portrayed as ritual acts performed around the perimeter of the world. On the Tizoc Stone this theme is more fully realized: below the sun on the top surface, a band of stars, the "eyes" of the night, surround the upper rim of the celestial level.

Another band frames the bottom edge, carved with upright pointed blades and four abstract masks of the earth deity, marking the four directions. Between the heavens and the earth, Mexica warriors are disposed in identical poses, grasping the submissive deities of foreign towns by the scalplock. As on the Stone of Motecuhzoma I, each town is named by hieroglyphs. The *tlatoani* Tizoc appears dressed in the regalia of Huitzilopochtli and Tezcatlipoca. On this monument the designer has eliminated the compartments separating each capture, thus developing the sense of a continuous procession. The triumphant Mexica all face to the right, moving counterclockwise around the perimeter, enclosing and claiming the world as a sacred space. Conquests are translated as ritual events, incorporating foreign communities into an ordered cosmos of which Tenochtitlan was the center.

The Stone of Tizoc

45–47 ABOVE and OPPOSITE (ABOVE) On top of the stone, the sun-disk and a band of stars represent the heavens, while pointed stones and four "earth-monster" masks on the bottom (not shown) symbolize the surface of the earth. OPPOSITE (BELOW) The sides of the stone depict Aztec conquests as a series of ritual "captive" scenes, with Tizoc (extreme left) and his minions grasping the deities of enemy towns.

The reign of Axayacatl: expansion and defeat

During the reigns of Motecuhzoma I and Netzahualcoyotl, an ambitious series of conquests set a standard that would challenge the talents and energies of the rulers to follow. Upon Motecuhzoma's death, the 19-year-old prince Axayacatl was elected *tlatoani*. Although hardly more than a youth, he had already proved himself a brave warrior and an able leader with important commands in Motecuhzoma's expeditions. He was to reign for 13 years, from 1469 to 1481. His principal military accomplishments began with his coronation war in the Isthmus of Tehuantepec, followed by a succession of campaigns in the Puebla Valley, on the Gulf Coast, in the Toluca Valley, and in Guerrero, as well as in lands north of the Valley of Mexico.[4] During his reign, long-standing tensions between the "sister" cities of Tlatelolco and Tenochtitlan erupted in a brief civil war on the island, ending with the permanent subjugation of Tlatelolco in 1473.

An early victory brilliantly won by Axayacatl against Toluca in 1475–76 led to further campaigns on the western marches in 1476–77 and 1477–78. These gains provided the logistical base for an Aztec thrust against the Tarascan dominions, probably in the dry season of 1478–79. The Tarascans still inhabit their ancestral homeland in the mountainous state of Michoacán. The archaeological ruins of their ancient capital Tzintzuntzan are still to be seen on a bluff above the colonial town of the same name, overlooking Lake Pátzcuaro. In the 15th century the Tarascans were organized as a confederation, and some scholars have seen them as a power that rivaled the Aztecs. Certainly they were sufficiently unified and militarily strong enough to repel two Aztec invasions. Historical descriptions of Axayacatl's invasion vary greatly, but all agree that

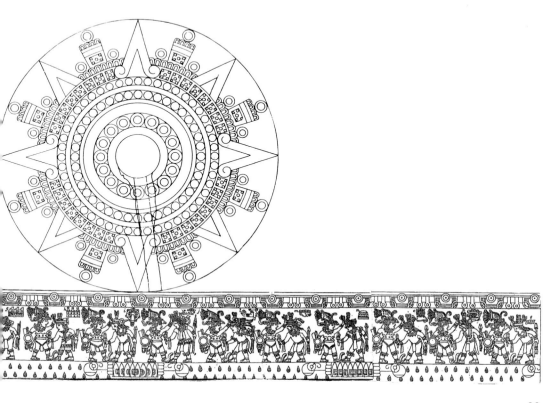

the Aztec force suffered an unprecedented defeat. In the vicinity of Taximaloyan (modern Tajimaroa) the Aztecs assembled some 32,000 warriors against an enemy host of about 50,000. Although Axayacatl sought to call off the battle, he was persuaded to press the assault. The Aztec squadrons broke and fled, but their commanders rallied and forcefully asserted their will to confront the enemy. The next day they were catastrophically defeated. It is said that only 200 Mexica returned to Tenochtitlan, Axayacatl among them; 400 Tetzcocans, 400 Tepanecs, 400 Chalcas, and 400 Xochimilcas as well as 300 Otomies are also said to have survived – a loss of some 1,100 men. Axayacatl's reign concluded with yet another expedition back to the Gulf Coast region to reconquer rebellious towns. This pattern of conquest and reconquest was to remain a feature of the empire until the Spanish arrival.

Failure and rebellion under Tizoc

When Axayacatl died in 1481 he was succeeded by his brother Tizoc, who had served as a member of the highest military council. From the outset his reign was marked by misfortune, first experienced in his coronation war. The Aztecs chose Metztitlán as their objective, located in mountainous country some 125 miles (200 km) to the northeast of the Valley of Mexico. To their surprise they found the enemy defending a narrow valley where maneuver was limited and the numerical advantage enjoyed by the Aztecs was much diminished. The battle went badly and the day was saved only when a formation of teenage warriors stood in the face of impending rout and succeeded in capturing 40 prisoners. This was to be the only visible token of victory brought home by the humiliated Aztecs. The coronation took place, but Tizoc's poor performance was perceived as an unfavorable omen.

48 The Dedication Stone of Tizoc and Ahuitzotl. The deceased king, Tizoc (left), confronts his successor Ahuitzotl (right). Dressed as priests, they draw blood from their earlobes with bone awls: the transfer of power from the dead to the living is legitimized by sacrifice to the sacred earth. The lower cartouche contains the date 8 reed (1486) when Ahuitzotl took power.

Thereafter Tizoc's wars aimed to suppress rebellions in areas previously conquered, mostly in territories where the Aztecs could count on logistical support. No significant ventures were extended by Tizoc to regions beyond the limits achieved by his predecessors. Tizoc had lost the offensive, and the longer his reign continued, the more the empire faced mounting antagonism, sedition, and rebellion. Tizoc's failure as an aggressive commander led to his death, seemingly by poison, perhaps by order of his brother Ahuitzotl, who held a post (the *tlaccatecatl*) on the high military council normally reserved for an heir apparent. Four days after Tizoc's death the elective council met formally and appointed this ambitious young prince to the office of *tlatoani* in 1486 (ill. 48).

Ahuitzotl's reign: expansion and renewal

Ahuitzotl was a born adventurer-conqueror who proved to be Tenochtitlan's most terrifying warrior. Tough and fearless, he lived and fought with his army and inspired the men with his personal valor. His campaigns were marked by swift, decisive action and murderous retribution against enemies. His first campaign – the coronation war – was to lead the allied army on a circuit into the Toluca Valley and northward to Xilotepec before turning back into the northern Valley of Mexico. This foray had the desired effect of suppressing rebellious communities and reasserting forceful leadership in the demoralized army. The success of these aims was underscored by the booty and prisoners obtained. Ahuitzotl's coronation was triumphant, with unprecedented gift-giving and feasting on a scale said to equal the tribute of an entire year. Having restored confidence in the imperial project with this expression of forceful resolve, Ahuitzotl set forth on another punitive campaign to the Gulf Coast where many towns had refused to send tribute. Once again the Aztec army returned victorious, this time with the intention of staging another grand ceremony to rededicate the Great Pyramid of Tenochtitlan.

The Great Pyramid was periodically enlarged during the reigns of successive rulers, in keeping with the ancient custom of adding new layers to mark important events such as the completion of a 52-year cycle of time, or to celebrate a major event in the life of the state. In addition, the leaders of Tenochtitlan were concerned with the idea of building their ritual center to match the grandeur of other cities from centuries past. An impressive layer had been added in 1454 at the turn of a new time cycle during the reign of Motecuhzoma I. Now, in 1487, another layer was completed to celebrate Ahuitzotl's reaffirmation of the imperial mission. The rededication of the looming structure was orchestrated by staging a mass sacrifice that would forever remain the most horrifying event in the ritualized life of Tenochtitlan. Prisoners of war were lined along the length of the causeways into the city, and in unprecedented numbers the sacrifices continued remorselessly for four days. The numbers have never been accurately determined. Appalled ambassadors from foreign nations were summoned to witness the dreadful slaughter, and the population of Tenochtitlan stood in awe in the plazas facing the pyramid. Streams of blood poured down the stairway and sides of the monument, forming great clotting pools on the white stucco pavement. The accounts of

49–51 Sacrifice was both a means of nourishing the deities and an instrument of political power. ABOVE A captive's heart is ripped from his body on the steps of a temple; from the Codex Magliabechiano. RIGHT Sacrificial knife, with a handle shaped as an eagle warrior and inlaid with turquoise, jade, and shell. BELOW Jaguar-shaped receptacle in which the hearts of sacrificial victims were placed.

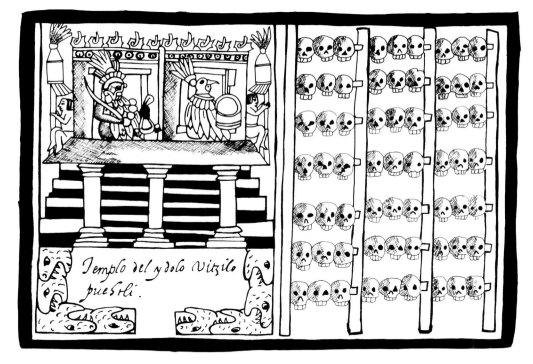

Human sacrifice and the skull rack

52, 53 ABOVE The Skull rack or *tzompantli* in the ritual precinct of Tenochtitlan, with the twin temples of Tlaloc (left) and Huitzilopochtli (right) on the platform atop the Great Pyramid. From Diego Durán's *Historia de la Nueva España*. BELOW The excavated base of a small skull rack by the foundations of the Great Pyramid in Mexico City.

the Aztec elders still conveyed a sense of horror 50 years later, when their descriptions were recorded by Spanish friars and historians. Ahuitzotl was determined to turn sacrifice into a powerful political lesson, instilling terror in the hearts of enemies and inuring the sensibilities of his own population to new thresholds of bloodshed.

The shock of calculated carnage, the sight of the streaming pyramid, and the skull rack strung with huge numbers of gory trophies, marked a turning point in Aztec rulership under Ahuitzotl. As he turned away from the model of Motecuhzoma I, the administrator-warrior, he assumed more of the character of Huitzilopochtli, the deified mythical warrior-hero. Ahuitzotl sought to instill the will to conquer, and the expansion of the empire continued without let-up. Year after year the Aztec armies departed to subdue the peoples and claim the riches of lands in Guerrero, Oaxaca, and the Isthmus of Tehuantepec. Yet as Nigel Davies has observed, this empire always remained more of an armature of lines and strongpoints in a vast terrain, for the Aztec armies hardly had time to penetrate the hinterlands.[5] Moreover, the Aztecs were not developing a strong, centralized administrative bureaucracy in the way of Rome or China. The hegemony established by the network of marriages, alliances, and political relationships always remained vulnerable and unstable; and great distances, broken topography, and the policy of leaving local chiefs in authority as long as the tribute flowed in, remained sources of weakness and potential rebellion. Nevertheless, the Aztecs under Ahuitzotl did develop additional ways to affirm their claims and assert control.

Symbolic appropriation and resettlement

The construction of ceremonial places in the homeland cities and around the Valley of Mexico had been a defining feature of the reigns of Motecuhzoma I and Netzahualcoyotl. These monuments quoted the forms and symbols of earlier artistic and architectural traditions, yet were sufficiently different to declare the unique identity of the new city-states and their ascendancy across the land. During Ahuitzotl's reign this endeavor was exported and expressed in conquered provinces, notably at Tepoztlán, Malinalco, and Calixtlahuaca. These sites were first explored during the 1930s and 1940s, and their archaeological monuments have continued to be sources of information that complement the written histories.

At Tepoztlán, a community high on the cliffs overlooking the Valley of Morelos, a new temple was commandingly sited upon a crag (ill. 54). Within the temple chamber a hieroglyphic inscription includes the name of Ahuitzotl. The monument was part of the Aztec intention to establish a permanent presence and affirm their claims on local resources. Local deities such as the Tepozteco *pulque* deity Mayahuel (ill. 66) were brought into the larger cycle of agricultural festivals celebrated in Tenochtitlan.[6]

The archaeological site of Malinalco is located in the high forested mountains southwest of Mexico City, in what is still Matlazinca Indian territory. The ruins lie on a high, easily defended promontory above the small valley where the colonial town of Malinalco was built after the Spanish Conquest (ills. 55, 56).

54 The Tepoztlán temple (rear view), built on a crag overlooking the Valley of Morelos. The temple affirmed Mexica–Aztec rule and the tributary status of this conquered community during the reign of Ahuitzotl.

Excavations by José García Payón in the 1930s disclosed an Aztec ceremonial center on a steep flank of the hill, partly carved from living rock and partly built on hillside platforms.[7] New excavations carried out in the late 1980s by the Instituto Nacional de Antropología e Historia, reveal the extent of the original Matlazinca settlement and ceremonial center. Malinalco and nearby towns were first subjected to Aztec rule by Axayacatl in 1476. Several rebelled during Tizoc's reign, although Malinalco was not among them. The rebellions were quickly suppressed, but it remained for Ahuitzotl to definitively reassert Aztec control in the region. His ruthless campaign against nearby Oztoman and Alahuistán, where wholesale ethnic cleansing of the native population took place, successfully re-established the imperial presence. In addition to having strategic importance as a base for operations and logistical support, Malinalco had historical significance for the Aztecs, for it was there, according to legend, that the dissident Malinalxóchitl had led her band after splitting from the Mexica tribe in the time of migration. Ahuitzotl visited Malinalco in the first year of his reign, and received the allegiance of local chieftains; but it was not until the final year of his life that the Aztec buildings were begun. Pages from the Codex Aubin record the project and the use of forced labor in 1501. The site is again mentioned as a place where "they went to excavate rock" in 1503. Malinalco was noted once more in the year 1515, when people were brought from Huexotzingo to work during the reign of Motecuhzoma II.

The circular rock-cut temple at Malinalco is one of the very few Aztec masterpieces combining architecture and sculpture to have survived the Spanish Conquest (ills. 57–60). The entrance to the monolithic chamber is framed by a carved mask in the form of the open jaws of a serpent, a symbol for "cave." A semicircular stone bench around the back wall of the chamber is sculpted with pelts of two eagles and a jaguar. Another eagle is carved on the floor. These were the seats of Aztec authorities – the "eagle chair," and the "jaguar chair." The four seats correspond to the positions of *tlatoani*, *tlaccatecatl*, *tlacochcalcatl*, and *etzhuanhuanco* (or *tillancalqui*), whose offices were replicated on the provincial level. The men who occupied this chamber were military governors from Tenochtitlan, or members of the local nobility appointed by the *tlatoani*. A small circular hole cut into the floor directly in back of the carved eagle pelt was a place for offerings to *tlalli yiollo*, "earth heart," or *tepe yiollo*, "mountain heart," location of the earth's regenerative power. However, the temple did not have an exclusively religious function as a place for the cult of the earth, for it was a place where religious and state concerns were intertwined. It must be remembered that when a ruler acceded to office, he was obliged to offer a sacrifice of his own blood, pricked with maguey spines from his ears and legs; this offering was made to the earth as a sign of truth and a bond with the land he was to govern. At Malinalco this offering would have been made in the hole cut in the floor. We have seen that such a ceremony was performed by the *tlatoani* himself as confirmation during coronation rites at another architectural "cave," the Yopico temple in the ceremonial precinct of Tenochtitlan. The temple at Malinalco replicated the Yopico temple, establishing a permanent center of Aztec rule.

The archaeological zone of Calixtlahuaca lies a few miles north of the city of Toluca, below a low hill in the open valley. It was originally a Matlazinca settlement, belonging to an occupation that may date to the 8th century AD. Calixtlahuaca was taken by the Aztecs during Axayacatl's campaign in the 1470s and, during Ahuitzotl's reign, it was assigned to colonists brought in from the Valley of Mexico in a project of resettlement and consolidation. Like Malinalco, the new Aztec buildings and sculptures projected the symbolic code of the metropolitan area. José García Payón's excavations during the 1930s revealed the ritual center including a structure he assumed to be a priestly school (*telpochcalli* or *calmecac*), but is now regarded by Michael Smith as a local ruler's palace. A circular temple-platform connected with the worship of Ehecatl, a deity of wind or storm related to Quetzalcoatl, yielded a basalt effigy of what is surely a masterpiece of Aztec sculpture, representing a standing male figure wearing the bird-bill mask of the deity (pl. XVIII). The effigy would have been dressed in the elaborate paraphernalia of the cult on festival occasions. The importation of such high-quality figures from metropolitan sculptural workshops, and the construction of the ceremonial buildings, are tangible evidence of Aztec intentions to establish a permanent colony in this conquered territory. Emily Umberger has noted that the presence of this and other fine sculptures and architectural monuments here and elsewhere in the Central Highlands, shows how aesthetic tastes and religious and political concepts were widely shared among the elite. The idea of claiming and holding new territory as opposed to simply exacting tribute, was also advanced along the Tarascan frontier. A series of forts was constructed by the Tarascans from north to south along their border with the Aztecs. These archaeological sites, identified by Dan Stanislawski in his 1947 study of Tarascan political geography, provide another body of evidence complementing the written sources.[8] The forts were strategically placed at locations commanding valleys where an invading force was likely to march.[9] The Tarascans also improved their defenses in this borderland by replacing local Matlazinca chieftains with their own rulers. Tarascan answers to the Aztec menace were apparently unique in Mesoamerica where fortifications were rudimentary, as in terraced hilltop sites, or in settlements placed on easily defended natural promontories or islands, or in urban areas where palaces or ritual precincts might be strengthened against assault. The Tarascan line of fortifications provided warning of enemy advances, acted as bulwarks to detain or hamper an invading force, and deterred the Aztec practice of encroaching on enemy territories by capturing frontier towns. The forts assured the Tarascans of a greater degree of stability along a fixed frontier. Control over territory was thus asserted by permanent military installations, as opposed to traditional reliance on political pressure, dynastic connections, and threats of violent action.

There is additional archaeological evidence, supported by historical texts, that the Aztecs themselves were building fortified sites at Alahuistán and Oztoman to the south of this frontier. Oztoticpac, another Aztec conquest, was partly surveyed and explored by Moedano Koerr in the 1940s.[10] These towns and their surrounding region had been taken by Ahuitzotl in his campaign of 1488–89, when all adults were massacred and the children were taken and redistributed throughout the empire. The towns were subsequently resettled by about 9,000 married couples from Tenochtitlan, Tetzcoco, Tlacopan, and neighboring cities.

Ahuitzotl's campaign of 1490–91 into Guerrero and northward along the Pacific coast may have been an initial effort to establish a series of tributary towns that would eventually have lent logistical support for an envelopment of the Tarascan region by outflanking the line of forts. The last conquests of this formidable *tlatoani* brought the Aztec armies far to the south, first to Tehuantepec around 1497, and again in 1499 or 1501 as far as Xoconochco, cacao-producing province of the Pacific coast of Guatemala. The latter expedition was largely commanded by Motecuhzoma II Xocoyotzin, who would be the new *tlatoani* within two years.

It is sometimes asked why the Aztecs did not advance in another direction, towards the lands of the Maya and Toltec-Maya in Yucatan and Guatemala. By the time of the Spanish Conquest there was an Aztec presence at Xicallanco in the Gulf Coast region at Laguna de Terminos, which could be interpreted as a presage of impending conquests into Yucatan, but no expedition had yet been sent. Nigel Davies ventures an opinion that the far-reaching network of trade based at Xicallanco, which brought much-prized jade and jadeite from highland Guatemala and beyond, would have been interrupted by outright

The ceremonial center at Malinalco

55, 56 The site of Malinalco overlooks the small Valley of Malinalco. The original settlement is located at the top of the hill, while the thatched roof of the reconstructed temple halfway down the slope on the right marks the site of the Aztec monuments. BELOW Plan of the excavated Aztec monuments at Malinalco; the circular rock-cut temple (labeled I) is to the left.

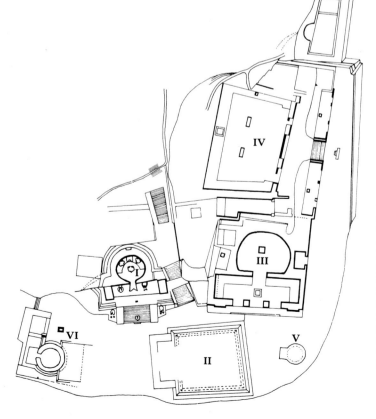

Opposite:
57–60 CENTER LEFT Façade of the rock-cut temple. CENTER RIGHT Detail from the Codex Borgia depicting the deity Tepeyollotl (Mountain Heart) approaching a circular earth temple similar to that at Malinalco. BELOW LEFT and RIGHT Interior chamber of the temple showing the eagle and feline seats of Aztec military governors. An orifice in the floor behind the central eagle was for receiving ceremonial blood-offerings.

conquest. Ahuitzotl may have chosen not to jeopardize this source of a most highly valued material.[11] By the end of his life, Ahuitzotl's campaigns had regained the imperial dynamic temporarily lost by Tizoc.

Motecuhzoma II: the last independent ruler

The final Aztec reign opened with Motecuhzoma II Xocoyotzin's coronation in 1502–03 (described in Chapter 1). Following tradition, his first military expedition was to procure prisoners for sacrifice at the confirmation ceremony. Soon thereafter the new ruler began a concerted effort to woo the nobility, since the threat of intrigues was always present. Sumptuary laws were proclaimed that further distinguished the nobles from the lower classes. Anthropologist Patricia Anawalt has disclosed how Aztec attire was traditionally used to identify different social ranks and ethnic groups (ill. 114). Matters of attire now grew in importance and related legislation was strictly enforced. Accomplished warriors among the commoners were no longer permitted to wear insignia or clothes different from those of inferior rank. At the same time Motecuhzoma II took care not to strip away the prerogatives of commoners who had attained high standing, but made the attainment of rank more difficult. Within the palace, elaborate court etiquette was enforced to affirm the new hierarchy, surrounding the new *tlatoani* with layers of ceremonial procedure. Many of the elaborate obeisances and expressions of extreme respect observed by the Spanish in the court of Motecuhzoma Xocoyotzin had their origin in his first years of tenure.

The new *tlatoani* also doubted the continued loyalty of Ahuitzotl's administrators and supporters, and as many new rulers often do, he moved rapidly to replace them with followers of his own. According to some accounts, many of the former were put to death. At the same time, he replaced all the existing servants in the palaces with junior members of the nobility from provincial towns. The young nobles thus brought into the palaces not only served, but were indoctrinated and kept as quasi-hostages to ensure the cooperation of their parents and relatives. By now the old system of dual administration was virtually defunct as the *cihuacoatl*, chief of internal affairs, came under the orders of the *huey tlatoani*.

Motecuhzoma II was a formidable warrior and his campaigns systematically enlarged the tribute domain and consolidated the conquests of former rulers. Only the stubborn Tarascans and Tlaxcalans remained undefeated. The Aztecs under Motecuhzoma Xocoyotzin were involved in no fewer than four wars against Tlaxcala and Huexotzingo, the last of which in 1515 proved disastrous. By the time Cortés arrived in 1519, a bitter, entrenched, and irreconcilable hatred existed between the Aztecs and Tlaxcalans which the Spanish invaders quickly learned to exploit. Yet Motecuhzoma's campaigns had also reached into Oaxaca, Puebla, Guerrero, the old Chichimeca, and south again to the Isthmus and Xoconochco, reaffirming old conquests and substantially advancing the Aztec position on all fronts. The empire was expanding. There is no evidence that the energy of Tenochtitlan and her allies was on the wane by the time the Spanish arrived.

PART FOUR
· · · · · · · · · · · · · · · ·
Aztec Religion and World View

6 · The Aztec Symbolic World

Since remote times the rhythms of life in highland Mexico had been deeply embedded in the land and the changing seasons. The annual alternation of rain and drought – periods of life and death – determined the cycle of farming peoples and hunter-gatherers before them. The pragmatic business of obtaining food went hand in hand with a sense of rhythm and periodic recurrence, and with the notion of belonging to the land. To the Aztecs, this interaction between humankind and nature was of profound significance, affirmed through a calendar of cyclic festivals performed at a network of sacred places in cities and throughout the surrounding natural landscape. The religious status and functions of rulers were critical in these relationships, for Aztec rulers and their priestly minions were obliged to ensure, by means of traditional rituals, the regularity of the seasons, the fertility of the soil, the productivity of the land, the abundance of plants and animals, and the wellbeing of the community from year to year.

The deities

When the Tepanecs, Chichimecs, Acolhua, and Mexica tribes first entered the Valley of Mexico, the old settled towns had their own religious cults centered on local nature-deities, deified ancestors, and legendary heroes. The 16th-century Spanish historian Juan Bautista Pomar remarked that "they had many idols, and so many that almost for each thing there was one." Yet there was no overarching idea of a court of gods controlling the forces of nature and capriciously intervening in human affairs, as in the ancient Mediterranean world. Instead, we find a widely shared spectrum of cult themes, each with different named deities belonging to different communities. Nevertheless, certain deities and their cults were very old in Mesoamerica and formed a core group centering on the worship of fire, the sun, the earth, rain and ground water, and vegetation. As the Aztec empire expanded, the principal deity of a conquered community was incorporated into the Aztec system. Indeed, conquest itself could be symbolically represented as the "capture" of an enemy town's tutelary deity, as we have seen illustrated by the Stone of Motecuhzoma I and the Stone of Tizoc (ill. 45–47). In Tenochtitlan, a special building in the great ceremonial precinct – the *coateocalli* – was assigned to house the captive religious paraphernalia and fetishes of conquered communities. The deities thus captured were extraordinarily diverse, but their fundamental characteristics often show strong similarities, for they were ultimately linked to the land and the sky or great ancestral heroes. When the Spanish friars called a meeting with the leading Aztec priests to inform them

that their old religion was to be renounced, the leading priest responded with
words that characterized their basic perception of these deities:

> They [the ancestors] said
> That it is through
> The sacred spirit
> That all live
> That they give us
> Our daily fare
> And all that we
> Drink, all that
> We eat,
> Our sustenance,
> Maize, beans,
> Amaranth, chia.
> They we supplicate
> For water
> For rain,
> With which
> Everything flourishes
> On earth.

Aztec religion is the subject of ongoing study, but Anthropologist Henry
Nicholson's research has suggested that most, if not all, the cults can be
grouped in basic clusters, which can be named for the dominant deity of that
grouping.[1] Complicating the matter is the fact that deity names can also occur
as titles of office, as in the notable case of Quetzalcoatl and Tezcatlipoca at
Toltec Tula. The following discussion summarizes Nicholson's approach, and
a list, "Principal Gods and Cults of the Aztecs," may be seen on pp. 116–17.

Tezcatlipoca, "Smoking Mirror," is often characterized as the most powerful, supreme deity associated with the notion of destiny or fate. He probably
embodies the idea of a mana-like numinous power inherent in all things. His
quintessential emblem, an obsidian mirror, was associated with divination and
ultimately reflects shamanistic origins, but there can be little doubt that this
cult was particularly identified with royalty; Tezcatlipoca is the subject of the
most lengthy and reverent prayers in the rites of kingship (ill. 65).

Tonatiuh, "Turquoise Lord," the sun, was another of the supreme forces
worshiped in ancient Mexico. The emblem of Tonatiuh was a solar disk, sometimes worn on the back of ritual impersonators, more often carved on
sculptural monuments. The sun was perceived as a primary source of life
whose special devotees were the warriors, charged with the mission to provide
the sun with sacrificial victims. A special altar to the sun was used for sacrifices
in coronation rites, signaling the importance of the sun cult for the *tlatoani* as
chief warrior.

Huehueteotl, the "Old, Old Deity," was one of the names of the fire cult,
which was among the most ancient in Mesoamerica. The idea of sacred fire
stems from its basic function in the domestic hearth (ill. 62), with its three

stones to support cooking vessels. Ceramic and stone effigies of an old man bearing a brazier on his back have been found at Teotihuacan, and one was also excavated from the circular pyramid of Cuicuilco, dating to *c.* 300 BC. Among the Aztecs, the maintenance of sacred fires in the temples was a principal priestly duty, and as we shall see, it was only during the last hours of the old year that the embers were extinguished throughout all cities. The renewal of fire was identified with the renewal of time itself.

The cult of Tlaloc, the rain deity, was another of the oldest and most universal cults in ancient Mexico. Although the name may be in Nahuatl, the idea of a storm god especially identified with mountaintop shrines and with life-giving rain was as old as Teotihuacan. Tlaloc's goggle-eyed mask was as ubiquitous there as it was at Tenochtitlan, 1,000 years later. Tlaloc (archaic spelling Tlalloc) means "He who is the Embodiment of Earth." This suggests that the ancient deity was also identified with the earth and ground water before evolving into a mountaintop rain deity. Indeed, an underground Tlaloc shrine has been discovered at Teotihuacan itself. The ancient appellations allude to the sight of mists welling up from canyons and collecting as clouds around mountaintops in the rainy season. Tlaloc's impersonators wore the distinctive mask and heron-feather headdress, often carrying a cornstalk or a symbolic lightning-bolt wand; another symbol was a water-jar. Tlaloc was also manifested in the form of boulders at shrine-sites. In the Valley of Mexico the primary shrine to this deity was located atop Mt Tlaloc.

Chalchiuhtlicue, "Jade Skirt," was connected with the worship of ground water. Her shrines were therefore by springs, streams, irrigation ditches, or aqueducts, the most important of these shrines being at Pantitlán, in the center of Lake Tetzcoco. Sometimes described as Tlaloc's "sister", Chalchiuhtlicue was impersonated by ritual performers wearing the green skirt that identified the deity. Like that of Tlaloc, this cult was intimately linked to the fertility and regeneration.

The name Quetzalcoatl, "Quetzal (feather) Serpent," had many associations. It was the name of a nature-deity; it was a royal title; it figured in Toltec times as a military title and emblem; it was the name of a legendary priest-ruler; and it was a title of high priestly office. Without attempting to review the complex manifestations of this major cult, we may point to an image that best explains its most fundamental significance. This is the sculpture of a plumed serpent coiled in conical form, rising from a base whose underside is carved with the symbols of an earth-deity and Tlaloc (ills. 63, 64). The image of the serpent rising from the earth and bearing water on its tail is echoed by a description of Quetzalcoatl from the text by Sahagún which describes the rise of a great thunderstorm with wind sweeping down, raising the dust before the rain.[2]

The cults of the earth were as protean as those of the sky. In its most basic form the earth was referred to as Tlaltecuhtli, "Earth lord" or Earth lady", represented as a crouching figure with an upturned, grinning mask, often wearing sacrificial symbols and a skull upon its back. Serpents, spiders, and centipedes were also associated with this deity as creatures close to the earth. The earth was not only a giver of life, it was also the ultimate recipient of all

61 The earth-deity Tlazolteotl, from the Codex Borbonicus. Crouching in parturition, the goddess wears a flayed human skin symbolizing a dried husk enclosing a living seed. Crescent moons signal periodicity and renewal, while the centipede, serpent, and spider carry associations with the earth and fertility.

that grows and moves on its surface. Other images alluding to the earth's regenerative powers depict the earth-womb, as in the famous Chicomoztoc page from the Historia Tolteca-Chichimeca (pl. III). Ritual impersonators of the earth-mother were especially identified with procreation and agricultural fertility. Their names, Teteoinnan, Tlazolteotl, Tonantzin, Itzpapalotl, Cihuateteo, and others, metaphorically alluded to earth's powers (ill. 61). There were many connections between the symbolic costumes worn by these figures and those worn by maize deities.

Maize was portrayed in feminine terms, and three deities were especially important. Xilonen, "Young Maize," was portrayed as an adolescent girl wearing

Principal Gods and Cults of the Aztecs

	NAME	TRANSLATION	MAIN ATTRIBUTES
PRIMORDIAL CREATORS	**Ometecuhtli**	Two Lord	Primordial male-female creative principle, parents of deities and humankind
	Omecihuatl	Two Lady	
	also known as		
	Tonacatecuhtli	Our Flesh Lord	
	Tonacacíhuatl	Our Flesh Woman	
FATE, DESTINY	**Tezcatlipoca**	Smoking Mirror	Omnipotent deity, associated with fate, both beneficial and destructive. His other metaphoric titles include **Moyocoyani** (Maker of Himself), **Titlacauan** (We His Slaves), **Yaotl** (Enemy), **Ipalnemoani** (Lord of the Near and the Nigh), and **Tloque Nahuaque** (Night, Wind). **Tezcatlipoca** figures prominently in coronation speeches and prayer and must be considered especially associated with rulership
SKY	**Tonatiuh**	Sun	Sun
	Metztli	Moon	Moon
	Tlahuizcalpantecuhli	Dawn Lord	Venus (the Morning Star)
WIND	**Quetzalcoatl**	Quetzal Serpent	Windstorms that bring rain (see also deified heroes and ancestral deities)
	Ehecatl	Wind, Air	
FIRE	**Huehueteotl**	Old, Old Deity	Fire
	Chantico	In the House	The hearth fire
	Xiuhtecuhtli	Turquoise Lord	Fire, hearth
EARTH	**Popocatepetl**	Smoke Mountain	Sacred mountains whose cult embraced various others associated with the earth, rain, groundwater, and vegetation
	Iztaccíhuatl	White Woman	
	Tlalocan (Mt Tlaloc)	Place of Tlaloc	
	Tetzcotzingo	Bald Rock Honorable Place	
	Matlalcueye	Blue Skirt	
	Tepeyollotl	Mountain Heart	Locus of the earth's regenerative powers
	Toci	Grandmother	
	Teteoinnan	Deities-their-Mother	
	Tonantzin	Honored Mother	
	Coatlicue	Serpent Skirt	
	Cihuacoatl	Woman Serpent	Female deities variously associated with the earth and its fertility
	Itzpapalotl	Obsidian Butterfly	
	Tlaltecuhtli	Earth Lord or Lady	
	Tlazolteotl	Sacred Filth	
	Ilamatecuhtli	Old Lady	

Principal Gods and Cults of the Aztecs

	NAME	TRANSLATION	MAIN ATTRIBUTES
RAIN, WATER	Tlaloc	He Who Is the Embodiment of Earth	The rain deity, also associated with the earth's fertility. The Archaic name indicates ancient origins as an earth and ground-water deity, the source of moisture that takes seasonal forms as rainclouds on mountains
	Tlaloque	Little Tlalocs	
	Tepictoton	Little Old Hills	
	Chalchiuhtlicue	Jade Her Skirt	Deity of springs, rivers, lakes, and the sea
	Iztlacoliuhqui	Obsidian (Blade) Curl	Deity of frost, snow, and cold; associated with snowcapped peaks
	Huixtocihuatl	Huixtotin Woman	Deity of salt
MAIZE, VEGETATION	Xilonen	Tender Maize	Deity of first tender maize
	Centeotl	Sacred Maize	Late-ripening maize
	Chicomecoatl	Seven Serpent	Seed corn
	Xipe Totec	Flayed Lord	Vegetable deity (especially seeds)
	Mayahuel	Maguey	Maguey plant deity
	Octli Deities		Variously named deities of *pulque* (fermented drink of maguey juice)
	Xochipilli	Flower Prince	Deity of flowers and plants, patron of song and dance
	Xochiquetzal	Flower Quetzal	Goddess of flowers and grains, patroness of weavers
	Macuilxochitl	Five Flower	Deity of flowers, plants, song, dance, and games
THE LAND OF THE DEAD	Mictlantecuhtli	Mictlan Lord	Deity of death, darkness, the subterranean regions
	Mictlantecacihuatl	Mictlan Woman	Female counterpart of **Mictlantecuhtli**
DEIFIED HEROSE AND ANCESTRAL DEITIES	Huitzilopochtli	Hummingbird on the Left	Mexica–Aztec ancestral tutelary deity, patron of war, associated with the sun
	Quetzalcoatl	Quetzal (feathered) Serpent	Ancient wind and storm deity. The name was also a title of rulers; historically associated with a celebrated ruler of Toltec Tula. At time of Spanish Conquest this cult was seated in Chollollan
	Yacatecuhtli	Nose Lord	Tutelary deity of traders
	Mixcoatl	Cloud Serpent	Ancient tribal deity of the hunt, especially revered in Tlaxcala, Huexotzingo, and other communities in Puebla Valley
	Camaxtli	Lord of the Chase	Chichimec deity whose cult was centered in Huexotzingo

The Aztec deities

62–64 LEFT The "Old, Old Deity" Huehueteotl (god of fire), recovered from the Great Pyramid. BELOW LEFT Quetzalcoatl; the green, iridescent feathers of the quetzal bird were an ancient symbol of royalty and of the sky. BELOW RIGHT The base of the coiled Quetzalcoatl portrays the rain god Tlaloc. The entire sculpture represents a great windstorm rising out of the mountains bringing the seasonal rain.

65–68 TOP LEFT An impersonator of
Tezcatlipoca, from the Codex
Ixtlilxóchitl. TOP RIGHT Mayahuel, female
deity of the maguey cactus, a plant highly
prized for its fiber and juice. ABOVE
Huitzilopochtli, the deified Aztec warrior-
hero and patron of Tenochtitlan, shown
with his hummingbird headdress, shield,
and darts. LEFT The sculpted mask of
Xipe Totec (god of vegetation),
representing a flayed human skin sewn
over the head of a living impersonator.
The mask alludes to a dry husk enclosing a
living seed.

the first tender maize of the rainy season on her headdress. Chicomecoatl, "Seven Serpent," was the title given to dried seed maize, harvested and kept for the next year; priestesses bearing ears of this seed maize appeared at the onset of the planting season. Cinteotl, "Sacred Maize-ear," was the more general term for maize eaten after the fall harvest season.

Other important cultigens were represented in the Aztec pantheon, among which the maguey agave was particularly important. In central Mexico these great blue-green agave are seen bordering the fields. They were the source of *octli* (*pulque*), the mildly fermented beer-like drink which, consumed in moderate amounts, was a staple part of the diet. The plant is also a source of fiber used to make cloth, netting, ropes, bags, and many other useful products.

Among the cults of deified ancestors, Huitzilopochtli was pre-eminent in Tenochtitlan (ill. 68). We have recounted the story of this legendary hero, and noted the possibility that he was actually a composite entity, fabricated by the primitive Mexica from other such figures identified with older towns in the Valley. The custom of deifying heroes and outstanding rulers can also be seen in Tetzcoco, where the ruler Netzahualcoyotl was posthumously enshrined at Tetzcotzingo, with his effigy carved in the rock among other shrines to the nature-deities. This is an instance of a revered "founder-father" figure attaining the status of a deified ancestral hero.

The concept of teotl

A basic feature of Aztec religious thought was expressed by the word-root *teo*, often written with the *tl* suffix as *teotl*. Difficult to translate, the word was recorded by the Spanish as "god," "saint," or sometimes "demon." Studies of the word *teo* show that it appears in Nahuatl texts in a variety of contexts. Sometimes it accompanies the names of nature-deities, but it was also used in connection with human impersonators of those divinities, as well as in association with their sacred masks and related ceremonial objects, including sculptured effigies of wood, stone, or dough. Such words as "mana," "numinous" or "sacred" have been used to suggest its significance. The word *teo* may be used to qualify almost anything mysterious, powerful, or beyond ordinary experience, such as great animals of prey, a remote and awe-inspiring snow-capped mountain, a phenomenon of terrible power such as the sun or a bolt of lightning, or the life-giving earth, water, and maize, or even a great *tlatoani*. Nor was its application restricted to good or ethical things, for malign phenomena might also be designated by *teo*.

The diverse contexts of the word *teo* suggest that the Aztecs regarded the things of their world – both transitory or permanent – as inherently charged to a greater or lesser degree with vital force or power. This reflects an outlook widespread among peoples of the pre-modern world, in which things of the physical environment were endowed with wills of their own, and even given, on occasion, a sense of personality. Aztec rituals offer many examples of this mode of perception. For example, during Ahuitzotl's reign in the late 15th century, he inaugurated a new aqueduct bringing water from Chapultepec to the center of Tenochtitlan. On that occasion his priests were dressed as the female water-deity Chalchiuhtlicue, "Jade Skirt." Attired as the deity, the priests waited by the channel to welcome the first flow of water. As the water rushed in they reached down to present incense, ground turquoise, and sacrificial quail to the flowing life-giving element; at the same time they spoke to the water itself as the living object of the offering. This rite illustrates the curious, inextricable equivalence of the deity, deity-impersonator, priest, and the natural element – a chain of associations alien to modern Western thought.

The myths of creation

The Aztec myths of creation were gathered in variant related versions by the 16th-century Spanish friars and members of the Indian intelligentsia who worked in different locations within the Valley of Mexico and neighboring regions. Cosmogonic myths describe the primordial beginning of the world and an ensuing sequence of eras whose transformations led to the present earth and its animal and human inhabitants. An understanding of the myths helped to explain the origin of the earth and the regularity of such phenomena as the sun, the moon, and the rainy season, as well as the cycle of vegetation and the presence of human beginnings. Myths also provided a way of learning sacred history and the principles governing cosmic and social existence. On many levels of meaning, the myths portrayed themes to which the Aztecs referred in their obligation to maintain a basic integration of the social and natural orders.

The primordial male and female force

According to one important text, before the world appeared there were primordial masculine and feminine creative forces, named *ome tecuhtli*, "two lord," and *ome cihuatl*, "two lady." They resided in *omeyocan*, "the place of two" (this is often translated as "the place of duality"; but as will be seen on the following pages, the concept of dual *opposing* forces was not strongly held in Aztec cosmological thought). Masculine and feminine forces were also personified as Tonacatecuhtli and Tonacacíhuatl, "Lord and Lady of our Flesh and Sustenance," denoting their association with the production of food. A page from the Codex Borbonicus depicts the primordial couple seated within a rectangular precinct surrounded by calendrical glyphs; they speak about time to each other (ill. 69). The two personified primordial forces had four sons, each of which was identified with one of the cardinal points. They were respectively colored red, black, blue, or white according to direction. Thus, the horizontal plane of the world was defined as having a living creative center around which the quadrants were symmetrically placed. Other cosmogonic accounts describe the vertical dimension of space, defined by an axis connecting the center of the plane of the earth to the celestial sphere and the world below. The heavens were divided into a series of layers – 13 by some descriptions, 9 according to others – and the underworld was similarly arranged. There was no juxtaposition of heaven versus hell in this cosmological schema, for the levels of the sky and those of the lower world carried no hierarchical moral value. The outer perimeter of the world was

69 One of the central pages of the Codex Borbonicus, showing the creator god and goddess, Ometecuhtli and Omecíhuatl. They sit in a sacred enclosure from which water flows, surrounded by day-signs and a series of associated ruling deities.

conceived as a circle (or sometimes a square), where the surrounding sea, *ilhuica-atl*, met the inverted bowl of the sky. One of the most ancient cosmological images preserved by the Aztecs likened the earth to an alligator floating in the primeval sea, with the scales and corrugations of its back corresponding to mountains and valleys.

The five ages

The idea of multiple, imperfect creations was very old and widespread in Mesoamerica, for it is also recorded in the sacred book of the Quiché Maya, the Popol Vuh.[3] The original creation of the earth was followed by destruction and a succession of four imperfect epochs, each ending in disaster, leading to the present fifth era[4] likewise prophesied to end in catastrophe. In the Aztec texts each of the five epochs formed an age called a "sun." The complete text of the Legend of the Suns is recorded in the 16th-century Codex Chimalpopoca, translated from the Nahuatl by John Bierhorst. The sequence of eras officially accepted in Tenochtitlan is recorded on such famous sculptural monuments as the "Stone of the Five Suns" (formerly known as the "Aztec Calendar") (ills. 70, 71), and the "Coronation Stone of Motecuhzoma II" (ills. 12, 13). We have reviewed the latter monument in the context of Aztec coronation rites (Chapter 1). Briefly re-stated, among the Aztecs the first era was called "four jaguar." At that time, giants walked the earth but did not till the soil or sow maize, only living by gleaning wild fruits and roots. This imperfect era ended when a jaguar devoured the giants. The hieroglyphic sign for the era was therefore a jaguar head. The second era, "four wind," was also flawed, and was destroyed by hurricanes that magically turned the imperfect existing men into monkeys – human-like, but not fully human creatures. The sign of this era was the mask of Quetzalcoatl, lord of the winds. The third imperfect era ended in a rain of fire, and its people either perished or were changed into birds. This happened on the day "four rain," therefore the sign of this sun was the mask of Tlaloc, lord of rain. The fourth era was one of rains so abundant and frequent that the earth was deluged and people were changed into fish. For this reason its sign was the head of Chalchiuhtlicue, "Jade Skirt," the deity of lakes, rivers, springs, and seas. The fifth, or present era, was prophesied to end in earthquakes, and its sign was the hieroglyph *ollin*, "movement" (of the earth). It was at the beginning of this era that the actual sun, moon, and human beings were finally created.

The eminent Mexican scholar Alfonso Caso pointed out that the succession of ages told in the Aztec myth is quite unlike the Judeo-Christian concept of an original paradise, followed by the fall and expulsion of the first human being.[5] Instead, the image of the Aztec creation myths is of a progression of worlds, as the creator-forces and deities strove to find a formula for a more perfect world and humanity. There is also the sense of a search for progressively better food-stuffs: in the first era the giants ate roots and wild fruits; the second era lists *acocentli*, pine nuts; the third era names *ace centli*, millium; and the fourth names *cencocopi*, or *teocentli*, a wild grass-like plant with seed similar to that of primitive maize.

The creation of the sun and moon

It will be remembered that the Aztecs regarded Teotihuacan as the mythic setting where the sun and moon were created. An account of this cosmic event at the beginning of the fifth era was recorded by Bernardino de Sahagún:

> It is told that when yet [all] was in darkness, when yet no sun had shone and no dawn had broken, it is said – the gods gathered themselves together and took counsel among themselves there at Teotihuacan. They spoke; they said among themselves: "Come hither, O gods! Who will carry the burden? Who will take it upon himself to be the sun, to bring the dawn?"[6]

In answer to this question, two gods volunteered to sacrifice themselves to become the sun. In preparation, the one named Tecuciztecatl laid out a sacrificial kit of the most costly materials: fir branches made of quetzal feathers;

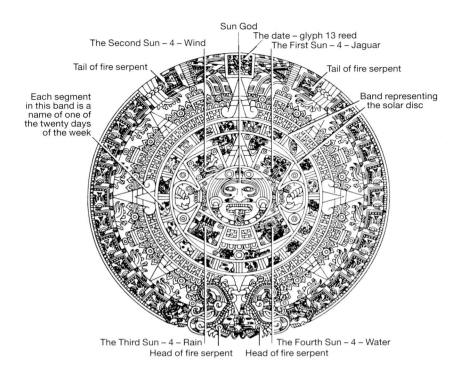

Sun God
The date – glyph 13 reed
The Second Sun – 4 – Wind
The First Sun – 4 – Jaguar
Tail of fire serpent
Tail of fire serpent
Each segment in this band is a name of one of the twenty days of the week
Band representing the solar disc
The Third Sun – 4 – Rain
The Fourth Sun – 4 – Water
Head of fire serpent
Head of fire serpent

70, 71 ABOVE and OPPOSITE The Aztec Sun Stone, found beneath the central plaza of Mexico City in the last decade of the 18th century. Carved at its center is the face of the sun, or perhaps the earth monster, Tlaltecuhtli. The monument is not a fully functioning calendar, but commemorates the five mythic world-creations ("suns"). The date-glyph cartouche 13-reed at the top denotes the mythical beginning of the present sun, but also marks the calendrical year 1427, when Itzcoatl rose to power. The conjugation of a sacred date and the historical year sanctified the authority of the Aztec rulers, and established a vital link between the cosmos and human society.

grass balls made of gold; maguey spines of greenstone; and the reddened bloodied spines of coral. His incense, moreover, was of the best kind. The other volunteer, an impoverished deity named Nanauatzin, could only afford green rushes, pine needles, actual maguey spines, and his own blood; and for incense, the scabs from his sores. Four nights of penance were spent atop the Moon Pyramid and the Pyramid of the Sun at Teotihuacan. On the fifth night the two volunteers were ceremonially dressed and brought before a hearth where a bonfire was blazing. It was midnight and the assembled gods said to Tecuciztecatl: "Take courage O Tecuciztecatl; fall – cast thyself – into the fire!" But the immense heap of glowing coals and the furious flames cast a heat so unbearable that four times he tried to throw himself in, only to turn away. Then Nanauatzin was called and, gathering his courage, he quickly cast himself in; then Tecuciztecatl took courage and followed.

After this, when both had cast themselves into the flames, when they had already burned, then the gods sat waiting to see where Nanauatzin would come to rise – he who fell first into the fire – in order that he might shine [as the sun]; in order that dawn might break.[7]

In all directions the gods looked and kept turning about, until those who looked east saw the first sunrise. The poetic parallel with the rising sun and the heat of the sacrificial bonfire the night before is especially striking:

And when the sun came to rise, when he burst forth, he appeared to be red; he kept swaying from side to side. It was impossible to look into his face; he blinded one with his light. Intensely did he shine. He issued rays of light from himself; his rays reached in all directions; his brilliant rays penetrated everywhere.[8]

Then, afterward, Tecuciztecatl rose as the moon, and to darken its first brilliance one of the gods threw a rabbit in his face – which is why in ancient Mexico the moon was perceived as having the imprint of a rabbit. But the sun and moon were still stationary: and it was only after all the gods had sacrificed themselves and Ehecatl (another name of Quetzalcoatl, the lord of the wind) blew and blew, that the sun and the moon were sent on their paths by day and night respectively.

The creation of humankind

The final episode of the creation myth is preserved in yet another account by Fray Gerónimo de Mendieta.[9] This describes Quetzalcoatl descending to the underworld regions of the dead, where he gathered a great heap of bones from past imperfect generations. These he sprinkled with his own blood and ground them up to create a new humanity.

It must not be imagined that myths such as these were told to provide entertainment or to exercise personal fantasy. Much less were they intended as rationally consistent and objective explanations of cosmic or human happenings. The stories provided poetic expression of the truths and principles that formed an underpinning to life and experience. The image of primordial male and female figures seated within an enclosure suggests a primal unity of complementary, generative forces. Myths describing a succession of cycles of creation and destruction show that death was but a condition for inevitable regeneration. The deities that offer themselves to the raging bonfire to be transformed into the sun and moon speak of the necessity of sacrifice to bring forth new forms of life. Similarly, the creator-god who offers his blood to be mingled with bones from the ancestors shows how something of value had to be offered to make something of greater value. These mythic events took place in a hallowed time, when models were established for subsequent activities. Thus the rising of the sun was seen as a sacred event because it was identified with the original sacrifice. And just as darkness was transformed into daylight, so too countless other changes experienced in the natural world could be traced to prototypes described in the mythic creation-time. The annual change from drought to rain, and the rebirth of vegetation; the passage of one stage of human life to the next, as in birth, puberty, marriage, and death; or the accession of a great chieftain, passing from a lower social role to a higher one, all reflect a basic aspect of the Aztec world view, which was marked by a tendency to focus on forces and phenomena not as fixed or static entities, but as things or existences in an eternal cycle of change.

Aztec cosmogony stands in contrast to that of ancient Mesopotamia, which stresses the struggle of dual powers of light versus dark, order versus chaos, life versus death, or good versus evil. In ancient Mexico by contrast, the myths seem not to lose sight of the observable seasonal process of birth, growth, maturity, and death, followed by sacrifice to ensure rebirth and renewal. As we shall see, it was the kings who were responsible for making the offerings essential to bring about new life: in the vast schema of cosmic events portrayed in Aztec myths, humankind was only a small part, yet it played a critical and active role in ensuring the progression of the seasons, the movement of heavenly bodies, and the periodic regeneration of nature as well as communal life. Whatever cosmic dualism existed in Aztec thought, it was a dualism of complementary forces in continual process of change, not a dualism of opposing forces struggling for each other's destruction.

The ritual calendar

Before describing Aztec religious festivals and buildings, their calendar system must be explained. The arrangement of time governed all important activities of individual life as well as the scheduling and performance of festivals and other state-organized events. Like many other peoples of antiquity in the New World and the Old, the Aztecs did not experience time as a succession of uniform movements, stretching monotonously from the indefinite past into the indefinite future. Nor was their time of indifferent, uniform quality. Time for the Aztecs was full of energy and motion, the harbinger of change, and always charged with a potent sense of miraculous happening. The cosmogonic myths reveal a preoccupation with the process of creation, destruction and recreation, and the calendrical system reflected these notions about the character of time.

There were two aspects of Aztec time-counting, each with different functions. The first was the curious *tonalpohualli*, "counting of the days," a 260-day cycle used for the purpose of divination. This repeating round of days formed a sacred almanac, widely used among Mesoamerican peoples long before the Aztecs. The *tonalpohualli* may have originated as far back as the Olmec period in the 1st millennium BC, or even before. The second part of the calendrical system was a 365-day solar count, known as the *xiuhpohualli*, "counting of the years," which regulated the recurrent cycle of annual seasonal festivals. These two counts were simultaneously in operation. They have often been explained as two engaged, rotating gears, in which the beginning day of the larger 365-day wheel would align with the beginning day of the smaller 260-day cycle every 52 years. This 52-year period constituted a Mesoamerican "century." The change from one 52-year period into the next was always the occasion of an important religious festival.

The 260-day count

It is thought that the 260-day *tonalpohualli* count originated in an observed astronomical phenomenon. Archaeoastronomers have noted that the sun, on its annual passage from south to north and back again, crosses a zenith point at a latitude near the Classic Maya city of Copán, in modern Honduras, at a 260-day interval. Did this interval determine the original planting-to-harvest season at an unknown time in history? Did it acquire a prestigious significance, hallowed from antiquity and preserved by custom as a time-count in later religious traditions? Answers to these questions are beyond our present reach. What may be described in greater detail is the organization of the *tonalpohualli* and some of the functions it served in ordering the lives of Aztec people.

The 260-day cycle was composed of 20 groups of named and numbered days. Each day received a name, such as rabbit, water, flint knife, alligator, jaguar, etc., visually represented by a hieroglyphic sign of a particular animal or object. The cycle of 20 days intermeshed with a rotating cycle of numbers, 1 to 13, each number denoted by dots. After every complete rotation, each number was engaged with a new day. Thus, within the 260-day period each day was identified by the combination of one of the 20 day-names with one of the 13 numbers (20 × 13 = 260).

The sacred 260-day cycle was then divided into 20 "weeks" of 13 days each, called *trecenas* by the Spaniards. Every *trecena* began with the number 1 and the day-name which came up in the sequence of rotation. Thus, each combination was unique within the *tonalpohualli* cycle, for no day in any one week could be confused with that of another.

The *tonalpohualli* counts were kept in screenfold books called *tonalamatl*. The books were made from a long strip of amatl bark paper, from which the word *tonalamatl* derives. This bark-paper was coated with white gesso upon which the fine drawing and brilliant painting were done. One of the most famous of these screenfold books is the Codex Borbonicus. The codex was made in Tenochtitlan or in the vicinity of Ixtapalapan-Culhuacan, very soon after the Spanish Conquest. At some time during the early colonial period it was taken to Spain, where it rested in the library of the Escorial Palace, near Madrid. It was removed to France probably around 1823 and bought by

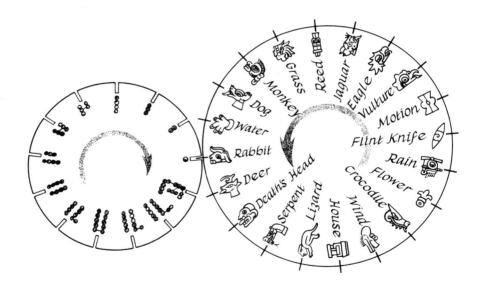

72, 73 ABOVE Schematic representation of the 260-day Aztec *tonalpohualli* calendar. The 20 named days intercalate with the numbers 1 to 13. OPPOSITE The first page of the ritual almanac Codex Fejervary-Mayer shows Xiuhtecuhtli (god of fire) in the central panel as the vertical axis mundi. The East lies at the top, where the sun-disk rises; West is at the bottom, shown as an earth-monster where the sun sets. The 13 days of each of the 20 *trecenas* are indicated by a continuous counterclockwise sequence of dots. The count begins with the day-sign crocodile, the first day of the first *trecena* at the lower right corner of the upper arm of the cross. Each of the remaining 12 days is indicated by a dot, until the 14th day, Jaguar, introduces the next *trecena*, and so on.

the Library of the Chamber of Deputies in the old Bourbon Palace in Paris: hence the name Borbonicus. The Indian artist worked in a virtually pure pre-Hispanic style, but spaces were ruled off to receive commentary written by the Spanish using Roman script.

Each of the screenfold pages in this codex is devoted to a 13-day *trecena*, and is also divided to show a regent deity presiding over the *trecena*. Individual days are shown in rectangular subdivisions, each with its own associated deity: there were 13 Lords of the Day, each with a particular bird or butterfly, and 9 Lords of the Night. These deities recur throughout the *tonalpohualli* in independent, repeating cycles. The *tonalpohualli* is thus revealed to be more than a system of numbers and days, for each *trecena* was influenced by a ruling deity, and each day was influenced by its own day-lord and night-lord.

It is clear from the writings of the Spanish chroniclers that the influences displayed by the *tonalpohualli* were interpreted by professional diviners. These specialists were called upon to make prognostications for newborn children, to give advice for different endeavors according to auspicious or inauspicious

days, or to determine the best days for planting and harvesting. The chronicler Alonso de Zorita describes the use of the *tonalamatl* for agricultural practices:

> These characters [of the *tonalamatl*] also taught the Indian nations the days on which they were to sow, reap, till the land, cultivate maize, weed, harvest, store, shell the ears of maize, sow beans and flax seed. They always took into account that it had to be in such and such month, after such and such feats, on such and such a day, under such and such a sign. All this was done with superstitious order and care. If chili was not sown on a certain day, squash on another, maize on another, and so forth, in disregard of the orderly count of the days, the people felt there would be great damage and loss of any crop sown outside of the established order. The reason for all this was that some signs were held to be good, others evil, and others indifferent, just as our almanacs record the signs of the zodiac.[10]

We may suppose that such prognostications were made in conjunction with known weather patterns and other environmental conditions, as well as social and economic factors. Unfortunately, most of the immense accumulated body of orally transmitted knowledge that accompanied the *tonalpohualli* was lost or diffused amid other recorded information during the Spanish colonial period. Nevertheless, Bernardino de Sahagún's Book Four, *The Soothsayers*, and Diego Durán's *Book of Gods and Rites and the Ancient Calendar* contain valuable records.[11]

Divination, the art of foreseeing future events or discovering hidden knowledge through supernatural means, was a standard feature of official and private life in many other ancient civilizations. All peoples seek to know the unknowable, to control the uncontrollable, or to make a confident choice about difficult decisions. Divination is one of the mechanisms by which this is attempted. Like the Greeks, Romans, and Chinese, the Aztecs believed in the portentous meaning of omens and auguries in the natural world. The pattern of diverse phenomena which appear to coincide were perceived as highly meaningful – auguring good or evil, success or failure for a proposed endeavor. In ancient Greece, no king or commander would dare take a major course of action without consulting one of the many famous oracles, such as that of Delphi; Alexander's career was deeply affected by the Libyan oracle at Siwah. Roman generals regularly sacrificed bullocks in order to read, from the configuration of their livers, the supernatural circumstances foretelling triumph or defeat in an impending campaign. Similarly in Shang China, oracle-bones of tortoise shell or the shoulder-blades of buffalo were carefully prepared, inscribed, and exposed to heat, so that cracks developing on the surface would reveal a hidden pattern of cosmic phenomena that could be interpreted. Another analogy to help understand the divinatory functions of the *tonalpohualli* is provided by the ancient *Chinese Book of Changes*, also known as the *I Ching*.[12] This book of wisdom was already old when Confucius wrote his commentaries on it around 500 BC, yet it continues to be widely consulted in the present day. To use the book, a question is posed and yarrow stalks or coins are thrown to produce a pattern which is recorded as a diagram of six continuous or broken lines. This hexagram in turn is interpreted according to the *I Ching* texts. The texts present a series of images describing changes and relationships observed in natural forces, interpreting them in terms of social circumstances. Thus, when a question is posed, those forces affecting the question at the moment it was formed can be taken into account in deciding a course of action. The *I Ching* texts, which reflect knowledge accumulated since great antiquity, are not intended to foretell fate as in ordinary sooth-saying or fortune-telling. What they offer the questioner is a picture of the cosmic circumstances surrounding a particular problem, and counsel for what may be done to arrive at the right course of action.

Another avenue to understanding the possible uses of the Aztec *tonalpohualli* is presented today by a traditional form of calendrical divination still practiced by Maya Indian diviners, called "daykeepers," at mountain shrines in Guatemala.[13] At such sacred places, candles are lit and copal incense is burned as an offering. Using crystals and seeds made of coral the day-keeper will make arrangements in lots of four, counting out the days of the 260-day calendar. One day is assigned to each lot, starting from the current day or the day the client's problem began. This is the beginning of a complex process of interpretation, through which the daykeeper's client will receive counsel on the course of action revealed by the time-count and the pattern of seeds and crystals.

Did the lost oral tradition accompanying the Aztec *tonalpohualli*, which was probably rooted in a very old agricultural cycle, have similar functions to those presented by these analogies? At present it is possible to say only that as a sophisticated system of divination, the *tonalpohualli* was undoubtedly the carrier of tradition and authority, a system woven into the fabric of Mesoamerican thinking. The *tonalpohualli* played an especially important role in the daily lives of the Aztecs, from the solving of personal perplexities, to serving the needs of rulers searching for counsel in matters of state, to prescribing the appropriate times for carrying out planting and harvesting.

The 365-day count

The annual ceremonial calendar of the Aztec city-states was governed according to the 365-day solar count, the *xiuhpohualli*. This period was divided into 18 "months" of 20 days each, called *veintenas* by the Spanish, plus a 5-day period between the old year and the new. The latter was a dangerous and inactive time of transition called *nemontemi*. Each *veintena* had its own festival, closely correlated to the agricultural year. The years were named after the "year bearer," one of four possible day-names of the *tonalpohualli* which could begin a new year with its accompanying number, according to the system of rotation. The possible year-names were rabbit, reed, flint knife, and house. The years were distinguished by their numbers – thus 1-rabbit, 2-reed, 3-house, 4-flint knife, until the 13 numbers and the 4 day and year-names began to repeat themselves every 52 years (13 × 4).

Curiously, the successive 52-year cycles were not calendrically differentiated. It is as if in the Christian world centuries were not distinguished as being before or after Christ. Thus the voyage of Columbus would have been recorded as '92, or the meeting of Cortés and Motecuhzoma as '19, the end of the Second

World War as '45, or the end of the 20th century as '99. In the Aztec system, only a knowledge of historical events would allow a person to place them in the appropriate 52-year cycle. It was customary in writing, or in sculptured inscriptions, to indicate year-names and their numbers by enclosing them in a square cartouche, as may be seen on the Coronation Stone of Motecuhzoma II (ill. 13). Day-names were ordinarily left unenclosed.

The conclusion of a 52-year cycle and the beginning of a new one was the occasion for special ceremonies. At that time the "binding of the years" took place, marked by the ceremonial tying of a bundle of 52 reeds, the *xiuhmopilli*. Stone sculptural representations of one of these objects have been recovered from Aztec ruins in the vicinity of the cathedral in downtown Mexico City. One example in the National Museum is carved with its date-hieroglyph corresponding to the year 1508, when a New Fire ceremony was also celebrated to ensure the beginning of a new cycle. Special importance was placed on the completion of two cycles (104 years), for at such times the solar count, the *tonalpohualli*, and the 52-year cycle coincided.

As mentioned above, there was an annual cycle of 18 festivals associated with the 18 *veintena* "months" of the 365-day solar year. These festivals were basically of three types: those directed to mountains and water in order to ensure rain; those directed to the earth, the sun, and maize, to ensure fertility and an abundant harvest; and those directed to special deities, particularly those identified as patrons of different community groups or of the community as a whole. The latter festivals usually had various purposes, among which the particular historical and cultural identity of a given group might be a special concern.

Just as the *tonalpohualli* seems to have functioned in a similar way in all areas, so too the same order of *veintena* festivals has been recorded in the ethnohistoric texts. Nevertheless there was great variation in the local practice of these festivals, due to different geographical and cultural conditions. For example, in the Valley of Mexico and its environs there are many micro-environments where rain may arrive at somewhat different times and with different intensity, and where the time for harvest is subject to variation due to altitude, local frosts, and so on. Such environmental factors would affect the timing of festivals concerned with agriculture. In addition, political factors and cultural change strongly affected ceremonial events, as the rulers of empires adapted old practices or invented new variations to express the new political, religious, and social needs. In this way, traditional agricultural ceremonies were often invested with new military and imperial themes. Old myths were thus fitted with new rites, and new myths might be created to accommodate old ritual procedures. Many adjustments of this kind were occurring in the Valley of Mexico at the time of the Spanish arrival. But no uniform practice of the festival cycle had yet been devised, hence the variety of descriptions recorded by the Spanish.

The chart of festivals found at the end of the book outlines the principal cult themes and local deities. But the festivals are best understood in the context of the landscapes, temples, or urban settings where they were celebrated. For this reason we shall now turn to the Aztec ordering of space, to see how the land was organized and equipped with monuments.

Sacred landscapes

It may be difficult for many who live in large cities today, removed from the natural environment that supports us, to fully realize the interconnections between ourselves, the land, and the cycle of the seasons. Our diverse activities within the city continue without interruption or significant change throughout the year, and our feelings about the natural setting are filtered through weather reports, documentary films, or news concerning the economic consequences of environmental degradation. But the Indian peoples of the Americas, including those who lived in the cities of antiquity, perceived themselves to be active participants in a ramifying network of connections that reached outward, into the natural setting and all its forces and phenomena. The physical forms of the land and its seasonal events were understood as primary sacred entities that came before the historic forms of their many deities. In Central Highland Mexico the most significant natural features were identified with some special spiritual presence. Many places used by the Aztecs had already accumulated mythical, historical, and religious meanings from centuries of earlier occupations. Topographic forms and man-made symbols were joined in certain locations to form a ritual network for communication between the social order, the natural forces and their deities, and a range of deified ancestral heroes. This articulation of the land outlined the structure of a sacred geography. As we will see on the following pages, the hill named Huixachtlán, the Great Pyramid of Tenochtitlan, the ritual Hill of Tetzcotzingo, and shrines upon the heights of Mt Tlaloc and at Pantitlán in Lake Tetzcoco were notable icons of Aztec sacred geography, designed to manifest the inherent powers of things seen and unseen in the natural environment.

The need to develop a system of sacred places was given impetus by an unprecedented natural disaster that affected the highlands between 1452 and 1454. This period marked the end of the 52-year cycle begun in 1402. The calamity started in 1447 with disastrous rains. Then, in 1450, a four-year sequence of frosts and droughts produced a terrible famine. In those years the clouds that usually appear on mountaintops failed to form with the expected summer rain. The long dry season that begins in late September and lasts until mid-June stretched into July and August. In the withering sun, scanty showers evaporated before reaching the ground, and maize fields yellowed soon after sprouting. Drought continued through the following year, and was repeated the year after that. At first, stocks of food were sufficient to ameliorate the worst effects, but soon the disproportion between reserves and the prolonged demand for them as sustenance became frighteningly evident. The drought affected a large highland region and tribute could not feed the entire population. The dry earth forced farmers and their families away from the desolate fields into the mountains in search of game, or to the lakeshores where they might find fish, birds, or other aquatic life. As maize, amaranth, and beans grew scarcer, houses and market stalls were abandoned and streets and canals of the cities became the last dwelling-places for those who could no longer move on. Country trails were also scenes of bitter desolation as men, women and children, weakened by hunger, were forced to lie by the wayside.

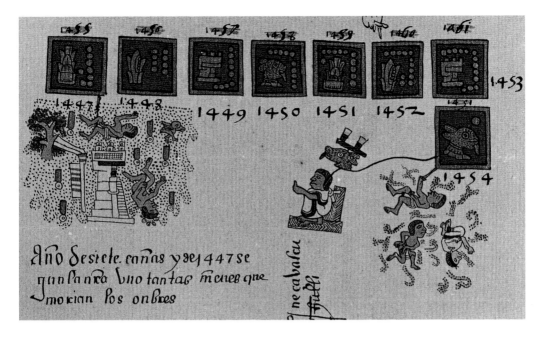

74 The year 1447 saw disastrous rains, heralding a period of climatic irregularity and crop failures culminating in the catastrophic famine of 1454. From the Codex Telleriano-Remensis.

Languor and exhaustion were followed by sickness, and thousands of starving and bewildered people slowly began to die.

The scale of the calamity grew in the third year because the last reserves of maize had disappeared and even the seed-corn was eaten. Parents sold their children into slavery for a few ears of maize, to Huaxtecs and Totonacs from the eastern coastland unaffected by the drought. At least the children would be fed and might therefore survive. In the atmosphere of corruption and despair suspicion abounded, and soon it was widely imagined that witches were abroad in the land. Some were seen by people in dreams, others were witnessed by victims predisposed to believe in them, while others actually confessed to witchcraft. The fear of those terrible years, like 20th-century memories of the great economic depression in the 1930s, was indelibly impressed on the Aztecs. The Codex Telleriano-Remensis, recording principal historical events, illustrates the year 1454 with the sign of diseased, famine-struck victims (ill. 74).

As the end of the old 52-year cycle drew near, preparations took place for the New Fire rites to bring in the new cycle. This was always a time of tension, for who knew what the future might bring when at present all seemed dark and uncertain?

The New Fire rites

Renewals celebrated every 52 years were especially critical, and none more so than the approaching year 1-rabbit (1454). On day 20 of the feast Panquetzaliztli

(10 December), dedicated to Huitzilopochtli, the last pink and turquoise light tinged the snowcapped peaks of Popocatepetl and Iztaccíhuatl, but in the deepening shadows below no evening fires were appearing. In towns and cities around the lakes, on pyramid temples, in palace kitchens and domestic hearths, and in goldsmiths' workshops and pottery kilns, all embers were being extinguished. The three hearthstones on which cooking pots rested, and stone pestles and figures of deities, were all thrown into water. Old pottery vessels were also thrown out and everywhere there was sweeping to remove all remnants of rubbish. These preparations gradually ceased as thousands of people went up to the flat rooftops or gathered in plazas and open spaces to wait in hushed expectation. Pregnant women wore blue-painted masks and were enclosed in granaries to be guarded by warriors lest they turn into fearsome beasts in the night. Small children were likewise masked lest they turn into mice. This was a time of ritual death, a transition in preparation and hope for renewal. As darkness filled the Valley, a procession of fire-priests and men dressed as gods departed from the ceremonial enclosure in the middle of Tenochtitlan, walking across the causeway to Ixtapalapan. Their destination was an ancient shrine on the hill named Huixachtlán, "thorn-tree place," a volcanic height commanding the headland between lakes Tetzcoco and Xochimilco. The summit is centrally located and visible from almost every-where in the Valley. This was the site of a temple-platform, hallowed long before the Aztecs had arrived in the region. At Huixachtlán, on the platform in front of the temple, an altar of firewood was stacked and waiting. Everyone looked toward the mountain's black shape and up to the millions of stars. Meteors were seen flitting in random dashes, and the gauzy belt of the Milky Way spanned the heavens. Perhaps in whispers the people would name the constellations: "the s-shaped stars"; "the scorpion stars." But the most anxiously awaited "fire-drill" had not yet risen from the eastern horizon. This would herald the new cycle, a sign of the renewal of time. The "fire-drill," *mamalhuaztli* in Nahuatl, corresponded in part to our constellation Taurus (Bull) and incorporated the bright reddish star Aldebaran. Apprehension touched the silent population, for it was widely believed that if the fire rituals failed, darkness would continue into infinity:

> Thus it was said: it was claimed that if fire could not be drawn, then [the sun] would be destroyed forever; all would be ended; there would evermore be night... and the demons of darkness would descend and eat men.[14]

As time grew shorter the masked procession of gods reached the steep slope of the Huixachtlán summit. Each came with their own peculiar gait, perhaps lightly trotting or slowly stepping, or seeming to glide on the pathway. Most of these deities are depicted in the New Fire rites page from the 16th-century Codex Borbonicus (plate XVI). Quetzalcoatl leads the procession, bearing a seashell emblem on his chest and wearing an elaborate plumed headdress with symbolic appendages. He was the ancient deity personifying the wind that brings rainstorms in its train. The deity Tlaloc is not shown in the manuscript, but is mentioned in Bernardino de Sahagún's account of the rite. Tlaloc, the deity of rain and agricultural fertility, wore a goggled blue mask with a crown of heron feathers, and carried a lightning wand in his hand. Then came Ixteocale, a deity of *pulque*, the staple fermented maguey sap drink. Xipe Totec was next, clad in a dried human skin, symbolic of a husk or shell enclosing a living seed; he was an agricultural deity of regeneration and plants. Ixtlilton followed, a deity whose black drink was used for curing children's illnesses. Then came Xochipilli, "flower prince," in waving plumes and a floral emblems, a deity of summer vegetation and feasting. The last two were great goddesses: Cinteotl, bearing on her back a rack with tasseled ears of maize, the staple upon which life depended; and Teteoinnan the ancient earth-goddess, with her spinning whorl and crescent-moon emblems, symbols of periodicity and renewal. The procession summoned the great powers of nature and the life of plants and the animal world. In their semi-human form, the procession of gods brought an enchantment beyond the boundary of ordinary experience and the memory of mythic events to the new fire altar at Huixachtlán.

Carmen Aguilera, of the National Library of Anthropology, INAH, has meticulously researched the Nahuatl texts describing the New Fire rites.[15] The constellation Tianquiztli, "marketplace," known to us as The Pleiades, began traversing the meridian dividing the sky from north to south at 10:03 pm, heralding the passage of *mamalhuaztli*. From the Huixachtlán temple the transit would be seen to occur almost straight overhead on a vertical axis. A fire-priest placed his drill-board flat on the chest of a sacrificial victim, and carried the flame to the wood on the platform. If the rite were successful Tianquiztli would be followed by Mamalhuaztli past the zenith. The sun would rise and a new 52-year cycle would begin. As Mamalhuaztli crossed the meridian at 10:44, the sacrifice was made and the heart was offered to the fire.[16] By midnight the pyre was fully burning and the body was placed on the altar as a glowing cloud of red sparks billowed into the night, visible to everyone watching in the towns far below. A great whooping arose as runners lit torches from the new fire. Soon they were seen as points of light moving quickly down the trails from Huixachtlán, carrying flame to fire-temple hearths in the cities below. From Tenochtitlan the torch could be seen coming across the length of the Ixtapalapan causeway toward the center of the city. The first fire was lit on the Great Pyramid altar of Huitzilopochtli, and the same torch was carried to the chief priest's house, the *calmecac* school, and the principal Fire Temple of the city. The Codex Borbonicus shows the spectacular conclusion of the ceremony as new fire blazed in the Fire Temple altar, where four priests lit brands to carry the flame to the four wards of the city. The fire was divided and taken to the local *calpulli* ward temples where the populace swarmed, jostling, blistering and burning themselves to carry new flame to their homes. New mats were laid out with new hearthstones and pestles as housekeepers appeared rejoicing. Men wore new capes and the women new skirts and embroidered *huipiles*. Incense and quails were offered to the household hearth, and amaranth-seed cakes with honey were eaten. Night was passing. As the dawn light turned yellow the blazing sun-disc rose above the dark indigo mountains. A fast was kept from dawn to midday, when feasts were spread in all homes. In the ritual precincts a bundle of 52 rods, *xiuhmolpilli*, was bound up in sign of the cycle's completion. At Huixachtlán in the darkness, the procession of gods and the making of fire, the burnt sacrifice, and the cycle's renewal and rebirth of sunlight, had magically suspended the sense of time, of ordinary duration, enacting a drama of primordial creation and the world's first sunrise.

The mountains of life: Mt Tlaloc and Tetzcotzingo

As the new year wore on and the season for rain drew closer, rites were performed to call the life-giving water. In the Tetzcocan heartland Netza-hualcoyotl had several temples refurbished or reconstructed, among which the Hill of Tetzcotzingo was especially important. Tetzcotzingo (which we saw depicted in the Codex Xolotl in the time of Acolhua migrations) rises to the east of Tetzcoco where the foothills of Mt Tlaloc meet the piedmont plain. Another extraordinary ritual place that figures in royal rain-making rites is located on the summit of Mt Tlaloc, a primary source of rain and springs for central Acolhuacan (ill. 75). Although little archaeological excavation has taken place at Tetzcotzingo and Mt Tlaloc, survey plans, aerial views, and surface explorations reveal the plan of the monuments, and the remains can be partly interpreted with the 16th-century historical texts. Conversely, the monuments in their natural settings reveal meanings and functions that texts alone do not mention. Tetzcotzingo and Mt Tlaloc disclose an essential religious role of Aztec rulers as priestly rain-makers, actively changing the long season of drought to the summer monsoon and renewal.

The temple on Mt Tlaloc stands far above the tree-line at the 4,000-m (13,000-ft) level. The site affords a splendid view of the snow-capped volcanoes Popocatepetl and Iztaccíhuatl and the Valleys of Puebla and Mexico. In the mid-1980s the site was first surveyed by Stanislaw Iwaniszewski, and a more detailed plan was prepared in 1989 by myself and Felipe Solís Olguín, Director of the National Museum of Anthropology, with a team from the INAH. Archaeoastronomical observations by Iwaniszewski indicate that the enclosure has orientation points leading to positions of the sun on the horizon at intervals of 20 days. These intervals marked by solar risings and settings were part of the site planning. Other sunrise alignments with prominent peaks to the east – Malinche, Orizaba, and Cofre del Perote – occur on dates of important rites on such high places.[17] Anthony Aveni also plotted a line of sight leading from the Great Pyramid of Tenochtitlan to a notch between Mt Tlaloc and its neighbor Mt Yeloxóchitl, where major springs rise in the Vale of Talocto, over which the sun is seen to rise on the equinox.

The temple on the summit of Mt Tlaloc is approached through a corridor-like processional way, enclosed by parallel walls of drystone masonry (ill. 76). These walls once rose approximately 3 m (10 ft). The approach leads east into a quadrangle enclosed by walls of similar height. Originally the visitor would have seen nothing of the surrounding spectacular view after entering the corridor or from the inner quadrangle floor. The enclosed yard is overgrown with coarse mountain grass; no building remains are visible today, but several large basalt boulders project upward in irregular positions roughly correspon-ding to the center, the east, and the intercardinal points. At the eastern side a rectangular shaft measuring 1.5 × 2 m (5 × 6.5 ft), is cut into solid bedrock to a depth of over 3 m (10 ft). A small shrine enclosed by a rough drystone wall toward the middle of the quadrangle is of recent origin.

Fray Diego Durán describes the Mt Tlaloc temple as a place of annual pilgrimage made by the rulers of Tenochtitlan, Tetzcoco, Tlacopan, and Xochimilco.[18] Their pilgrimage was made in April or May at the height of the dry season, to perform a ceremony to summon rain from the mountain. This was a seasonal rite of passage to initiate the transition from the time of death to the time of rebirth. Durán says that the quadrangle originally contained a finely made temple of impermanent materials – probably a house-like structure with a thatched roof. He also describes "idols," the principal of which was an effigy of Tlaloc, surrounded by others named after neighboring peaks on this range of mountains. No trace of the Tlaloc effigies remains today, although a Tlaloc fragment was photographed in the quadrangle in the 1920s and 1950s. The location of the main projecting boulders shows that they were part of the symbolic layout. Other rocks and quantities of earth were removed when the site was constructed, leaving these particular stones in approximate positions corresponding to the four-part cosmic order governing cities and urban ritual centers. Pictorial manuscript pages are often designed according to this principle, as seen on a page from the Codex Borgia depicting four Tlalocs at the intercardinal points, and another Tlaloc standing in the center (ill. 77). Each figure rests upon a female figure symbolizing the earth. The affinity between this illustration and the Tlaloc temple layout supports the notion that the quadrangle formed a symbolic landscape, a microcosm of Mt Tlaloc and adjacent peaks. In keeping with this abstract schema, the large rock-cut shaft on the eastern side of the enclosure corresponds to a place of offering and communication leading to *tlalli yiollo*, "earth heart," the regenerative mountain interior.

While surveying the temple, a question arose concerning the original height of the enclosing walls. Why was it important for these walls to have been built to a height of 3 m (10 ft)? Once inside, the visitor would have seen only the symbolic landscape and the empty void of the sky. Only upon reemerging at the entrance of the long processional corridor would the outside world be seen again. The separation of exterior and interior space was intentional. By this token, what was the purpose of the narrow processional way? Why did the kings, as chief ritualists of their nations, walk down this narrow corridor to reach the precinct interior? Fray Diego Durán describes the royal processions in detail. The assembled kings first entered with gifts, following rank order, and then proceeded to dress the stone idol in Tlaloc's splendid regalia, just as new rulers were dressed by royalty at the time of their coronation. In effect, Tlaloc was being inaugurated into office. The four rulers then withdrew from the temple, but soon reentered as a magnificent feast was laid out. It is said that during the famine of the early 1450s, children of royal lineage were also sacrificed on mountaintops. Lengthy prayers were spoken during all stages of these acts. The rite concluded as the feast was spread for Tlaloc, and the kings withdrew to attend another feast laid out for themselves and their retinue outside the sacred precinct.

Considering the form of the temple-enclosure in the context of the landscape, and the movement of the ritual processions, the enclosure and the processional way may be seen as a symbolic womb of the mountain – the womb of mother earth. The well-known page from the Historia Tolteca-Chichimeca (pl. III), depicting the mountain Culhuacan, illustrates this concept. The temple on Mt Tlaloc may similarly be considered a symbolic earth-womb, architecturally drawn on the summit. At this pivotal place between inside and outside, where the earth meets the sky, the Aztec kings recycled food and energy between the social and the natural orders. Soon afterwards in early June, the first clouds of the rainy season are seen to collect around the mountains. The monsoon arrives. Dark storms take shape with lightning and peals of thunder, renewing life in the Valley. No one who has lived in this part of the world can forget the annual drama of this seasonal change.

Aztec rulers were not abject supplicants, fearing a punitive deity, but active agents performing an essential role in calling the change of seasons. A long pilgrimage had brought the kings from the floor of the Valley, across the lake and through mountain chasms to the place of ritual danger. In this sacred enclosure above the line of forest life, the rulers entered the place of contact between the earth and the heavens. Offerings were made and the kings returned home, bringing the gift of life-giving water. This ritual process has the archetypal structure of a mythical happening. In some distant time of genesis, a hero emerges from a dry land – the earth still incomplete. He undertakes an arduous journey in quest of a supernatural boon. The place is found, offerings are made, and he returns to the point of departure bearing the gift of life. Rain arrives, plants spring forth, and the fruits of the earth are given. Such a myth was never recorded by the Spanish friars, but its "text" may be read in the topography, the design of the temple, in the ritual performance, and in the seasonal renewal that followed.

As the events on Mt Tlaloc were taking place, another part of this complex ritual process was unfolding in the main ritual center of Tenochtitlan. A large tree, cut and transported in a sacred manner, was erected in the courtyard on the Tlaloc side of the Great Pyramid. This tree was named Tota, "father," and was surrounded by four smaller trees, forming a symbolic forest. A maiden attired as Chalchiuhtlicue, "Jade Skirt," the deity of ground water, was brought to sit within this arbor as a living personification of the lake. A chant was begun to the rhythm of drums, until news was received that the lords had completed the rites on Mt Tlaloc and returned to the eastern shore of Lake Tetzcoco. In Tenochtitlan the Tota-tree was taken up and carefully bound on a raft. It was then taken out upon the lake to a place called Pantitlán, accompanied by Chalchiuhtlicue, musicians, priests, and a vast crowd of singing people in a fleet of canoes. Pantitlán was the place of a great spring (or a sump-hole according to some accounts), surrounded by banners attached to poles stuck into the muddy bottom of the shallow lake (ill. 79). At this place in the middle of the water, the rulers returning from Mt Tlaloc met the procession in their own fleet of canoes As the assembled nobility and populace watched, the Tota-tree was unbound and set up by the spring as a "tree of life" – the symbol of plant regeneration. The Chalchiuhtlicue-maiden was then sacrificed and her blood poured on the water, along with greenstone jewelry. The rite concluded and everyone departed, leaving the tree standing with others from

The temple at Mt Tlaloc

75, 76 ABOVE Access to the rectangular Temple of Tlaloc was through a long, narrow, processional way. The volcanoes Iztaccíhuatl and Popocatepetl can be seen in the distance. BELOW The stone walls enclosing the processional way and ritual precinct once rose to a height of *c*. 3 m (10 ft).

77 ABOVE Tlaloc stands in the central panel of this scene from the Codex Borgia, between the cloudy sky and the cultivated earth. Four other Tlalocs are placed at the intercardinal points, indicating "rain in the four directions." The format of his illustration echoes the design of the Mt Tlaloc temple.

78 RIGHT Temple to Tlaloc the rain deity (left) and Chalchiuhtlicue the female diety of ground water (right), upon a mountaintop with a ceremonial paper banner. From the Codex Borbonicus. Mountains were seen as containers of water, to be called forth as rainclouds by royal rituals at the end of the annual dry season. Compare the drawing of the sides and the base of the mountain in this codex of *c.* 1525 with the design framing the doorway in 8th-century Cacaxtla (ill. 22).

79 Pantitlan,"Banner Place," shrine to the water goddess in Lake Tetzcoco, from Sahagún's Florentine Codex. An outer ring set with banners encloses the inner quadrangular basin with steps to the four directions. Water jars, seashells, pieces of jade and an effigy are represented in the water as offerings.

previous years.[19] While the rites performed on distant Mt Tlaloc acknowledged the male sphere of clouds and rain, the sacrifice of Chalchiuhtlicue was addressed to the female sphere of springs, streams, lakes, and the surrounding seas. Lake Tetzcoco was spoken of as *Tonanhueyatl*, "mother great water," a provider of moisture to *chinampas*, teeming with edible plants and algae, and the home of myriad aquatic and avian creatures. The lake was a sustainer of life, regarded as a mother by the peoples of the Valley of Mexico. The rites at Pantitlán expressed their perception of water as the element that precedes solid form, the support of all earthly creation. In these ancient rites we also find an expression of the old two-part moiety system embedded in the changing imperial order. The *tlatoani* may be said to have traditionally been responsible for external relations and dry season activities, principally embracing trade, travel, foreign relations, and war. Yet on Mt Tlaloc at the height of the dray season, at the temple on the far periphery, on the border of foreign lands, he is also seen to be responsible for enthroning Tlaloc and bringing the season rain. The seating of Chalchiuhtlicue in the symbolic forest and the sacrifice offered to the lake completed this seasonal obligation to ensure the cycle of fertility.

Following these themes, other ceremonial centers in the city and in the country were designed as symbolic landscapes. The Hill of Tetzcotzingo is one of the places where a new ceremonial center was built (ills. 80–82). Following the famine of 1454, the *tlatoani* Netzahualcoyotl designed – or redesigned – Tetzcotzingo with symbolic works of art and architecture. It is likely that the hill had long been a place of worship, for it was a stopping point when the Chichimecs first settled and the first location of the Acolhua capital. A major system of farming terraces extends northward from the hill in a huge natural amphitheater. The towns of this terraced district still bear their Nahuatl names, and are supplied with water by aqueducts from springs on Mt Tlaloc. Although the monuments at Tetzcotzingo were almost entirely destroyed by the Spanish in 1539, remaining fragments can be decoded by means of ethno-historic texts, pictorial manuscripts, and related works of sculpture and architecture as well as the topography itself.

I had the good fortune to map Tetzcotzingo in 1979[20] with a grant from the National Geographic Society. The plan reveals how the upper hill was organized in a cosmological design. The ritual zone is demarcated by a walkway cut around the hill about 55 m (180 ft) below the summit. Four baths or shallow basins are still seen on this path at points corresponding to the cardinal directions (ill. 82). As manifestations of Chalchiuhtlicue's aquatic domain, these receptacles served purposes of ritual purification, supplied with water by an aqueduct built upon the circular path. The path itself was for circumambulation, dividing the upper area from the world below.

Another important shrine is the cave located immediately below the circumscribing path on the southern side of the hill. Rock-cut steps lead to a system of lower terraces where Netzahualcoyotl's villa and a botanical plantation were built. The cave has lost all trace of its original sculpture, for in addition to the destruction ordered by Bishop Zumárraga in 1539, Tetzcotzingo was subject to generations of treasure-hunters whose depredations by blasting completed the damage. Nevertheless, the cave can be assumed to have had a specific religious purpose. The ritual use of natural caves, or architectural temple-caves such as Malinalco, as places of communion with the earth is well known. Caves also had historical associations, as illustrated by a page from the Mapa Tlohtzin showing Chichimec chieftains within a cave identified with Tetzcotzingo and Tetzcoco. These are the tribal ancestors who established Netzahualcoyotl's lineage. The picture records an historical event, while also evoking the widespread genesis myth of people emerging from the womb of the earth. The Mapa Tlohtzin affirms the legitimacy of Netzahualcoyotl's descent, simultaneously suggesting the time of creation. Such themes were surely expressed by the cave on the side of Tetzcotzingo.

Another shrine on Tetzcotzingo is placed high on the western axis. Two effigies are carved in the living rock, with a view of terraces and planted fields in the sweeping agricultural crescent. Both sculptures are severely damaged, but fragments of a headdress and the outline of their shape show that they were maize deities. The Codex Borbonicus depicts such figures with trapezoidal outline, holding multicolored ears of maize and wearing others in their headdresses (ills. 83, 84). Sahagún's *Book of Ceremonies* and Durán's *Book of the*

The ritual hill of Tetzcotzingo

80–82 ABOVE Tetzcotzingo overlooks the
terraced hillside and fields of central
Acolhuacan. RIGHT The rock-cut bath
on the south side of the hill, used in
ceremonies of ritual purification. OPPOSITE
Plan of the ritual zone at Tetzcotzingo.

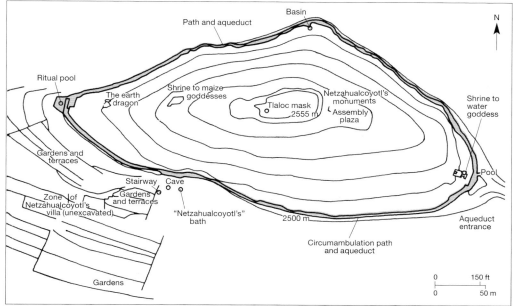

Basin

Path and aqueduct

N

Ritual pool

The earth
dragon

Shrine to maize
goddesses

Tlaloc mask
2555 m

Netzahualcoyotl's
monuments

Assembly
plaza

Shrine to
water
goddess

Gardens and
terraces

Stairway   Cave

Pool

Zone of
Netzahualcoyotl's
villa (unexcavated)

Gardens
and terraces

"Netzahualcoyotl's"
bath

2500 m

Aqueduct
entrance

Circumambulation path
and aqueduct

Gardens

0   150 ft

0   50 m

83, 84 ABOVE Destroyed figures of
maize deities on a rock face at
Tetzcotzingo. The fragment of a
headdress is visible in the foreground.
LEFT Detail of a maize and earth deity,
from the Codex Borbonicus.

85 OPPOSITE The Tlaloc mask
petroglyph at the summit of the
ritual hill of Tetzcotzingo.

Gods, Rites, and the Ancient Calendar describe a sequence of three festivals in which these deities appeared.[21] The first was Huey Tozoztli, a festival celebrated in the high dry season, when seed corn was consecrated by Chicomecoatl priestesses for the coming season for planting. Chicomecoatl, "seven serpent," was the Aztec deity of dried seed corn. The second festival was Huey Tecuilhuitl, in the middle of the rainy season. Attention centered on the female deity Xilonen, whose named derives from the word *xilotl*, "corn silk." The term was also given to the first tender sweet maize to appear in the growing period. A young girl impersonating Xilonen was the focus of a first-fruits offering. The last maize festival was Ochpaniztli, with a sequence of ceremonies featuring the deities of earth and maize, signaling harvest and the onset of the dry season.

Another sequence of shrine stations is aligned on the east–west axis, following the natural ridge of the hill. This alignment reflects the path of the sun, indicating that Tetzcotzingo had astronomical and calendrical functions at equinoctial and solstitial times. The summit shows traces of foundations, and an image of Tlaloc engraved on a boulder offers testimony of a rain cult temple in this location (ill. 85). An early colonial description of the ruined site by Juan Bautista Pomar mentions a narrow enclosed way leading up to the temple, recalling the design of the temple on Mt Tlaloc.

The last shrines at Tetzcotzingo are Netzahualcoyotl's personal commemorative monuments, located below the summit on the eastern slope of the hill. A broad assembly platform was constructed facing an exposed rock-face where the sculptures were located. The monuments are destroyed, but texts from Fernando de Alva Ixtlilxóchitl, Juan Bautista Pomar, and *The Titles of Tetzcotzingo* describe what was there. The first monument was a large circular relief sculpture, recording the principal deeds of Netzahualcoyotl as the founder of the Tetzcocan city-state. The format of this monument was related to the 16th-century pictorial document known as the Boban Wheel, recording the history of Acolhuacan within a circular calendar of festival

signs. Next to Netzahualcoyotl's biographical relief sculpture there stood a three-dimensional seated stone coyote, the hieroglyphic name of Netzahual-coyotl, "fasting coyote." The remnants of this monument still stand as a mutilated upright bedrock boulder. These vanished historical monuments faced east, linking the memory of the great *tlatoani* with the rising of the sun and the eternal round of the seasons. Although Netzahualcoyotl was an historical figure, he was deified after death and enshrined on the sacred mountain, a founder-father corresponding to the position of the mythical warrior-leader Huitzilopochtli in Tenochtitlan.

Tetzcotzingo also functioned as a place of administration where water and land rights in central Acolhuacan were confirmed. *The Titles of Tetzcotzingo*, a 16th-century legal document, describes in detail how Netzahualcoyotl at Tetzcotzingo allocated water sources and aqueducts to specific towns and to his relatives, appointees, allies, and their children. The action of assigning water in a ceremony held at Tetzcotzingo, with the ruler standing on the assembly platform in front of his own commemorative monuments, speaking directly to the notables of central Acolhuacan, is another example of an increasing tendency toward centralized control and the personal role of the *tlatoani* in distributing resources.

Before leaving Acolhuacan, we must note a symbolic expression of water and mountain left in the time of Teotihuacan. The colossal stone "Tlaloc" placed in front of the National Museum of Anthropology in Mexico City was originally a sculptured bedrock boulder in a wide ravine near Coatlinchan, at the foot of the Mt Tlaloc range. Periodically flooded during the rainy season, this was surely a shrine to the water goddess and was undoubtedly made, although never finished, in the heyday of Teotihuacan. This testimony of a Teotihuacan presence also opens a question as to when and by whom the temple of Tlaloc was constructed. None of the detailed ethnohistorical records attribute the making of the temple of Tlaloc to any of the rulers of Tetzcoco or Tenochtitlan, whereas other notable monuments such as Tepoztlán, Calixtlahuaca, Malinalco, and Tetzcotzingo – as well as the Great Pyramid of Tenochtitlan – are accounted for in terms of when and by whom they were commissioned. Fray Toribio de Benavente (Motolínia) mentions that Netzahualcoyotl commissioned temples on hilltops in Acolhuacan, and the Codex en Cruz notes temples in addition to Tetzcotzingo, built at the time of the famine and the turn of the 52-year cycle in 1454. But the question remains, why is the major temple of Tlaloc not specifically attributed to any particular Aztec ruler?

There is archaeological evidence that the mountaintop site was held sacred in the time of Teotihuacan if not before, for a surface collection of pot sherds includes specimens from Cuicuilco dating to the late 1st millennium BC. The plan of the temple of Tlaloc also echoes the plan of the Processional Way at Teotihuacan, leading into the quadrangle below the Pyramid of the Moon where a monolithic goddess was enshrined, all against the backdrop of the sacred mountain Tenan, "Stone Mother." That temple of Tlaloc may have first been laid out by Teotihuacan architects is a possibility that future archaeology stands to resolve.

The Great Pyramid at Tenochtitlan

The final site to visit is the urban ritual center where sacred landscape was replicated by the Great Pyramid of Tenochtitlan. Continuing a project begun by his immediate predecessor Itzcoatl, Motecuhzoma I enlarged the precinct and Great Pyramid with building materials and labor supplied by tributary communities. This work continued during the worst of the great famine, 1452–54, as the end of the 52-year cycle drew near. The principal original approach to the ceremonial enclosure was by a long east–west avenue, again echoing the Processional Way at Teotihuacan. The pyramid rose in the middle of the precinct as the social, religious and geographical center of the Aztec world.

The design of the Great Pyramid was not a unique Mexica invention, for precedent can be seen at Teopanzolco (within today's Cuernavaca) and Tenayuca where the old Acolhua-Chichimec chieftain Xolotl first settled in the Valley of Mexico. At Tenayuca the dual pyramid is surrounded on three sides by rows of serpents, constructed of masonry and with stone monolithic heads, once all plastered and brightly painted. Two large fire-serpents with crested heads are coiled on separate platforms to the sides (ills. 86–88). The sculptured features are of a style more rustic than the monuments of Tenochtitlan and likely belong to the period of Atzcapotzalco's ascendancy. Their presence suggest that this pyramid was an earlier expression of Coatepetl, "Serpent Mountain," a symbolic mountain of victory, an image and a mythic theme incorporated and adapted by the Mexica in their own Coatepetl at Tenochtitlan.

We have previously briefly described the outer appearance of the Great Pyramid in the context of coronation rites for Motecuhzoma I, as a monument rising in four superimposed tiers with the upper platform extending before the temple of Tlaloc to the right and the temple of Huitzilopochtli to the left. The building was aligned east–west, so that people climbing the dual stairway would be facing east, with the line of sight between the two temples leading to the Vale of Tlalocto on distant Mt Tlaloc and to the equinoctial sunrise beyond.

The location of the pyramid foundations in downtown Mexico City was long known and small-scale archaeological excavations began during the early 20th century. In 1978 the chance discovery of the monolith, 3.25 m (10.5 ft) in diameter, representing the goddess Coyolxauhqui led to one of the most extraordinary archaeological projects in the history of Mexico. The excavation, directed by Eduardo Matos Moctezuma, offered an unprecedented opportunity to answer questions about the pyramid and the dynamic role it played in the development of the imperial state (ills. 89–91).[22] The first phase of the project was to demolish and remove 19th-century and colonial buildings superimposed on the site. Gradually, the Aztec foundations appeared. The structure seen by Cortés, razed soon after the Conquest, was revealed to have been constructed in a succession of layers. Each of these layers completely enclosed an earlier version of the pyramid. As excavations continued to disclose the concentric foundations, vast quantities of offerings buried in foundation-caches were also unearthed.

86–88 OPPOSITE The Tenayuca Pyramid. Prefiguring the Great Pyramid of Tenochtitlan, the dual monument supported twin temples. An alignment of snakes around the base correspond to the name Coatepetl, "Serpent Mountain," and a coiled, crested serpent, Xiuhcoatl, "turquoise serpent" represents the power of the sun and deified warrior-heroes.

The problem of interpretation was to understand the pyramid in symbolic and functional terms, particularly its connection with agricultural production and military expansion. Three related themes have emerged in considering this problem. The first theme concerns state patronage as revealed by the growth of the pyramid during consecutive reigns, and particularly during the time of Motecuhzoma I and his successor Axayacatl. The second theme concerns the symbolic organization of the pyramid as a man-made mountain. The third theme concerns the pyramid as a stage for mythic drama, expressed in rites offered to Tlaloc (similar to those at the distant mountain, but also performed in the city at various times of the year); in sacrificial triumphs devoted to Huitzilopochtli, especially at the successful conclusion of a war; and in the coronation rites of the *tlatoani* of Tenochtitlan.

One of the unique features of Mesoamerican pyramids is that they were frequently built in enveloping layers over decades or centuries. In this way an original foundation would become completely enclosed by later superimposed structures. Containing vast accumulations of offerings, sculptures, and diverse deposits, such buildings became massive architectural fetishes in the minds of their makers. The Tenochtitlan pyramid reflects this tradition of construction. A primitive platform, perhaps dating from the time of the founding of Tenochtitlan in the first half of the 14th century, has been found within a platform dated by a hieroglyph 2-rabbit, AD 1390, attributed to the reign of Acamapichtli. A sacrificial block in the platform in front of the remains of the Huitzilopochtli temple, and a crude but colorful recumbent sculpture found on the Tlaloc side, confirm that the two deities were installed at this early time (ills. 92–94). Few changes were made to the Tenochtitlan pyramid during the reigns of Huitzilihuitl (1396–1417) and Chimalpopoca (1417–26), when the Mexica were still paying tribute to the Tepanec city of Atzcapotzalco. It was after the formation of the Triple Alliance in 1428 that Itzcoatl commissioned a more ambitious temple for the Aztec capital. A date-glyph 4-reed (1431) marks this construction phase. The pyramid grew and was equipped with stone "guardian" and "fealty" figures, reflecting Tenochtitlan's rising power and status.

The next additions to the pyramid correspond to the reign of Motecuhzoma I, indicated by the date-glyph 1-rabbit (1454) incorporated in a new rear wall of the Huitzilopochtli temple. At this time the pyramid was embellished with large-scale incense braziers and stone offering-cysts on all four sides, and a new grand stairway was added over the old one on the west façade. The next excavated date-glyph 3-house (1469) corresponds to the year of Axayacatl's coronation. It is probable that during his reign (1469–81) a platform was extended in front of the stairway, set with the powerfully expressive sculpture

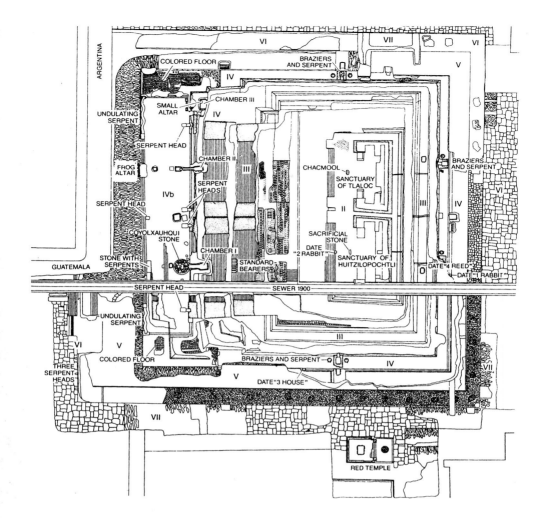

ARGENTINA

VI VII VI V

COLORED FLOOR
IV
BRAZIERS AND SERPENT

CHAMBER III
SMALL ALTAR
IV
UNDULATING SERPENT

SERPENT HEAD

FROG ALTAR

CHAMBER II

III

CHACMOOL

SANCTUARY OF TLALOC

BRAZIERS AND SERPENT

VI

IVb

SERPENT HEADS

II

III

IV

SERPENT HEAD

STONE WITH SERPENTS

COYOLXAUHQUI STONE

CHAMBER I

SACRIFICIAL STONE

DATE "2 RABBIT"

SANCTUARY OF HUITZILOPOCHTLI

DATE "4 REED"

GUATEMALA

STANDARD BEARERS

DATE "1 RABBIT"

SERPENT HEAD

SEWER 1900

UNDULATING SERPENT

III

VI

V

COLORED FLOOR

BRAZIERS AND SERPENT

IV

VII

THREE SERPENT HEADS

V

DATE "3 HOUSE"

VII

RED TEMPLE

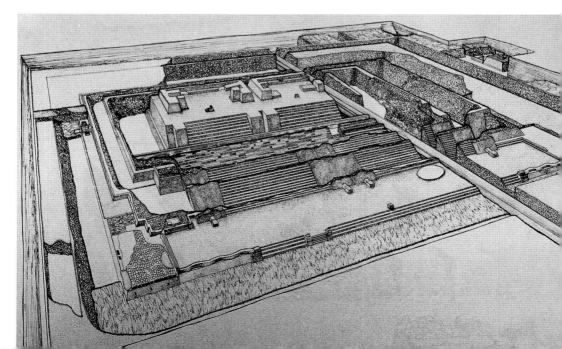

Excavating the Great Pyramid

89–91 OPPOSITE ABOVE Plan of the foundations of the Great Pyramid, showing successive enlargements. OPPOSITE BELOW Drawing of the excavated foundations. ABOVE View of the excavations in progress. The earliest dual pyramid–platform (Temple II) lies under the temporary protective roof on the right, and the Coyolxauhqui Stone (ills. 96–98) is beneath the scaffolding near the center of the picture.

The dual shrines of the Great Pyramid

92–94 OPPOSITE LEFT The chacmool sculpture from Tlaloc's shrine. Dating from around 1390, this crude, polychromed sculpture strongly echoes Toltec prototypes (see ill. 24). BELOW General view of the foundations of the dual shrines of Temple II. RIGHT The pyramid of Tlaloc and Huitzilopochtli in Tetzcoco followed the style of the Great Pyramid in Tenochtitlan. From the Codex Ixlilxóchitl.

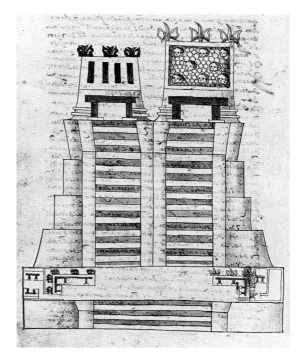

of Coyolxauhqui, carved in high relief with an assurance of design and a technical virtuosity not previously seen at the pyramid (ills. 96–98). Although the Coyolxauhqui Stone almost certainly dates from Axayacatl's reign, the theme was already sculpturally expressed by the time of Motecuhzoma I if not well before – as shown by another, stylistically more primitive Coyolxauhqui carved on a greenstone slab discovered beneath the larger Coyolxauhqui disk. A third Coyolxauhqui, represented by a famous greenstone head in the Museum of Anthropology (ill. 95), was carved at a later date and discovered elsewhere in downtown Mexico City early in the 19th century.

Coyolxauhqui is represented with dismembered limbs in a dynamic pose, and her attire is carved in meticulous detail. This fearsome image shows the Aztec genius for translating two-dimensional figures of manuscript paintings into monumental sculptural forms. Eduardo Matos Moctezuma first noted that the placement of the sculpture at the foot of the stairs was to commemorate the legend of Huitzilopochtli defeating Coyolxauhqui in the battle on Mt Coatepetl. Positioned on the landing of the stairway leading to Huitzilopochtli's temple, the sculpture of Coyolxauhqui presented a forbidding sign to the enemies of Tenochtitlan.

The north side of the Great Pyramid supported the temple of Tlaloc, and the structure was therefore also identified with Tonacatepetl, Tlaloc's sacred mountain of sustenance. An effigy filled with seeds from all the important cultivated plants was placed in the Tlaloc shrine. The pyramid foundations on both sides contained offering-caches with thousands of artifacts. Tlaloc-masked pots and ceramic vessels with the image of the water-deity Chalchiuhtlicue were used as containers of ritual water, and hundreds of seashells, different coral species, and a splendid necklace of mother-of-pearl and jade, carved with figures of aquatic animals, also alluded to these cults.

The Coyolxauhqui Stone

96–98 OPPOSITE ABOVE Details of Coyolxauhqui's right foot and severed head. OPPOSITE BELOW The Coyolxauhqui Stone. Placed at the foot of the Huitzilopoctli stairway, this huge disk represented the defeat of the Aztecs' enemies.

95 LEFT Head of the goddess Coyolxauhqui. Carved in green diorite, this superbly finished sculpture is stylistically late, dating from the reign of Ahuitzotl (1486–1502). The theme of the dismembered Coyolxauhqui, represented opposite by flat sculptural reliefs, was continued in three-dimensional form.

Also recovered were miniature fish of mother-of-pearl, model canoes of green-stone, equipped with model paddles, fish hooks and bird-hunting spears, as well as skeletons of water-birds and fish. A crocodile skeleton evokes an ancient mythic image of the earth floating in the primordial sea. The skeleton of a jaguar alluded to rulership, for the jaguar was lord of the forest. Trophy objects from conquered regions, antiquities such as an Olmec mask, and another mask carved in the manner of Teotihuacan (ills. 99, 100), alluded to the pyramid as

99, 100 ABOVE Olmec mask (left) and Mixtec mask (right) recovered from the foundations of the Great Pyramid. Both are symbolic of conquered regions incorporated into the Aztec empire.

101 LEFT The earth deity Tlaltecuhtli, squatting in a parturition position, with an upward-facing mask and opened jaws with rows of teeth. A circular diadem surrounded with round pieces of jade indicates "center" and "precious." The earth is depicted as a giver of life, yet also the eventual receiver of life, hence the skull-and-crossbones skirt, clawed hands and feet, and upturned, open-jawed mask.

102 OPPOSITE The Codex Telleriano-Remensis depicts the death of Ahuitzotl (he is shown wrapped in a funerary bundle below his name-glyph) in the year 10-rabbit, 1502. Motecuhzoma, identified by his royal diadem, is immediately seated in office. In the following year 11-reed, 1503, the same year the coronation process of Motecuhzoma was completed, snow was reported in Tlachquiaco.

an imperial symbol and to the Mexica as heirs to the past. Analyzing these objects, Matos Moctezuma, Johanna Broda, and David Carrasco showed that the pyramid was at once a replica of Huitzilopochtli's mountain of victory and Tlaloc's mountain of sustenance.

The principal archaeological excavations at the Great Pyramid site continued from the late 1970s through the 1990s, and several restricted projects since have revealed additional features and monuments. In October 2007, new explorations at the landing in front of the Huitzilopochtli stairs added by Motecuhzoma II uncovered a large rectangular monolith (pls. XII, XIII), measuring some 4 m (13 ft) square, estimated to weigh 12 tons. The slab was badly fractured under the pressure of a colonial building that suffered earthquake damage and had been demolished. Debris and mud were cleared from the surface. The stone was revealed to have been carved with an image of the earth-goddess Tlaltecuhtli, squatting in the parturition position, wearing her skull-and-crossbones skirt, with a grinning mouth issuing a stream of blood, and her clawed hands and feet held open and ready. The right-hand foot holds a date-glyph 10-rabbit, corresponding to 1502 – the year of *tlatoani* Ahuitzotl's death. This date has led archaeologist Alfredo Lopez Luján to speculate that the monument may mark the burial of Ahuitzotl's ashes and funerary offerings; but as the great stone slab was lifted, as the large waterlogged boxes of offerings are slowly and painstakingly unpacked, and as more is understood about associated architectural features such as an unexcavated staircase leading beneath the colonial building close by, this initial hypothesis may change.

Diego Durán's detailed account of Ahuitzotl's funeral begins by noting that when this most feared of Mexica *tlatoanis* returned from the successful campaign to Xoconusco, he fell ill with a strange wasting disease that proved incurable. From full vigorous health he was slowly reduced to skin and bones. Presently he died and the eerie sound of wailing and moaning arose throughout Tenochtitlan (ill. 102). The lamentations were led by women of the same

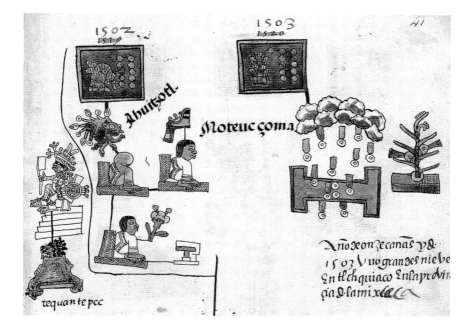

lineage as the *tlatoani*, joined by others customarily hired to wail at the death of rulers, nobles, and those lost in war. As they screamed they continually bowed to the earth and clapped their hands. The news of Ahuitzotl's death was carried to the allied capitals and quickly spread throughout the Valley of Mexico and into the distant provinces. Delegations of chiefs and rulers began arriving in Tenochtitlan with loads of rich offerings and slaves to accompany the dead *tlatoani*. The funeral opened with all the panoply of a great state occasion. The body of Ahuitzotl was laid out in the palace and guests stood before the bier to make eloquent speeches ritually expressing their sadness and condolences. Then, echoing the process of a coronation, the corpse was borne by the principal rulers to a "first station" (presumably in the ceremonial precinct) where dirges and chants were sung. Next, the *tlalcochcalli* was visited, where the body was dressed in full royal attire by Netzahualpilli, *tlatoani* of Tetzcoco. Then, anointed with pitch, Ahuitzotl's remains in all the regalia were carried up the stairs of Huitzilopochtli's temple to rest on the landing before the idol, where high priests incensed the body. As the sun set behind the mountains, all the war captains assembled in panoply of ceremonial battle-dress, and the lords and dignitaries from other cities stood by as a bonfire was lit. The corpse was placed on the flames and slaves were sacrificed, assured that they would be reborn as nobles in the land of the deceased. Their hearts were cast on the burning body together with many offerings, as the cremation continued into the night and a pillar of fire rose from the platform. Dawn light slowly suffused the Valley, as ashes still drifted and eddied around the pyramid temples. The ashes and all that had not burned were gathered in an urn to be buried near the *cuauhxicalli*, beneath the pavement at the base of the pyramid. Archaeological excavations at the site are continuing to examine and conserve the offering caches beneath the Tlaltecuhtli monument, and it remains to be seen whether in fact they commemorated Ahuitzotl's achievement in renewing the imperial project.

The New Fire platform at Huixachtlán, the Great Pyramid of Tenochtitlan, the Hill of Tetzcotzingo, the temple on Mt Tlaloc and the Pantitlán shrine in Lake Tetzcoco were all designed to address the eternal forces and phenomena seen and experienced in the natural environment. The fundamental purpose of the elaborate rites and blood sacrifices was to fulfill an obligation to recycle food and energy from human society to the earth, the sky, and the waters. The Nahuatl word for sacrifice is *uemmana*, composed of the term *uentli*, "offering," and *mana*, "to spread out," as has been pointed out by historian of religions Kay Read.[23] Aztec rulers and priests played an indispensable and active role in renewing the cycles of time and ensuring the rebirth of life. Religion, history, and economy became part of the land at these ritual sites, and the Aztecs affirmed their charter to the land as established since the primordial beginnings.

PART FIVE
Aztec People and the Cycle of Life

7 · The Family and Education

Birth and childhood

The Aztecs were devoted to children, and parents were expected to take special responsibility for their discipline and instruction. From the day of birth, children were brought up to respect their elders, to revere the deities, and to be obedient, well-mannered and productive. While Aztec society offered opportunities for individuals to rise socially and professionally, especially in the military and priesthood, children tended to inherit the profession and status of their parents. Education did not emphasize individualism as it is understood in modern Western culture. Rather, the individuality of a person was always subordinate to the life of the family, the school, the *calpulli*, the professional organization, and society as a whole. In this respect Aztec culture more closely resembled that of traditional China or Japan.

The arrival of a newborn child was a special occasion. Upon delivering the baby, the midwife shouted war cries to honor the mother for having fought a good battle, for having become a warrior who had "captured" a baby. The midwife then spoke to the baby, as if addressing an honored but tired and hungry traveler, exhorting it to rest among its parents and grandparents, and telling it of the transitory nature of life. The umbilical cord of a male child was kept and eventually taken by an adult warrior to be buried on a distant battlefield; the female cord would be buried by the hearth. The ceremonial cutting of the cord was also accompanied by formal speeches describing the roles of men and women and exhorting the infant to work hard and do its duty. Then followed the child's first bath, during which the midwife spoke in a low voice to the baby about the purifying water deity, Chalchiuhtlicue:

> Approach thy mother Chalchiuhtlicue, Chalchiuh Tlatonac! May she receive thee! May she wash thee! May she remove, may she transfer, the filthiness which thou has taken from thy mother, from thy father! May she cleanse thy heart! May she make it fine, good! May she give thee fine, good conduct![1]

More speeches were given by the midwife as she proceeded with the first cleansing, and then she spoke to the mother while many guests from the extended family arrived. Aunts and grandmothers would speak in turn, honoring the midwife, and the midwife would formally reply. In these speeches there is always a sense of reverence for the mother and especially for the infant. Such speeches were an essential aspect of the midwife's professional training and qualifications. Among the nobles or wealthy merchants, the arrival of a child was the occasion for even more elegant formal addresses and visits. Many pages from Bernardino de Sahagún's texts are devoted to these ceremonial addresses, which often include admonitions to the baby as a responsible member of the ruling classes.

The most powerful families received visitors – even ambassadors – from near and far, sometimes for as long as 20 days after the birth. The most important guests were greeted with gifts of fine clothing – beautifully woven capes, skirts, or huipiles, as many as 20 or 40. And even the most humble visitors were given food, drink, or the mildly alcoholic *pulque*. At all levels of society, the hosts provided for visitors in proportion to their economic status.

One of the most important events after childbirth was the visit of soothsayers, who would be summoned with their Book of Days, the *tonalamatl*. They were responsible for reading favorable or unfavorable day signs, and for determining the configuration of cosmic forces that would affect the child's life. It would be important to know the very instant in which it was born; the books would be opened and, if it were a bad day, perhaps the dominant ill effects would be modified by other, more beneficent signs associated with that moment. The soothsayer would then assign a time four days hence for the baptismal rite to take place. But if that time also had bad auguries he would skip to find another day. In this way the soothsayers sought to ameliorate adverse conditions and to exert a measure of control over the hidden forces affecting each child's destiny. In the readings it would be pointed out that unfavorable signs could be compensated for by the child through hard work and dedication. The *tonalamatl* was thus regarded not so much as a book of fate or predetermination, but rather as a guide to action.

The final episode in the newborn's rite of passage was the formal baptism. This differed from the first washing mentioned before. The baptismal ceremony was prepared by placing a basin of water upon a reed mat, and by laying out instruments appropriate to the sex of the baby. If male, there would be a miniature bow and arrow laid upon a "shield" made from a tortilla of amaranth-dough; or there would be the tools of the carpenter, featherworker, scribe, goldsmith, or potter, according to the family profession. If a girl was to be bathed, they laid out a spinning wheel, a batten, a reed basket and spinning bowls, and other weaving instruments, as well as a miniature skirt and huipil. The Codex Mendoza depicts this layout and other aspects of the baptismal rite (ill. 103). The midwife is shown walking counter-clockwise around the basin, talking to the child. The child was bathed, massaged, and presented four times to the sky and to the cleansing water. Older children would then run through the neighborhood crying out the name of the newborn, and the baby was returned to the cradle. A feast and gifts were then offered by the parents to the assembled relatives.

The Codex Mendoza also shows that between the ages of three and four, children were introduced to basic household chores. Boys carried light loads of water and girls were given elementary instruction in weaving or the preparation of food. Later, boys carried heavier bundles, and by the age of six or seven they were involved in activities outside the home, such as practicing with fishing nets or gathering reeds. Knowledge of specialized crafts such as

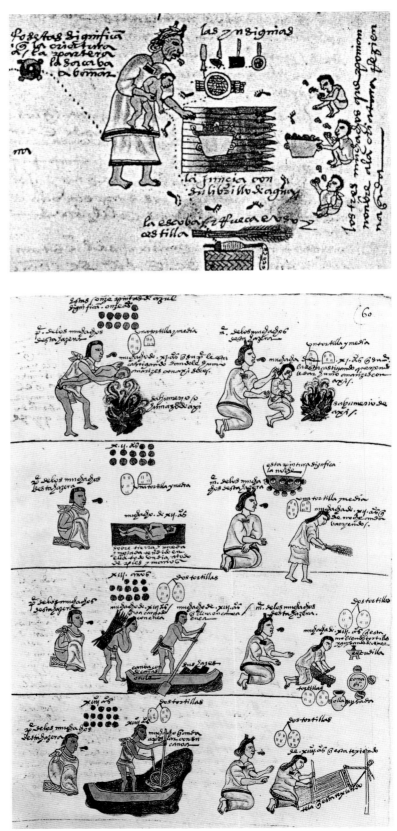

103 Detail of a newborn child's first bath, a rite of passage into the world. The midwife circles the sacred water vessel of Chalchiuhtlicue, placed upon fresh rushes. Female symbols (broom, spindle and weaving implements) and male symbols (miniature shield, darts, and other objects) are placed on either side.

104 The upbringing of Aztec children emphasized discipline and hard work. This page from the Codex Mendoza shows how children between the ages of 11 and 14 (signified by rows of dots) endured such punishments as inhaling the fumes of roasting chilies; on the left boys are taught by their fathers to carry loads and to fish, while on the right girls are trained in the arts of cooking and weaving.

pottery, metalworking, and basketry was transmitted from father to son and mother to daughter, beginning between the ages of eight and ten. Disobedient or recalcitrant children were not (in theory) severely punished until this time. The Codex Mendoza depicts pinching the arms or ears, or more unusually, pricking with maguey thorns. In extreme cases children could be spanked, held over a fire of roasting chile peppers, or bound and left to lie outside in the cold or on muddy ground (ill. 104).

Schools and education

Children were promised to schools when they were still infants, but the formal entrance and presentation did not take place until they were of age (variously estimated to have been at 7, 10, or 14). Both the promising and the actual entrance ceremonies were marked by lengthy admonitory speeches, in which the children were urged to obedience, deportment, diligence, humility, self-discipline, and cleanliness. There were two types of school, neither of which was co-educational, for they were designed to perpetuate sexual and social distinctions. The first type of school was the *telpochcalli*, "youth house." Each ward or *calpulli* had its own *telpochcalli* attached to the local temple. These schools were for the education of commoners. Emphasis was placed on basic moral and religious training, knowledge of history, ritual dancing and singing, as well as rhetoric. Public speaking from memory was essential in Aztec life, and both men and women were expected to be proficient in this art. Boys entering the *telpochcalli* would be given military training, while girls would learn to participate in the religious cults they would serve in later life.

The second type of school was known as the *calmecac*. Its purpose was to train the most promising boys and girls from the nobility for leadership in religious, military, or political life. Rarely, some of the most intelligent children of the lower classes were chosen for this school. There was only one *calmecac* for boys and another for girls in each city. Discipline was strict, obedience was enforced, and students underwent periods of rigorous abstinence with penances, prayers, and ritual baths. The atmosphere was akin to that of a military academy or a monastery. Since religion was a pervasive force in all aspects of life, the curriculum included basic calendrical calculation and the use of the *tonalamatl*; the significance and timing of the annual *veintena* festivals were taught, and students were expected to learn a range of ritual performances and how to address the deities. History, arithmetic, architecture, astronomy, agriculture, and warfare were also part of the curriculum. Since *calmecac* graduates were to be appointed as judges and to other key administrative posts, instruction included a basic knowledge of law.

The art of speaking was interwoven with the teaching of all these subjects, because the learning of technical skills, accounts of history, the reciting of stories and poetry, the conduct of lawsuits, and bargaining, were all primarily accomplished through oral means. To be educated was to be a master of expression, a dialectician, and an orator. An educated person had to be able to deliver artful or moving speeches on a diversity of occasions with all the etiquette prescribed by the ritualized pattern of life.

There were no books in the sense of today's textbooks, manuals, or novels. Aztec hieroglyphic writing had a restricted field, where individual glyphs appear embedded in large pictorial compositions, communicating names, places, dates, and tallies. Such "texts" on monuments and in painted manuscripts had a mnemonic function, for their complex messages were meant to be filled out, amplified, or otherwise qualified by knowledge transmitted orally. Memorization played a critical role in this oral mode of learning, facilitated by repetitive rhythms and the percussive beat of musical instruments as well as the meter and cadence of poetry and song. Such devices also helped to recall information during delivery of a speech. To be thoroughly literate also implied knowledge of hundreds of metaphors, set phrases, and sequences of repetitive verses or strophes.

Poetic language, music, and dance

Metaphors had a mnemonic function as well as being the very substance of Nahuatl poetry. The Nahuatl language employed a particular form of extended metaphor which has been curiously likened to the "kennings" of old Norse poetry.[2] An example of this convention is the term Chalchiuhtlicue, "Jade Skirt," which we have already seen as the name of the deity of lakes, springs, and rivers. If we say "the lake's water is like jade," we are making a simile or direct comparison; if we say "the lake's jade water," we are making an implied comparison, or metaphor, by not likening the water to jade, but calling it jade; however, if we say "jade skirt" without mentioning either the lake or the water, then we are making a comparison by substitution, or kenning: the water *is* "jade skirt" and by implication it is personalized as "she." To understand the meaning of this extended form of metaphor the listener must know that in ceremonial or courtly language it is customary to refer to the water of lakes, rivers, or springs as "skirt of jade." Among the Aztecs, the names and attributes of deities and heroes were expressed in many such extended metaphors and were often translated into plastic form as hieroglyphic or figural elements. Thus, sculptural effigies of Chalchiuhtlicue would be shown wearing a jade-covered skirt or, as in the Codex Borbonicus, the skirt would be painted jade-green. When a ritual performer appeared as the personification of lake water and the female deity, their skirt would thus visually name Chalchiuhtlicue. In Aztec society everyone witnessing the performance would know how to "read" the element of ritual costume.

In his book on the life of Netzahualcoyotl, ruler of Tetzcoco, José Luis Martínez points out that Nahuatl poetry routinely used extended metaphors, not only for the names of deities but also for places, actions, heroes, and objects or concepts of special significance.[3] Thus, Tenochtitlan was variously known as "the place where darts are made," "the place of the white willows," or "the place of the eagle and the cactus." Warfare was "the song of shields," "where the smoke of shields diffuses," or "flowers of the heart upon the plain." Huitzilopochtli was spoken of as "the blue heron bird," "the lucid macaw," or "the eagle." Something precious or valued was "precious stones, gold, jade, flowers, fine feathers." Poetry was "flowers and song." The place where poetry was recited was "the house of flowers," "the house of springtime," "the flowering patio," and so on. Scores of other metaphors were employed in ceremonial speech and in the visual metaphoric language of manuscripts, sculptural monuments, and ritual costumes.

Many of the hymns and speeches recorded by Bernardino de Sahagún have archaic and hermetic forms of metaphor that seemed so unclear that he commented, "they would sing without understanding what was said." Durán, on the other hand, recognized that these forms of expression masked age-old mysteries and had a liturgical purpose:

> All the songs of these [Indians] are composed of metaphors so obscure that there are only few who understand them, without taking pains to study and discuss them to grasp their meaning. I have given myself the purpose of listening with great attention to that which is sung, and between the words and terms of the metaphors, while they may first seem nonsense, but afterward, having spoken and conferred, they are admirable sentences, as much in the divine ones they compose as in the human songs composed.[4]

It would be difficult to underestimate the importance of music, song, and dance in Aztec society, and the *telpochcalli* and *calmecac* took pains to instruct students in these subjects. Everyone from the *tlatoani* down to individual family members took part in dances held on all festival occasions. The Spanish friar Gerónimo de Mendieta attests:

> One of the principal things that was in all this land were the songs and dances, both to solemnize the feasts of their demons which they honored as gods and for private enjoyment and solace. Each lord had in his house a chapel with composer-singers of dances and songs, and these were thought to be ingenious in knowing how to compose the songs in their manner of meter and couplets that they had. Ordinarily they sang and danced in the principal festivities that were every twenty days, and also on other less principal occasions. The most important dances were in the plazas; on other occasions in the houses of the lords, as all the lords had large patios; they also danced in the houses of the lords and magistrates. When there had been some victory in war, or when a new ruler was assigned, or when a marriage was made with a high-ranking lady, or for any other novel event, the master would compose a new song, in addition to the general ones they already had for the festival of the demons and the deeds of antiquity and of past lords.[5]

Mendieta also refers to the careful rehearsals of songs and dances, and Durán describes the trouble taken in giving instruction to girls and young ladies. Teachers would set their drums in the center of the patio and the children, often paired, would dance around them (ills. 105, 106). Extra instruction was given to those who could not follow the steps or body movements. The dancers were simultaneously required to sing, and rhythms and speech were guided both by the percussion and the tones of the singing. The Aztec songmasters

modeled themselves on the "Toltec" ideal: artists who knew that the most
creative levels of expression welled up from the deepest personal sources:

> The Toltecs were truly knowledgable,
> they knew how to speak to their own hearts
> they sounded the drum, the rattles,
> they were singers, they composed songs,
> they made them known,
> they learned them by memory,
> they made divine with their hearts
> the marvellous songs they composed.[6]

In the *telpochcalli* schools, which were located by the *calpulli* temples, a special
patio with surrounding rooms was designated as the *cuicacalli*, "house of song."
Here were taught the songs of heroes, elegies to princes, lamentations, war songs,
love songs, and all that might fall under the classification of "profane." In the
calmecac schools, on the other hand, emphasis was placed on songs and dances of
a ritual nature. The role of music, dance, and ritual performance was to become
increasingly important as adulthood and marriage approached.

105, 106 ABOVE A wooden *teponaztli* drum
of early colonial date, carved in the Aztec
manner. Two tongues cut into the back
emitted different tones when struck. LEFT
A standing drum *huehuetl* is carved with
birds of prey and the hieroglyph *atl-
tlachinolli*, "water, fire," meaning "deluge
and conflagration."

107 OPPOSITE A marriage ceremony from
the Codex Mendoza. The bride is carried
to the groom's house (bottom), and (above)
the garments of the couple are knotted to
signify union.

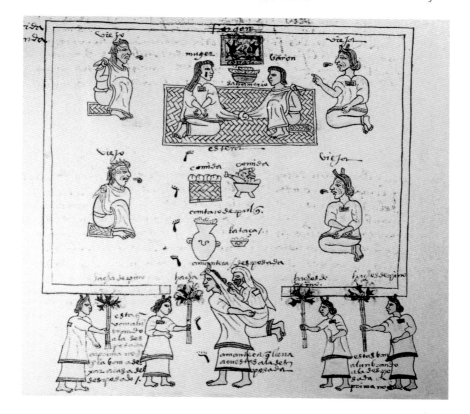

Marriage

Marriage took place in the late teens or early twenties. When a youth arrived at the marrying age, his parents looked about for a suitable partner. A meal was prepared and the young man's schoolmasters were invited, to be told that his schooldays were over. Then another council was called and the assembled kinsmen decided which young woman was the most eligible – perhaps indeed someone who had already taken the youth's fancy at one of the great public festivals. Matchmakers were sent to the parents of the maiden to solicit her hand in marriage. The next day they would go again, and so on until the fourth day when her parents would give an answer.

Elaborate preparations preceded the marriage ceremony: cacao was bought, smoking tubes prepared, flowers set out, sauce bowls and pottery cups acquired. Then maize was ground and *tamales* (corn husks filled with a mixture of meat and corn dough) were made, sometimes over two or three days, and honeyed *pulque* was bought for the elders. As the evening of the appointed day approached, the bride was ceremonially bathed, dressed, and pasted with red feathers on her arms and legs; her face was painted with glittering ground pyrites. She was counseled by her kinswomen, one of whom bore her on her back in a torchlit procession to the groom's house. Once inside, the bride and groom were seated upon a mat. A fire was lit in the hearth and copal incense laid out. After the groom's mother presented gifts of fine clothing, the elder matchmakers tied the groom's cape to the bride's shift (ill. 107). Then the groom's mother fed the bride four mouthfuls of *tamales* in a special sauce, and another four mouthfuls to the young man. After that the bride and groom were led into their bedchamber. Four days of feasting followed, at the conclusion of which the elder women of the groom's family admonished and counseled the bride as to diligence, humility, and trust, and the bride's mother spoke to the groom of his duties and obligations, exhorting him to hard work, conscientiousness, and self-sacrifice. These speeches, preserved by Bernardino de Sahagún, present an admirable picture of the ideals of Aztec upbringing, if not always the reality.

Matters concerning the hearth and home were central to women's activities, yet their sphere also embraced a much wider range of endeavors. The place and role of women in Aztec society has been charted by Elizabeth Brumfiel, who observes that this matter was generally defined in terms of the principle of gender complimentarity. Male and female were held as distinctive but equal and interdependent parts of a larger productive whole. Men and women regarded themselves as equally related to their mother's and father's families. They could own houses and movable property. And they inherited assets equally. Women also held parallel positions of public authority in the market, in the *calmecac* schools, and temple organizations. Women worked as professional market vendors and participated in agricultural activities and in gathering foods in their season. Other areas of professional activity included healing and medicine and crafts manufacturing, especially spinning and weaving. In the cosmological order of Aztec society, women's temple obligations were linked to the cults of female deities of the earth, ground water, maize and plant cultivation. Interestingly, childcare was not exclusively for women, since men remained largely responsible for the upbringing of their sons. As the Aztec empire evolved and men gained markedly in prestige, power, and economic importance as warriors, high administrators and priests, a tendency gained strength to affirm a male gender hierarchy. This tendency was surely reinforced by the myth of Huitzilopochtli defeating his sister Coyolxauhqui at the summit of Mt Coatepetl – the principal subject of the symbolic configuration of the Huizilopochtli side of the Great Pyramid, and the subject of triumphal ritual reenactment with sacrificial prisoners following successful conquest campaigns.

8 · Farmers, Traders, and Artisans

An ancient agricultural tradition

Anyone visiting the big open markets in Mexico today will find a palimpsest of fruits and vegetables from all over the globe, among which are found an exceptional variety of edible plants that were domesticated in Mesoamerica and elsewhere in the New World. There will be heaps of fresh green ears of maize, avocadoes arranged in geometric piles, baskets of tomatoes and trays of squash flowers; stacks of *nopal* cactus leaves and the sweet, juicy *tuna* fruit; bins of dried beans of many kinds, and stalls heaped with different kinds of pumpkins; booths with red, green, and yellow chiles as well as chile pastes in mounds of different flavors, and booths selling bowls of hominy stews and corn-husk *tamales*, frying tacos of every kind, fresh mushrooms gathered wild in season, and turkeys roasted with green pumpkin-seed sauce. Native fruits include mameyes, papayas, chirimoyas, zapotes, guavas, and big carrying baskets of huamuchil pods, all in great color and abundance. The list stretches on, for the different altitudes of highland valleys, the proximity of tropical coasts, and the meeting-ground of northern and southern ecological zones, make Mexico one of the world's most favored places for the variety of domesticated and seasonally gathered wild edible plants. Many more varieties of plants were domesticated in the Americas than in the Old World, and the Aztec farmers and horticultural specialists were heirs to a knowledge of cultivation transmitted for millennia.

When the primitive Mexica were run out to the swampy islands in Lake Tetzcoco by the angry lords of Culhuacan, they were obliged to fall back on their old skills as hunters and gatherers. Native chroniclers describe them successfully living on roasted and stewed snakes and other stews and soups of fish, frogs, turtles, and the eggs of insects, including the "flies that sprang from the foam on the water," as well as ducks and other waterfowl that lived and bred in the rushes. But soon enough the Mexica and their immigrant neighbors were learning the farming and horticultural skills practiced for centuries by the older town-dwelling peoples. In the Nahuatl text of his *General History of the Things of New Spain*, Bernardino de Sahagún distinguishes between "farmers" and "horticulturalists." Farmers are described as general field workers charged with preparing the soil, weeding, breaking up clods, hoeing (with the *coa* digging stick), leveling, setting boundary markers, planting, and irrigating, as well as winnowing and storing grains (ill. 108). Horticulturalists were more specialized, with much wider knowledge of seeding, transplanting, and the planting of trees. These specialists would have needed thorough understanding of crop sequences and rotations necessary to ensure continuing high levels of production. Horticulturalists are known to have played a managerial or supervisory role, and they were also expected to read the *tonalamatl* almanacs to determine the best times for planting and harvesting.

It will be recalled from previous discussions of land tenure in the Valley of Mexico that the *calpullis*, at the base of Aztec society, held communal land that was assigned to individual families according to need. In the new *chinampa* zones, however, considerable numbers of farmers were not *calpulli* members but resident tenants tied to the land of estates, who paid rent in kind to owners residing in Tenochtitlan. These laborers were essentially dependents and were supervised by state-appointed administrators. The estates were owned by the *pipiltin* (nobles) or the *tlatoani* himself, and were also awarded to distinguished warriors whose tenure tended to become hereditary. Food was thus supplied to Tenochtitlan by tenant farmers living outside the traditional *calpulli* framework; additional food was acquired from non-tenant *calpulli* farmers who brought their surplus to market, and from individual producer-vendors from towns around the lake basin. The final source of food was provided by tribute exacted from conquered communities.

Chinampas, terraces, and experimental gardens

Archaeological evidence of extensive *chinampa* farming in the Chalco-Xochimilco basin was found in surveys carried out between the 1950s and early 1970s. The archeological surveys initiated by Jeffrey Parsons in the 1970s have continued, now revealing to greater extent the natural resources of the Valley of Mexico and the rural economy in Aztec times and its varied survivals in the 20th and even the early 21st century.[1] This information is supported by the 16th-century ethnohistoric sources.[2] The beginnings of *chinampa* agriculture in the Valley of Mexico remain unclear. There is suggestive evidence that *chinampa*-like cultivation was practiced in well-watered fields around Teotihuacan during the middle of the 1st millennium AD, and it is highly likely that fossil *chinampa* fields from centuries before may underlie present ones still under cultivation around Cuicuilco, Xochimilco, and vicinity.

Archaeological surveys indicate that during the 13th and 14th centuries *chinampa* zones were restricted, bordering islands and shorelines of the Chalco-Xochimilco lakebed. At that time most of the surface would have remained essentially a wetland. By the 15th century, during the reign of Motecuhzoma I, older *chinampa* zones were being incorporated in larger drainage and water-control systems that included large-scale construction of new *chinampa* fields. Aerial surveys show an overall uniformity in *chinampa* size and orientation, indicating a planned program of construction probably carried out over a short period of time. Plots were built by staking out a long, narrow rectangular enclosure approximately 30 m (100 ft) in length by 2.5 m (8 ft) wide, into the swampy shallows (ill. 109). The stakes were joined by wattles and the fence thus formed was filled with mud and decaying vegetation. Another plot was next constructed parallel to the first, leaving a narrow canal between for the passage of canoes. In this way, lines of *chinampas* were extended in a regular pattern. To stabilize plots, tall slender willows were planted around the

Aztec horticulture

108, 109 ABOVE Planting, cultivating, harvesting, and storing maize and amaranth; note the use of the digging stick or *coa*. From Sahagún. BELOW Cross-section of a *chinampa* plot showing how the long narrow pots were constructed with stakes, willows, and a wattle fence, which were then filled with sediment. (For a plan of *chinampa* plots, see ill. 36.)

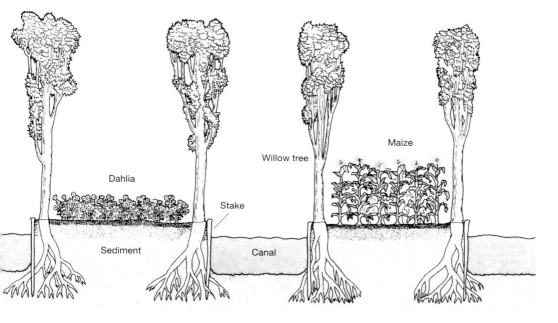

perimeter. In time the willows developed dense root systems that anchored the retaining walls, and constant pruning kept the trees from casting excessive shade. The Chalco-Xochimilco basin was watered by abundant springs along the base of the Ajusco mountains, and a sophisticated drainage system was installed including dams, sluice gates, and canals. This water-control system was interconnected throughout the *chinampa* zone, another factor suggesting central state management. Central control of the water supply was essential to ensure good harvests throughout the year. It was also important to control the level of water in order to avoid flooding during the rainy season, and to maintain moisture during the dry season. In the dry months, irrigation of plants was done by hand, water being carried in containers from the canals to the seedbeds on the *chinampa* platforms. The gardens were fertilized with decaying muck and vegetation dredged up from the canals, and with human excrement collected in canoes from Tenochtitlan and other cities and transported to the fields.

Chinampa development during the reigns of Itzcoatl and Motecuhzoma I was paralleled in central Acolhuacan by the construction of terrace systems during Netzahualcoyotl's long reign. Concentrations of potsherds and traces of domestic refuse found during archaeological surveys disclose that the piedmont and foothills of the Mt Tlaloc range were becoming heavily populated by the early 15th century.[3] Prior to that time, and continuing into the period of Netzahualcoyotl's military campaigns of consolidation, the leaders of Acolhuacan began efforts to increase food production. Early Chichimec chieftains had directed, or perhaps even forced, immigrant tribes to adopt "Toltec" ways that included agricultural practices and settlement in villages. Netzahualcoyotl continued this trend as he extended control over the central region, encouraging the construction of an extensive system of aqueducts from mountain springs to towns and agricultural terraces of the piedmont and foothills. Copious springs in the Vale of Tlalocto below the temple on Mt Tlaloc, were channeled to supply Netzahualcoyotl's ritual baths, terraces, and villa on Tetzcotzingo, as well nearby towns of central Acolhuacan. Another major spring near Santa Catarina del Monte supplied towns around the terraced agricultural crescent between Tetzcotzingo and La Purificación. A third spring rises north of San Gregorio Amanalco, running northwest before branching down to the towns of the north-central district.

Sophisticated hydraulic engineering was required to build these watercourses over broken terrain, and in three locations large embankments were constructed to bridge ravines and saddles. In a number of places the aqueducts are associated with agricultural terracing, most notably in the Tetzcotzingo crescent and vicinity. When the aqueduct system was first investigated in the late 1940s and early 1950s, it was thought to have been primarily a state-sponsored project; but subsequent enquiries have questioned this assumption.[4] It seems likely that local communities were encouraged and supported but not necessarily coerced by the central administration. Calculations have shown that the flow of water through this system was insufficient to have maintained intensive farming as well as household use for so many people throughout the year. The hydraulic system is now thought to have mostly supplied the towns with household water, with some left over for irrigating household gardens and orchards during the dry season. The aqueducts effectively permitted permanent year-round settlement, while the vast terrace systems were used to create new farmland, whose crops were still largely dependent on seasonal rain.

Large-scale irrigation projects were built in the northwest Valley of Mexico, where the Cuauhtitlan River was diverted and its channel enlarged, widened, and straightened with graded embankments. Water was conducted through diversionary channels to flood a broad area of open fields. Elsewhere, archaeological explorations by Michael Smith and his associates at village sites in the Valley of Morelos have also yielded evidence of agricultural terracing, with small-scale check dams built across streambeds where the action of water would gradually level and widen a field suitable for farming. At the village site of Cuexcomate, the pattern of settlement shows some 150 houses, storehouses, and temples dispersed along a sloping rise; evidence of house occupation from *c.* 1200 to *c.* 1550 shows a dramatic increase in population in the final century – a regional reflection of the population explosion that also took place in the Valley of Mexico. Smith points out that it is highly likely that the original population greatly exceeded the production of rainfall agriculture, thus propelling efforts toward more intensive cultivation by building check dams on the local level. Excavations at Cuexcomate and Capilco also reveal that the rural peasant population were not just full-time farmers, for they also produced textiles, pottery, stone tools, and rope. Excavations also revealed remains of many goods originating elsewhere in the highland regions, showing that villages participated in a widespread network of market trade.

We cannot leave the subject of farming and agriculture without mentioning special experimental botanical gardens and pleasances. During the reign of Motecuhzoma I, an old garden that once belonged to "the ancestors" was discovered by the Aztecs at Huaxtepec in Morelos. It was decided that this warm, well-watered place in the shadow of Popocatepetl would be rebuilt, and Motecuhzoma commissioned an overseer named Pinotetl to inspect and restore the fountains, springs, streams, reservoirs, and irrigation system. At the same time Motecuhzoma dispatched messengers to the coast of Veracruz, with a request to the Lord of Cuetlaxtla for plants of the vanilla orchid, cacao trees, and other valuable species. He asked that these be carefully transported to Huaxtepec by native gardeners, who would be capable of replanting and tending them in the proper season. The treasured plants were duly dug up with their roots encircled in earth, wrapped in textiles, and dispatched to Huaxtepec. Before planting the gardeners carried out a planting rite. Success was apparent before three years had passed, for the transplants began to blossom luxuriantly. The Cuetlaxtla gardeners were amazed to see that these plants could flourish away from their original home. Motecuhzoma took delight in the successful experiment and gave thanks to the Lord of the Heavens and of the Day and the Night.

The botanical gardens at Huaxtepec, and a similar garden established by Netzahualcoyotl at Tetzcotzingo, combined practical considerations, ritual use, and pleasure. Dr Hernandez, a Spanish botanist who visited New Spain between 1570 and 1577 on commission by Philip II, wrote an extensive botanical

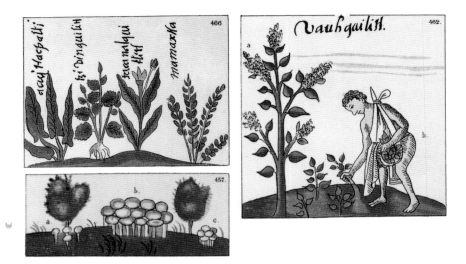

110 Wild plants and herbs were cultivated in botanical gardens for food and medicinal purposes. From Sahagún.

study of native plants and mentions valuable medicinal trees in the Huaxtepec garden (ill. 110).[5] Netzahualcoyotl's garden at Tetzcotzingo was also a source of therapeutic plants.[6]

Pleasure gardens were also a feature of Aztec ruling-class houses. The most detailed description of such a garden was written by Cortés in his second letter to Charles V in 1520. This garden was at Ixtapalapan, where Cortés and his staff were quartered on their way to Tenochtitlan in November 1519:

> Its Lord or chief has some new houses which, though still unfinished, are as good as the best in Spain; I mean as large and as well constructed, not only in the stonework but also in the woodwork, and all arrangements for every kind of household service, all except the (carved) relief work and other rich details which are used in Spanish houses but are not found here. There are both upper and lower rooms and very refreshing gardens with many trees and sweet-scented flowers, [and] bathing places of fresh water, well constructed and having steps leading down to the bottom. He also has a large orchard near the house, overlooked by a high terrace with many beautiful corridors and rooms. Within the orchard is a great square pool of fresh water, very well constructed, with sides of handsome masonry, around which runs a walk with a well-laid pavement of tiles, so wide that four persons can walk abreast on it, and 400 paces square, making in all 600 paces. On the other side of the promenade toward the wall of the garden are hedges of lattice work made of cane, behind which are all sorts of plantations of trees and aromatic herbs. The pool contains many fish and different kinds of waterfowl.[7]

The fruits of the earth: Aztec diet

Sophie Coe's thoughtful book, *America's First Cuisines*, presents an especially informed view of the history of food among the Aztecs, the Maya, the Incas and their predecessors, including a host of insights on the way these foods were eventually incorporated in the diet of Europeans, Africans, and Asians. Among the Aztecs and their neighbors, the dog, turkey, and muscovy duck were the only domesticated livestock in addition to a species of stingless honey bees. Sheep, goats, pigs, bovine cattle, and horses were introduced by the Spanish. The Aztecs' basic diet therefore strongly inclined toward vegetables and fruits, supplemented by game animals, fish, turkeys and other birds, and various kinds of insects. Maize was the principal staple, forming the traditional basis of the Aztec diet together with beans, squash, and chile. Maize was prepared as it still is in Mexican villages, by soaking the dried grains, boiling them with lime or wood ashes, and removing the transparent skin of the grain (the pericarp) before grinding. At this stage of preparation the grain is called *nixtamal*. The process of making nixtamal also greatly enhances the protein value of maize, far more than when the grain is simply ground like wheat to make meal or corn-bread. Today, nixtamal is almost universally ground in a local electric mill, but traditionally it was ground by women using a smooth stone slab metate and a long cylindrical mano. The dough is patted into thin round tortillas for baking on a large flat griddle, or wrapped in corn-husk *tamales* and steamed with meat, sauces, and other flavorings. Nixtamal dough is a versatile foodstuff used to create a great variety of dishes. Popcorn was also a significant part of the diet.

In the Americas, beans of the genus *Phaseolus* were domesticated, of which the species *Phaseolus vulgaris* has myriad varieties. Coe notes that the protein profile of beans complements that of maize, so that a basic diet of nixtamal-processed maize together with beans provides all the protein requirements for working males, although not enough for lactating mothers or infants.[8] In terms of squashes of the species *Cucurbita*, several were domesticated as important food plants. They may be eaten in various stages of development, beginning with the fresh yellow flowers and shoot-tips, to the immature fruit, the ripe fruit (fresh or dried in strips), and also the ripe seeds. Acorn squash, zucchini, summer squash, and certain decorative gourds as well as some pumpkins are all of the species *Cucurbita pepo*. Two other species, the pear-shaped *Cucurbita Mixta* or cushaw, and the *Cucurbita Moschata*, of which the butternut squash is especially well known, are also Mexican domesticates.

Huautli (amaranth), a very high-protein grain, was second in importance only to maize. Amaranth lost much of its appeal in colonial times, but is now making a comeback. Red tomatoes, *xictomatl*, were domesticated from wild species the size of large peas on a vine. Green husk tomatoes, *tomatl*, were lightly boiled, ground and made into sauces. White sweet potatoes, *camotli*, were roasted, although in Mesoamerica potatoes never held the primacy they have always enjoyed in the Andean world. The jícama, a turnip-like root, was eaten raw with salt and chile (and with lime juice today), and is also steamed or stewed with other ingredients in a variety of dishes. The chayote, also known as the vegetable pear, grows in three varieties on dense shady vines; the large, medium-green type covered with a spiny rind has an especially delicate, sweet flavor often complemented by sauces. Peanuts also figured in the diet, although not as significantly as in Peru. The Aztecs chewed gum (chicle), bitumen, and other natural gums to clean their teeth; but public chewing of gum was considered ill-mannered: prostitutes were noted for walking through the marketplace at Tlatelolco, brazenly chewing and loudly snapping their gum. Many fruits were cultivated including the mamey, white and black zapotes, chirimoyas, guavas, papayas and custard apples. Another important vegetable crop was the nopal cactus, and even today villages have extensive nopal orchards which are regularly harvested for tender paddles and the sweet, succulent fruit. Nopal cactus groves were also the habitat of myriad cochineal bugs, gathered periodically and dried for their intense red color used as a textile dye. Tall, pleated stalks of the *Pitaya* cactus were and still are tended in orchards and harvested for their succulent fruit. Maguey agaves (not a cactus) whose fermented sap provides *pulque*, and whose baked leaves and boles become a candy-like sweet, still line the sides of maize fields throughout the highlands. Maguey leaves and cotton were the principal sources of fiber for weaving.

The well-known condiments of Mexico include epazote, a chenopodium whose pungent, serrated leaves are used to flavor beans and a host of other dishes; avocado leaves, toasted and ground; and achiote, the deep red seeds of the annatto tree, used as a base for seasoning pastes for fish and meat. Annatto trees were probably not grown by the Aztecs, for they are native to lowland tropical climes. Then there are the incomparable chiles – serranos, poblanos, piquines, jalapeños and more, fresh, dried, and sometimes smoked in their many flavors, were all used in infinite combinations as in Mexican cuisines to this day. Chiles are important sources of vitamins A and C, and are still considered basic to the diet as well as serving as condiments and stimulants. Vanilla, extracted from the pods of a species of orchid, was among the most esteemed flavorings, but chocolate was the most esteemed of all. Chocolate comes from the roasted beans of cacao pods, growing from trees that require a warm, humid climate. In antiquity the most extensive cacao plantations were in the Xoconusco region along the Pacific slope of Guatemala. The large fleshy pods sprout directly from tree trunks or large branches, in groves shaded by larger trees. The seeds are extracted, fermented, cured, and toasted; chocolate was overwhelmingly consumed as a beverage, prepared by grinding the seeds into powder, mixed with hot water and sometimes ground maize. This mixture was beaten with a wooden whisk until foamy. Bernardino de Sahagún describes the process:

> The seller of fine chocolate [is] one who grinds, who provides people with drink, with repasts. She grinds cacao [beans]; she crushes, breaks, pulverizes them. She chooses, selects, separates them. She drenches, soaks, steeps them. She adds water sparingly, conservatively; aerates it, filters it, strains it, pours it back and forth, aerates it; she makes it form a head, makes it foam; she removes the head, makes it form a head, makes it foam... She sells good, superior, potable [chocolate]: the privilege, the drink of nobles, of rulers – finely ground, soft, foamy, reddish, bitter; [with] chile water, with flowers,

with uei nacaztli, with teonacaztli, with vanilla, with mecaxochitl, with wild bee honey, with powdered aromatic flowers. [Inferior cholocate has] maize flour and water; lime water; [it is] pale; the [froth] bubbles burst. [It is chocolate with water added – Chontal water [fit for] water flies.[9]

Like tea and coffee, chocolate is rich in caffeine and was very highly prized throughout Mesoamerica. The Codex Mendoza reveals that cacao was a primary item of tribute, and was also used as a form of money. Cacao was a highly valued item of long-distance trade since the time of Teotihuacan.

This is but a token list of Aztec cultivated plants and foods, which have become subjects of special interest to ethnobotanists as well as historians and contemporary authors of Mexican cookbooks. Mexican cuisine, long regarded in terms of a few simple dishes from the reaches of New Mexico or Texas, is becoming known for its distinctive regional traditions and deep range of ingredients, second in complexity only to Chinese cuisine.

The market at Tlatelolco

The Valley of Mexico had flourishing markets located near the main temple at the center of every community. According to Diego Durán, a law made it obligatory to go to market and bring supplies to town; no one could sell anything on the way to the market, first under penalty of law and second for fear of angering the market god.

But it must not be imagined that secular and supernatural sanctions were the only stimuli to commerce, for markets were certainly more than mere centers for the exchange of material goods. As Durán says, "the markets are so appetizing and friendly that a great concourse of people come here," and he describes at length the powerful attraction exerted by markets upon the population. Then as today, the great markets of Mexico were places for meeting people and gathering information and gossip: more than once, Aztec women overheard rumors of impending rebellion or attack by neighboring peoples, particularly during the formative years of the empire.

The principal market of Tenochtitlan was at the annexed sister-city of Tlatelolco. Another was located adjacent to the great ceremonial precinct of Tenochtitlan, where the Zócalo of Mexico City lies today. Elsewhere small local markets were scattered throughout the city to serve the various *calpulli* wards. Canoes supplied the markets via the system of main canals and lesser waterways, many of which continued to operate in Spanish colonial times, and some even into the late 19th century. It is probable that the small-scale markets of Tenochtitlan were held on a temporary basis by producer-vendors from around the lakeshore or local peddlers re-selling goods obtained in the larger markets at Tlatelolco and Tenochtitlan.

The great market at Tlatelolco was described by the Conquistador Anónimo as being thronged daily by some 25,000 people. A special market was held every fifth day, when the crowd increased to about 40,000–50,000. This roughly tallies with Cortés' estimate of 60,000, probably made on an unusually crowded occasion since at the time the Spanish had only been in the city for four days.

The size, organization and the variety of goods astonished the Spaniards. The lively scene is described by Bernal Diaz:

> When we arrived at the great marketplace, called Tlatelolco, we were astounded at the number of people and the quantity of merchandise that it contained, and at the good order and control that was maintained, for we had never seen such a thing before. The chieftains who accompanied us acted as guides. Each kind of merchandise was kept by itself and had its fixed place marked out. Let us begin with dealers of gold, silver, and precious stones, feathers, mantles, and embroidered goods. Then there were other wares consisting of Indian slaves, both men and women; and I say that they bring as many of them to that great market for sale as the Portuguese bring Negroes from Guinea; and they brought them along tied to long poles, with collars around their necks so that they could not escape, and others they left free. Next there were other traders who sold great pieces of cloth and cotton, and articles of twisted thread, and there were *cacaoteros* who sold cacao. In this way one could see every sort of merchandise that is to be found in the whole of New Spain. There were those who sold cloths of hennequen and ropes and the sandals with which they are shod, which are made from the same plant, and sweet cooked roots, and other tubers which they got from this plant, all were kept in one part of the market in the place assigned to them. In another part there were skins of tigers and lions, of otters and jackals, deer and other animals and badgers and mountain cats, some tanned and others untanned, and other classes of merchandise.
>
> Let us go and speak of those who sold beans and sage and other vegetables and herbs in another part, and to those who sold fowls, cocks with wattles, rabbits, hares, deer, mallards, young dogs and other things of that sort in their part of the market, and let us also mention the fruiterers, and the women who sold cooked food, dough and tripe in their own part of the market; then every sort of pottery made in a thousand different forms from great water jars to little jugs, these also had a place to themselves; then those who sold honey and honey paste and other dainties like nut paste, and those who sold lumber, boards, cradles, beams, blocks and benches, each article by itself, and the vendors of ocote firewood, and other things of a similar nature. But why do I waste so many words in recounting what they sell in that great market? – for I shall never finish if I tell it all in detail. Paper, which in this country is called *amal*, and reeds scented with liquidambar, and full of tobacco, and yellow ointments and things of that sort are sold by themselves, and much cochineal is sold under the arcades which are in that great market place, and there are many vendors of herbs and other sorts of trades. There are also buildings where three magistrates sit in judgment, and there are executive officers like Alguacils who inspect the merchandise. I am forgetting those who sell salt, and those who make the stone knives, and how they split them off the stone itself; and the fisherwomen and others who sell some small cakes made from a sort of ooze which they get out of the great lake, which curdles, and from this they made a bread having a flavour something like cheese. There are for sale axes of brass and copper and tin, and gourds

and gaily painted jars made of wood. I could wish that I had finished telling of all the things which are sold there, but they are so numerous and of such different quality and the great market place with its surrounding arcades was so crowded with people, that one would not have been able to see and inquire about it all in two days.[10]

Cortés noted in his letter to Charles V that everything was sold by counts and measures but not by weight. Sahagún describes the ordering and administration of the marketplace by appointed directors drawn from the principal merchants, the *pochteca*. These officials pronounced harsh judgment upon those who cheated customers. Anyone caught stealing would be sentenced to death, as would those found selling stolen goods. The directors were also responsible for assigning each type of merchandise to a particular section of the plaza, and for fixing prices. Barter was a means of effecting exchange. Cacao beans were widely used as money in the market, though they may not have had a standardized value from region to region. Other items were also used as currency, such as gold in transparent quills, tropical feathers, or small copper axes and pieces of tin.

Arts and crafts

The range of goods displayed in Aztec markets deeply impressed the Spaniards for their variety and artistry. These manufactures reflected traditions that reached back in some cases to the remotest periods of human occupation in the Americas.

Stoneworking

Stoneworking had been a fundamental industry since the earliest times, for metallurgy only arrived in Mesoamerica around the 9th century AD and was mainly used in jewelry-making. Obsidian ranked as one of the most useful stones. This brittle volcanic glass occurs in gigantic natural deposits in several places in the Central Highlands, where mines were established in antiquity. During the early centuries AD, Teotihuacan controlled a prime obsidian source near Pachuca in the State of Hidalgo, and traded the material as far south as Guatemala. Using technologies that were essentially developed in Upper Paleolithic times, a multiplicity of cutting and puncturing implements were made from obsidian for specialized purposes. Razor-sharp blades were flaked off larger "blanks" of stone in a sophisticated "unwrapping" process; single-edged and double-edged knives were also made, as were scrapers, v-shaped gougers, dart-points of various dimensions, and heavy striking blades. The refinement achieved in working this natural glass is evident from objects such as polished obsidian mirrors, earspools as delicate and thin as if machined with precision instruments, and even whole vessels (ill. 112). Yet making such admirable objects, and others of crystal, amethyst, jade, and turquoise, depended on knowledge of how to employ hard stones against softer ones, how to use sand and pumice-powder as an abrasive for cutting with cords or in polishing surfaces, how to use simple hand-held pump-drills, and how to

111, 112 ABOVE An exceptionally fine example of mosaic work. This ritual mask with turquoise inlay is thought to have been included in the first shipment of gifts and trophies sent by Cortés to Europe. BELOW Parts of an obsidian wand, carved as a rattlesnake. Found at the Great Pyramid.

apply the right pressure and where to strike a stone in knapping operations. In Mesoamerica the techniques and skills of stone technology reached their fullest flowering. Other aspects of stonework are seen in the extraordinary inlaid masks and other ritual objects completely covered with a delicate mosaic of the finest craftsmanship, including turquoise, jet, pyrites and colored shell (ill. 111; pls. XXI, XXII). It is widely assumed that such masterpieces were manufactured by Mixtec craftsmen residing in Tenochtitlan, although the turquoise was imported from several locations, some as far away as New Mexico. The custom of bringing foreign artisans to reside in special sections of cities had its origins in Teotihuacan.

At the other end of the stoneworking scale, Aztec craftsmen were employed by the state to make colossal basalt sculptures. Such figures as the great Coatlicue (see frontispiece) and the disk of Coyolxauhqui are examples of the Aztec genius for carving in high relief (ills. 96–98). Aztec sculptors less often ventured into the realm of "liberating" figures from the block of stone as did the sculptors of Mediterranean antiquity, although works such as the seated Xochipilli and the Ehecatl from Calixtlahuaca show that by the end of the 15th and the beginning of the 16th centuries, master sculptors were increasingly venturing in that direction (ill. 113; pls. XVII–XX). The technologies of quarrying,

113 Figures of "guardians" (right arm raised) and others expressing "fealty" (hands held on chest), from the third enlargement of the Great Pyramid of Tenochtitlan, 1430s. The slab-like character of these effigies gave way to increasing naturalism in Aztec sculpture by the second half of the 15th century.

transporting, and working large monoliths were very well developed in Olmec times, *c.* 900 BC, and had reached new levels of achievement in Teotihuacan (during the early centuries AD) where sculptural monuments weighing up to 40 tons were brought from distant quarries (presumably using log rollers) to be set up in the ceremonial center. The Aztecs acquired the tradition of monumental stone carving first from Atzcapotzalco, and later from the Huaxtecs of the Gulf Coast. Their ability to develop a signature Aztec style is evident when we compare the slab-like sculptural figures featured on Itzcoatl's pyramid, dating to about 1430, with figures such as the Xochipilli probably made between the 1450s and early 16th century.

Basketmaking

Basketry was another ancient manufacturing art inherited by the Aztecs. Like methods of making stone tools, basketry had been a feature of early hunting-and-gathering societies. The extensive reedbeds in the highland lakes provided an inexhaustible source of prime material, but other fibers were woven from palmleaf, cane slats, various cacti, and especially from fibers of the long broad leaves of maguey agave. At the market in Tenochtitlan, baskets of many sizes and shapes were used and sold, for carrying produce, storing grains, and as special containers designed for different foods. Fine baskets of very tight weave were intended for personal use, holding valuables such as jewelry or family keepsakes. Larger square or rectangular baskets with lids were used as chests for clothing. Closely related to the basketmakers were the weavers of reed mats, *petlatl*, and the makers of reed seats. In ancient Mexico, furniture was limited to stools, litters, and low small tables. Mats, like Japanese tatami, were an essential item in both royal and humble households where activities took place upon or close to the floor. The mat was an old symbol of rulership and one of the appellations for the *tlatoani* was "he who is seated upon the mat." Reed mats are still produced, especially in the Toluca Valley, but they are fast becoming a residual art from what was once a major industry, producing mats both coarse and fine for all levels of society.

Jewelry and metallurgy

The golden ornaments worn by Aztec officials and nobles were largely made by Mixtec craftsmen working in Tenochtitlan. Their manufacturing techniques and design had been developing in Oaxaca since about the 10th century AD. The famous discovery of a royal Mixtec burial in Monte Albán tomb 38 by Alfonso Caso in the 1930s, revealed to the modern world the extraordinary craftsmanship of the Mixtecs, seen in rings, cast pendants, ear-danglers and necklaces. The Aztecs coveted this artistry and their own jewelry strongly reflected the tradition of Mixtec goldworking. But it must be remembered that the Mixtecs themselves acquired this knowledge from lands farther south. Beginning around 2000 BC, the sophisticated techniques of metallurgy had slowly diffused northward from their place of origin in the Andes of South America, eventually reaching Panama and Costa Rica by overland routes and coastal trade. In Mexico the earliest and most developed metalworking centers were on the Pacific side – among the Mixtecs, and also at sites in Guerrero and

XII, XIII The monumental Tlaltecuhtli "Earth Lady" sculptural relief was discovered in 2008 in front of the Great Pyramid of Tenochtitlan. Archaeologist Ximena Balderas cleans the imposing slab broken under the weight of a Spanish colonial mansion damaged by earthquake and now demolished. Ongoing excavations have revealed offering caches beneath the sculpture, but whether or not the site contains buried ashes of the ruler Ahuitzotl remains to be seen in 2009.

XIV OPPOSITE Crowned with a colorful headdress, a figure of the deity Chicomecoatl, "Seven Serpent," holds ears of maize. Attached to a large incense-burner, the effigy presided during annual planting, first-fruits, and harvest rituals devoted to securing agricultural success.

XV RIGHT ABOVE The earth deity Tlazolteotl holds ears of maize, attended by four Tlaloc rain-priests attired in colors of the four cardinal directions. The name Tlazolteotl, "Sacred Filth," refers to the deity as the recipient of personal confessions as well as fertilizer during the time of cultivation. The Codex Borbonicus, c. 1525.

XVI RIGHT New Fire Ceremony, from the Codex Borbonicus, c. 1525. A procession of deities bearing unlit torches (left and lower left) approaches the hill Huitzachtlán identified by a thorn-bush place-glyph (upper right); a fire-drill rests on the summit. Within houses, women and children wear blue masks and a pregnant woman is guarded in a granary (below right). The figure of Huitzilopochtli appears before his temple (above). At center, four priests light torches at the Fire Temple of Tenochtitlan, to distribute new fire in the wards of the city.

OVERLEAF, LEFT TO RIGHT (NOT TO SCALE)

XVII An impersonator of the agricultural deity Xipe Totec "Our Flayed Lord," is represented attired in a flayed human skin, representing a living seed within a dried husk or shell.

XVIII The duck-billed masked effigy of the deity Ehecatl, "Wind," recovered from a temple at the Aztec colonial site of Calixtlahuaca in the Toluca Valley. The marked tendency toward naturalism shown by this imposing figure was increasingly seen in major Aztec sculpture of the late 15th and early 16th centuries. Like many other sculptural effigies, this figure would have been ceremonially dressed with a headdress, cape, and items of jewelry for ceremonial presentations at prescribed times of year.

XIX Masked effigy of the deity Xochipilli, "Flower Prince," seated upon a throne-like dais ornamented with jade roundels alluding to value, and flowers and butterflies associated with festivals and the idea of regeneration. Late 15th or early 16th century.

XX Inlaid shell and obsidian eyes and teeth intensify the rapt, naturalistic facial features of this effigy. Emblems carved on the back identify the figure as an impersonator of the solar deity Xiuhtecuhtli, "Turquoise Lord," also associated with the power of the deified Mexica-Aztec hero, Huitzilopochtli, and by extension the warriors. Of metropolitan Aztec workmanship, the sculpture was excavated in the provincial site of Coxcatlán in the Tehuacan Valley, Puebla.

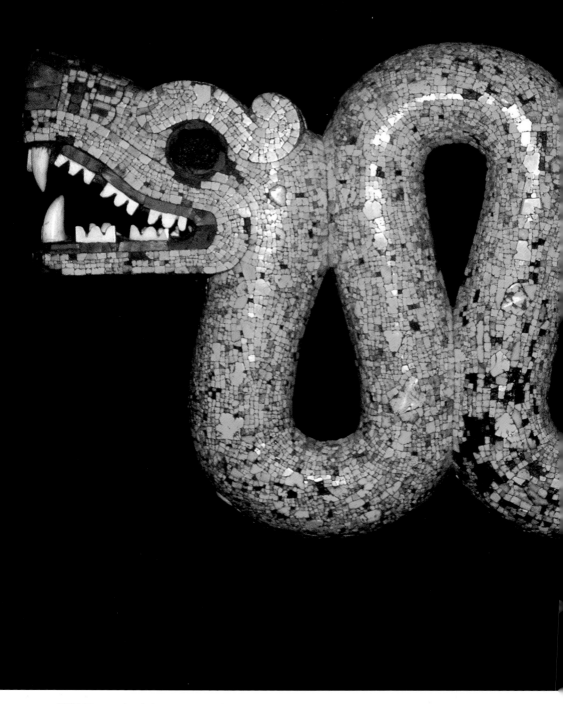

XXI The two-headed serpent was a sky symbol in Mesoamerica from the early centuries AD, appearing above royal personages in sculptural reliefs, or held diagonally across the body as a cosmic emblem of rulership. Snakes shed their skin and were therefore associated with renewal, and their movements evoked a sense of flowing water

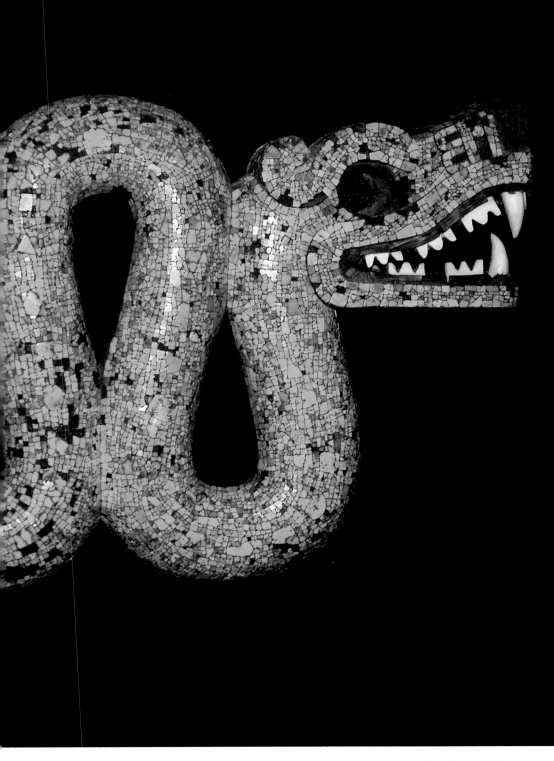

and wind. This Aztec snake of carved cedar, covered in turquoise mosaic and inlays of white, red, and orange shell and mother-of-pearl, undoubtedly served similar symbolic purposes, alluding to the ruler's religious responsibilities as chief intermediary between human society and the forces of nature associated with the sky and cyclic renewal.

XXII Possibly associated with the omnipresent creator deity Tezcatlipoca, commonly translated as "Smoking Mirror," this famous mask features bands of turquoise and lignite mosaics superimposed on a human skull. A vivid red spondylus shell nose-piece and pyrite eyes with shell rims complete the visage. The lower jaw remains moveable, hinged to a leather lining. This masterpiece summarizes the fearsome theatricality of Aztec ritual imagery.

Michoacán. Near Zihuatanejo on the Guerrero coast, pieces of slag were archaeologically recovered with hundreds of metal objects, indicating a flourishing copper-smelting operation between AD 900 and 1100. The Tarascan peoples of Michoacán developed a copper-working industry that included such trade items as cast bells for dance costumes, tweezers, needles, axes, and small figurines. The manufacture of bronze was also known. Yet the Mixtecs of Oaxaca remained the most celebrated artisans, and it was through them that the art of jewelry was brought to Tenochtitlan. Gold was panned and collected as nuggets from riverbeds, and smelted in furnaces heated by men blowing through tubes onto charcoal embers. Casting was accomplished by the lost-wax method, and methods evolved in South America were used for gilding copper, and mixing copper and gold to produce an alloy known as tumbaga. Jewelers working at Tenochtitlan combined cast and filigree goldwork with other materials such as crystal, turquoise, and jade. Even though most Aztec goldwork was lost in Spanish melting-pots after the Conquest, the few pieces that survive in museums show the trend towards achieving a new and distinctive style, and a quality of workmanship that matches the finest goldwork from elsewhere in the ancient Americas (pl. VIII).

Cloth and clothing

The beginnings of the textile arts are unclear in Mesoamerica, because climatic conditions rarely permit the survival of cloth and clothing. This is unlike the coast of Peru, where the most splendid textiles of the ancient Americas were preserved in the desert environment. Our record of Aztec textiles stems from Spanish descriptions, pictorial manuscripts, and details of finely sculpted figures showing the intricacy and variety of cloth made throughout the empire (ill. 114). Each region had distinctive designs, woven, embroidered, dyed or painted on male and female garments. Clothing was highly emblematic of place as well as social status and function. Sumptuary laws were enforced to regulate the wearing of clothes according to social and official position. The most common cloth was made of maguey or hennequen fiber for capes, loincloths, skirts, and *huipiles* (mantles worn by women). Maguey fiber was a stiff and uncomfortable material, but the techniques for weaving could produce highly flexible and delicate cloth. Cotton had long been cultivated in Mesoamerica, and was raised in warm lowland Morelos since the time of Teotihuacan. Even at the highest levels of Aztec society, men and women wore the same types of garments as the lower orders – only the materials, the fineness of weave, and the manner of ornamentation varied. There was no tradition of tailoring clothes to fit the limbs and body. Pictorial and sculptural sources show that textiles were predominantly decorated with geometric designs, but some were embroidered with patterns reflecting local flora and fauna. Dyes were made from mineral sources such as blue clay and yellow ocher, and vegetal dyes were derived from a multitude of plants. Red color was obtained from cochineal insects, and violet was obtained by dyeing skeins of cotton thread with a secretion from coastal mollusks.

Feather garments were a specialty of weavers called *amanteca*, whose brilliant products were reserved for the nobility and the highest-ranking officials.

114 OPPOSITE ABOVE A messenger (left) wears a plain shoulder-mantle and loincloth. A nobleman (center) wears quetzal-plume tassels, a mantle with conch-shell designs, and gold and jade jewelry. Prince Netzahualpilli of Tetzcoco (right) wears the royal turquoise mantle and loincloth, quetzal plumes, a jade necklace and gold earplugs and legbands.

115, 116 OPPOSITE BELOW Ceremonial shield (left) with feather decorations and gold trim, sent to Europe by Cortés. The coyote in the center has the speech-glyph *alt tlachinolli*, "water, fire," i.e. deluge and conflagration, the metaphor for war. To the right a feather-worker dyes and glues feathers; from Sahagún.

Feathers for these most prized garments were gathered by professional hunters who netted birds in the tropical forests, but colorful plumage was also obtained from birds raised in captivity. The art of feather-working was old in Mesoamerica and consisted of tying the stems of feathers into the fabric during the weaving process. Several Aztec ceremonial shields have survived, demonstrating the bold effects achieved by these artisans, who were not only superb technicians but also unsurpassed colorists and designers (ills. 115, 116; pl. VII). The Spaniards speak of admirable featherwork cloaks and elegant *huipiles*, as well as sumptuously ornamented loincloths.

Ceramics

One of the most extensive sections of the Tlatelolco market was assigned to the pottery stalls. Pottery began in ancient Mexico with the appearance of village agricultural life, and like others before them the Aztecs had developed their own styles of ceramics. The potter's wheel was not used in the Americas before it was introduced by the Spaniards, so vessels and figures were handbuilt. Coiling strips of clay and then scraping and paddling to thin down the walls, joining slabs of clay, or assembling pieces from molded sections were well-known ways of manufacture. Neither the Aztecs nor their predecessors developed the technology of vitreous glazes, high-fired stoneware, or porcelain. Rather, ancient New World ceramic traditions were of low-fire earthenware. Yet, as with stoneworking, relatively simple methods produced some of the most remarkable, varied, and beautiful ceramics in the world. In the 15th century Aztec pottery was characteristically a thin-walled, finely proportioned, cream-colored or red-and-black slipped ware, decorated with fine-line geometric designs that often have the quality of calligraphy. By the early 16th century Aztec potters were beginning to favor more naturalistic motifs, depicting flowers, fish, and other animals in combination with fine-line designs. Coarse utilitarian vessels were made in a variety of specialized shapes and sizes for cooking, including large flat clay griddles for baking the indispensable tortillas. Prized ceramics, such as those used in royal palaces, were made in Chollollan in the Valley of Puebla. This was a polychrome earthenware, painted with mineral-colored slips and burnished when "leather-hard" before firing. The lustrous, warm surfaces were covered with designs related to manuscript illuminations, in another aspect of what has been called the Mixteca-Puebla "international style" (ill. 117).

Aztec potters also made special pieces for temples, sometimes using techniques and shapes that followed earlier ceramic traditions. A famous pair of blue Tlaloc vases, found in a Great Pyramid offering-cyst, are painted in a fresco medium that recalls the brilliant frescoed pottery of Teotihuacan (pl. X). Also recovered from the Great Pyramid were a pair of cylindrical vessels, carved while still leather-hard with detailed reliefs of Aztec deities. Such forms recall an antique tradition combining Classic Maya and Teotihuacan styles, pointing to a deliberate historicizing intention. Other forms of ceremonial ceramics, such as large standing incense-burners with attached figures of deities, are distinctively Aztec yet ultimately echo longlasting traditions of Oaxaca and the Maya region (ill. 118; pl. XIV). These composite figures were fashioned from mold-made and handbuilt forms, brilliantly painted with colors illustrating the spectacular costumes worn by Aztec ritual performers. Such items were designed to be seen at a distance in architectural settings. They are unlikely to have reached the marketplace, for they were commissioned especially by temple organizations and patrons.

117, 118 LEFT Highly prized ceramic cup from Cholollan, with polychrome depiction of a feline. BELOW An incense-burner with a deity figure, from an offering in the Great Pyramid of Tenochtitlan.

An archaeological area of household workshops

One of the most telling archaeological projects of the late 1980s revealed specialized craft workshops near the town of Otumba, southeast of Teotihuacan. The original "Aztec" Otumba is now a zone of plowed fields bordered by rows of maguey close by the modern town. Archaeologists Thomas Charlton, Deborah Nichols, and Cynthia Otis Charlton gathered surface collections showing concentrations of specific types of artifacts and object fragments in specific areas of the site.[11] A pattern emerged, indicating the distribution of craft production centers within the old town. Principal manufactures included obsidian blades, basalt implements (metates and manos for grinding maize), scrapers, polishers, fine lapidary products (ear spools, lip plugs, beads, and disks, including fragments showing the entire sequence of production for these objects). Households specializing in obsidian core-blade manufacturing were found in both the central elite zone of Otumba as well as in scattered residential areas. Mold-made ceramics (incense holders, figurines, rattles, stamps, spindle whorls and pellets) were also recovered, as well as evidence of cotton and maguey-fiber textile production, indicated by concentrations of small and large spindle-whorls. Subsequent excavations revealed that manufacture took place close by or within houses, and not in separate workshops. The distribution pattern shows that whole neighborhoods specialized in certain products. The period of highest production fell between the mid-15th century and the mid-16th century. Did the Otumba industries supply a local market area, or were their products more widely traded in the Valley of Mexico and beyond? Such questions remain to be answered, yet it is apparent that the Aztec provinces as well as the capitals participated in networks of raw material sources, manufacturing, and trade.

Long-distance traders

Not all the merchandise available in markets was produced locally: much of it came from neighboring highland basins, from the most distant confines of the empire, or from exotic lands beyond. Most of these goods were brought by long-distance merchants known as *pochteca*. The *pochteca* handled long-distance trade on behalf of the Aztec nobility, as well as acting as independent traders. The importance of the *pochteca* in the expansionist policies of the Aztec state, their role within the religious system, their association with the nobility, and their journeys to distant "ports of trade" form a unique and fascinating chapter in the story of the Aztec economy.[12]

The difference between long-distance *pochteca* trade and the predominantly local character of regular market trade is reflected in the fact that regular markets continued to exist throughout the colonial period and up to the present, whereas long-distance trade disappeared within about five years of the Spanish Conquest. This disappearance was due to the fact that the trade network dealt primarily in the importing of luxury items such as the feathers of tropical birds, greenstones, and exotic animal hides, which had high value for the Aztecs but not for the Spaniards.

According to the early colonial historian Alonso de Zorita, the *pochteca* enjoyed a privileged position with the nobility, as they paid tribute to the rulers in the form of merchandise but were not obliged to render personal services; he also writes that theirs was an occupation that could only be inherited.[13] It is probable that the *pochteca* were organized as a *calpulli* kin unit, living on the land owned by their lineage. There were seven merchant wards in Tenochtitlan-Tlatelolco, of which the most famous was named Pochtlán. The other wards with important long-distance trading communities were Tepetitlán, Tzonmolco, Atlauhco, Amachtlán, and Itztotolco. Significantly, these names appear widely dispersed in regions far beyond the Valley of Mexico, and it has been suggested that some of these sites may have been trading centers as far back as Toltec times. Other towns in the Valley of Mexico with notable trading communities were Tetzcoco, Atzcapotzalco, Huitzilopochco, Huexotla, Cuauhtitlan, Coatlinchan, Chalco, Otumba, Xochimilco, and Mixcoac.

The term *pochotl*, from which *pochteca* and Pochtlán derive, was the name for the Bombax ceiba, a towering, sheltering tree of the tropical forests, traditionally regarded as a sacred "tree of life." In a figurative sense, *pochotl* means father, mother, governor, chief, or protector. This meaning of the ancient title is important because it suggests that *pochteca* occupied very high positions in Mesoamerican societies before the Aztecs, as we shall see.

The origins of long-distance trading in Tlatelolco and Tenochtitlan probably date to the 1380s. According to Sahagún, the first two merchants sold only red macaw feathers and blue and scarlet parrot feathers. But in the early 15th century, cotton garments began to appear, as well as quetzal feathers (not yet the large ones), turquoise, and green chalchihuite stones. By the 1470s the list of imports had grown to include luxury garments, a wider variety of precious feathers, stone jewelry, and cacao. The close association between rulers and merchants continued after the last of the independent Tlatelolcan rulers and the absorption of Tlatelolco into Tenochtitlan.

There were four types of *pochteca*, each with specific duties and obligations. The highest officials were referred to as *pochtecatlatoque*, commanders of the *pochteca*. These august personages were appointed by the ruler, selected from the oldest, most prestigious of *pochteca*. They were seasoned travelers who now stayed at home to serve in an administrative capacity, advising and admonishing younger traders, and also commissioning outgoing trading groups to exchange goods in the distant centers of trade. Upon the return of the expedition, the gains were shared by both parties. Another duty of these elder merchants was to sit in judgment on miscreant *pochteca* and to deliver the appropriate sentences; the merchants' courts were held separately from those of the state, and no state authorities had the right to intervene. These principal merchant rulers were also assigned the important task of administering the marketplace.

The second group of *pochteca* comprised the slave traders, known as *tlaltlani*, "bather of slaves." This title referred to the ritual bathing of slaves, required before their use as sacrificial victims. According to Sahagún the slave traders were the richest merchants, and they were also accorded special privileges by the rulers. Slave traders were considered particularly devout and played a central role in the annual Panquetzaliztli festival devoted to the deified hero, Huitzilopochtli.

Certain merchants were specially commissioned by the rulers to conduct their personal trade. These were the *tencunenenque*, "royal travelers, passengers." They also served on occasion as tribute-collectors. These royal trade officials may have constituted a special category among *pochteca*, but it is more likely that they were simply particularly able or trustworthy *oztomeca* "vanguard merchants," who carried out the bulk of long-distance trade. The fourth group were the *naualoztomeca*, or "disguised merchants," trader-spies whose development as a special type of merchant at the service of the state forms a most interesting theme in Aztec trading. *Naualoztomeca* began as ordinary travelers who were obliged to disguise themselves as natives when entering enemy territories in search of rare goods:

> When they entered land under which they were at war, and went among people who were far distant, they became like their enemies in their garments, their hair-dress, their speech, that they might mimic the natives.
> And if they came to an evil pass, if they were discovered, then they were slain in ambush and served up with chili sauce. But if any – even one, even two – escaped alive, such a one informed Motecuhzoma.[14]

The gossip of the marketplaces and the network of commercial contacts yielded vital information to the trader-spies. As the empire evolved during the 15th century, the *naualoztomeca* were regularly employed as spies by the state before the initiation of hostilities.

By the reign of Ahuitzotl (1486–1502), merchants had attained particular prominence in the Aztec hierarchy. Following their remarkable actions in the conquest of the province of Xoconochco, the *pochteca* were publicly acclaimed by the ruler in Tenochtitlan and were awarded special capes and breechcloths, although these items might be worn only on special occasions since it was a privilege of the nobility always to wear fine capes. The *tlatoani* of Tenochtitlan also gave certain traders the privilege of handling his personal trade. The *pochteca* thus became increasingly involved in the work of the imperial state; new categories of *pochteca* developed; and the *pochteca* in general were brought into close commercial association with the military aristocracy.

Trading centers

By the time of the Spanish Conquest, the *pochteca* were trading far beyond the limits of the Aztec empire. Most of what is presently known about this trade concerns the southern Gulf of Mexico, but it is also probable that Aztec merchants were also operating to the northwest, in the ancient mining districts of Hidalgo and Querétaro, and even further north, in Zacatecas and Durango. From these parts, a down-the-line system of trade led farther afield to turquoise sources in New Mexico and Arizona. To the south, the trade routes led down from the central plateau to Tochtepec, where the trail forked. One branch continued into Oaxaca, the Isthmus of Tehuantepec, and Xoconochco. The other branch led to the Gulf Coast at Coatzacoalco. Inland from Coatzacoalco was the powerful Nahuatl-speaking town of Cimatán, strategically located on the Grijalva River – a major trade route leading into the sierra of Chiapas, which was a source of amber. To the east of Cimatán lay the populous, tropical region known as the Chontalapa, the location of some 25 towns where Aztec traders kept warehouses and representatives. Potonchán lay beyond, above the confluence of the Grijalva and Usumacinta Rivers. The Usumacinta River had been a trade artery since Classic Maya times, and gave Potonchán ready communication with the inland forest region known as Acalán and beyond through a network of trails and waterways to the Petén region of lowland Guatemala and the trading center Nito on the Gulf of Honduras. However, Potonchán was not frequented by Aztec *pochteca*, for it was controlled by powerful Maya traders. On the other hand, the trading center of Xicallanco, located at the outlet of the Laguna de Términos, was almost certainly a headquarters for Aztec *pochteca*. The rulers of Xicallanco spoke Nahuatl, although the population was Chontal Maya, so it is probable that Aztec traders ruled this important town. In this respect they followed the Maya tradition in which traders and rulers were one and the same. Xicallanco also enjoyed access by trail and canoe to the Petén forests in Guatemala and occupied a ward in Nito on the Gulf of Honduras. The principal trading center of Itzamkanac on the Candelaria River in the Petén was visited by Cortés on his Honduras march of 1523. Five years later a lieutenant under the command of Francisco de Montejo, the conqueror of Yucatan, arrived and reported that although there were some 500 limestone and stucco buildings, the former prosperity had fallen away. This was of course due to the collapse of the *pochteca* system after the Spanish Conquest. Itzamkanac was also probably an outlet for trade from the rich cacao-producing valleys of the Sarstoon, Polochic, and Motagua Rivers of Belize and Guatemala.

The principal commodities exported by *pochteca* from Tenochtitlan, Tlatelolco, Tetzcoco, and other highland cities were sumptuary items manufactured from imported raw materials or materials acquired as tribute. These commodities were supplied to the traders by the nobility from their tributary towns, or by the *pochteca* network itself. Other trade wares included obsidian, copper bells and ornaments, needles, obsidian ornaments, combs, red ocher, herbs, cochineal, alum, and rabbit-fur skins. Many such items were supplied by commoners, who purchased them in the marketplaces of the metropolis. Finally, slaves were exported to Cimatán and the forests of Acalán and the Petén region, to meet the need for canoe paddlers and porters in the riverine trade routes, and perhaps to act as laborers in the cacao groves, since cacao is a crop requiring year-round care. In return for these commodities the *pochteca* received feathers of various kinds, valuable stones, animal skins, cacao, gold and related luxury goods. Cacao was carried by the *pochteca* en route to the trading centers, serving to purchase supplies along the way.

The southern centers of trade do not seem to have had open markets, for transactions took place directly between *pochteca*, their local representatives, and the native rulers of the region. In the highlands, however, thriving traders' markets existed at Coixtlahuaca, Tochtepec, and Tepeaca, suggesting that the differences between long-distance and marketplace trade that were so marked at the time of the Spanish Conquest may not always have applied in every region.

Religious functions of the pochteca

Traders played a central role in the religious life of Tenochtitlan, especially during the annual Panquetzaliztli festival dedicated to the patron deity, Huitzilopochtli.[15] This was celebrated on the 15th *veintena* of the *tonalpohualli* cycle. The priesthood began preparing for this most significant festival 40 days in advance, and singing and dancing began on the second day of the *veintena*. Long before this, young traders seeking professional status had begun preparations with a visit to the Atzcapotzalco slave-market, to purchase four slaves destined to be sacrificed during the culminating ceremonies of the festival. Time and effort were also spent accumulating expensive gifts for the guests – especially for the other merchants and nobles who would be invited to attend a huge banquet. Soon thereafter the young prospective traders made a long ceremonial trip to Tochtepec, where they personally extended invitations to the Aztec merchant elders – the *pochtecatlatoque* – residing in that town. On the ninth day before the festival the four slaves were ritually bathed with sacred water from the springs at Huitzilopochco and ceremonially dressed. On the eve of the festival the slaves were given a drink of cacao, "to comfort them," and were led by the young initiate traders in a procession to the ward temple in Pochtlán, where ceremonies were conducted in honor of Yacatecuhtli, the traders' patron deity.

Meanwhile, the image of Paynal (or Painalton) had begun a ceremonial circuit of Tenochtitlan-Tlatelolco:

> Paynal was "the delegate," "the substitute," "the deputy;" because he represented Huitzilopochtli when there was a procession. He was named Paynal because he pressed and urged them ahead. And the people followed [the impersonator], jostling, howling, roaring. They made the dust rise, they made the ground to smoke. Like people possessed, they stamped upon the earth. And one man carried the image in his arms.[16]

In touring the city, and running across the causeway to the western shore, turning south all the way to Huitzilopochco and over the causeway to Ixtapalapan before continuing back to Tenochtitlan, Paynal was ritually "purifying" the area within the circuit boundaries, rendering it sacred and marking off the crucial, most essentially Mexica space in the empire. On completion of Paynal's circuit the procession arrived before the temple of Huitzilopochtli on the summit of the Great Pyramid. On the 20th and final day the four slaves were brought and led around the building four times, performing on a smaller scale the symbolism of the larger processional circuit. A vast crowd had now assembled in the plaza and the *tlatoani* himself arrived to witness the conclusion of the festival. First there came many sacrifices of prisoners captured by warriors on conquest campaigns, and finally, as dusk approached, Paynal personally sacrificed the four slaves and cast their bodies down the steps of the pyramid. The young traders, now officially initiated, stored their ceremonial attire in boxes which were to be kept until the end of their lives and would be cremated with them at death. Parts of the body of one of the slaves were taken home to be cooked and ritually eaten with maize and salt as part of a sacramental offering. A great banquet followed, with lavish distribution of gifts to the guests.

A similar ceremony was held by traders of the city of Cholollan during the festival of the patron deity of that city, Quetzalcoatl. Comparison of those events and those at Tenochtitlan, indicate that the traders' ritual had a very old history in Mesoamerica, and that at Tenochtitlan it was grafted onto the festivals of Huitzilopochtli; throughout the empire, traders were admitted to office during the special festival celebrating a particular city's patron deity. This was another instance of syncretism, in which the practices and beliefs of different ethnic groups were integrated into the larger ceremonial system. The *pochteca* were far from being a rising mercantile middle class in the Aztec empire. Rather, they formed an ancient guild-like organization of high-class commoners ranked below the nobility itself. Before the rise of a warrior aristocracy, they may well have been one and the same with the ruling class in the older societies of Mesoamerica.

Summing up the ethnohistoric descriptions of metropolitan markets and trade, and the archaeological evidence from excavations at provincial sites such as the crafts-manufacturing city of Otumba, and remains of trade items from trash middens in the small town of Cuexcomate in the Valley of Morelos, Michael Smith states that the marketplace system was an institution that linked together the various sectors and regions within a highly commercialized, dynamic economy. Yet it was not a capitalist system. There was no wage labor, land was not to be bought or sold (except under restricted circumstances), and investment by wealthy commoners or the nobility was limited to *pochteca* expeditions. Although the extensive network of marketplace trade afforded opportunities for commoners and merchants to improve themselves economically, they could not advance to higher social levels. The economy in general, and the markets specifically, were contained in a system of social classes with barriers no one could cross.[17]

9 · Priests, Scribes, and Warriors

The priests: servants of the gods

When the Spanish expedition first came to Tenochtitlan and Cortés and his party were shown the sacred precinct, they were shocked by the sinister appearance of the Aztec priests. Bernal Diaz del Castillo writes:

> They wore black cloaks like cassocks and long gowns reaching to their feet. Some had hoods like those worn by canons, and others had smaller hoods like those of Dominicans, and they wore their hair very long, right down to the waist, and some had it even reaching down to the ankles. Their hair was covered with blood, and so matted together that it could not be separated, and their ears were cut to pieces by way of penance. They stank like sulphur and they had another bad smell like carrion. They were the sons of chiefs and abstained from women. They fasted on certain days and what I saw them eat was the pith of seeds. The nails on their fingers were very long, and we heard it said that these priests were very pious and led good lives.[1]

What Bernal Diaz described were priests engaged in special duties, requiring long penances and behavior contrary to normal life, in the course of service to the deities. Behind these men there lay an organization that was heir to a tradition of great complexity and sophistication, for religion was a unifying and pervasive force in all manifestations of Aztec culture. The priesthood that supervised the religious establishment and all its activities also directed Aztec intellectual and artistic life in great part. They governed the schools, they managed the many deity cults, and coordinated and choreographed the public rites and performances.[2]

We have seen in previous chapters that the offices of *tlatoani* and *cihuacoatl* were respectively concerned with external and internal affairs of government, with the *tlatoani* in the dominant position. Both offices also held indispensable religious obligations. Strictly speaking, the *tlatoani* and the *cihuacoatl* were not priests, yet they performed as key ritualists on numerous occasions. The *tlatoani* was invested with a measure of divine power at his coronation, although he was not considered a god as were the pharaohs of Egypt. His titles included *yiollo altepetl*, "heart of the city," and *inan ita altepetl*, "the mother, the father, of the city," for his overarching religious responsibility was for the maintenance and renewal of human society as an integral aspect of the renewal of nature. His "external" ritual duties took him on the long annual pilgrimage to the remote shrine high on Mt Tlaloc, to perform the annual dry-season rites calling for rain and renewal (ill. 119). As chief warrior, he personified the

119 Priestly duties included night-time pilgrimages to mountain shrines where incense was burnt and drumming and singing reached the gods of rain and fertility. From the Codex Mendoza.

hero-ancestor Huitzilopochtli, whose cult was especially associated with sun worship. The *tlatoani* also made regular appearances in many other crucial festivals of the ceremonial cycle. He was required to perform penances and retreats, and directed matters of state after weighing the auguries in ritual almanacs and seen in the portents of nature.

The *cihuacoatl*, chief of internal affairs, was still an especially powerful office during the reign of Motecuhzoma I, when his brother Tlacaelel filled the post. The *cihuacoatl* governed the city, particularly when the *tlatoani* was away at war; he was the domestic counselor, and also a military strategist and aide. He also arranged triumphs when the *tlatoani* returned, and saw to the prisoners' sacrifice. The office of *cihuacoatl* is recorded in Tenochtitlan, Tetzcoco, Atzcapotzalco, and Culhuacan. Yet this office, filled by a man, held the title of the female deity Cihuacoatl, "woman serpent," essentially associated with the earth, agricultural fields and crops, and with the "war" of parturition, when women were likened to warriors. Cihuacoatl was the chief diety of Xochimilco and perhaps Chalco and Culhuacan. A man dressed as the deity Cihuacoatl (perhaps the *cihuacoatl* himself) appeared in major festivals of the Aztec calendar devoted to the earth and vegetation, as illustrated in the Codex Borbonicus. The religious obligations of the *cihuacoatl* were thus identified with priestly agricultural matters of the "female" wet season.

The term for priest was *tlamacazqui*. Although priests could come from any social class, even the poorest levels, the highest priests were drawn from the ranks of the *pipiltin* – the hereditary nobility. Immediately under the ruler were two supreme priests whose titles and dual functions reflect a pre-Aztec system of organization. The *Quetzalcoatl totec tlamacazqui* and *Quetzalcoatl tlaloc tlamacazqui* were respectively associated with the cults of Huitzilopochtli and Tlaloc. Quetzalcoatl was the ancient title inherited from the Toltecs and their predecessors. Totec was similarly an old cult name from a time before the Aztecs in the Valley of Mexico. The second priest's title included the name Tlaloc and was clearly connected to the prominent history of that deity in Mesoamerica. The dual high priesthood may well find its roots in an old moiety type of social division, in which the cult responsibilities alternated according to the dry and rainy seasons.

The next priestly rank was the *Mexicatl Teohuatzin*, described as a general commander and overseer of ritual, and the superintendent of the *calmecac* school. He was assisted by the *Huiznahua Teohuatzin* and *Tecpan Teohuatzin*, who governed the rest of the priestly orders. The latter were in charge of par-ticular temples and attending to the communal festivals and worship pertaining to the cults of their temple deity. They had important duties in administering the temple lands, *teopantlalli*. They oversaw the selection of deity-imperson-ators who wore the sacred masks and other regalia in public performances and processions, and they might also on occasion wear the regalia themselves. Certain priests were also warriors, and their duties included carrying effigies of deities in the vanguard of Aztec armies during campaigns. These warrior-priests also captured enemies, and made sacrifices in the field. Women fulfilled priestly duties, especially in connection with the numerous earth-mother cults

120 Restored temple at Santa Cecilia Acatitlan. Burnished white plaster trimmed with red and polychromed roof-panels distinguished local temples from the wattle-and-daub walls and thatched roofs of residential compounds in the densely populated wards of Aztec towns.

and maize goddesses, their responsibilities included the instruction of young girls and women in the service and impersonation of these deities.

All priestly officials were assisted by *calmecac* students and by postulants to the priesthood. In the *calmecac*, postulants lived under strict supervision. Meditation and the learning of prayers were accompanied by periods of fasting. Long vigils were kept and marked by periodic offerings and purifying baths; food was usually taken in meager amounts at midday and midnight. Special occasions demanded auto-sacrifice; blood would be drawn by pricking the legs and arms with maguey spines, by cutting the earlobes with obsidian blades, or by running a cord through the tongue or the penis.

As in the monastic orders of Europe, the Aztec priesthood had a place for every kind of talent and interest. Some priests were codex painters and scribes. Specialized knowledge included the reading and interpretation of almanacs in connection with calendrical calculations and the observation of the night sky and the sun's travels from north to south and back again during the course of the year. The progression of the sunrise each day along the eastern horizon was the index to naming the right day for festivals and to attuning the vast apparatus of religious life in Aztec cities to the regular movements of the heavenly bodies, and ultimately to the round of the seasons and their scheduled economic and military activities. Certain priests engaged in prophesies and the interpretation of visions: these could be induced by psychotropic plants – jimson weed, *Psilocybe* mushrooms, or peyote cactus buttons. Perhaps the most highly esteemed priests were the teachers called *tlamatini*, a term which may be translated as "wise man." Bernardino de Sahagún's informant speaks eloquently of these individuals:

> The wise man [is] exemplary. He possesses writings; he owns books. [He is] the tradition, the road; the leader of men, a mover, a companion, a bearer of responsibility, a guide.
> The good wise man [is] a physician, a person of trust, a counselor; an instructor worthy of confidence, deserving of credibility, deserving of faith; a teacher ... He lights the world for one; he knows of the land of the dead; he is dignified, unreviled.[3]

Aztecs scribes and Nahuatl hieroglyphic decipherment

In the palaces, law courts, temples, schools, and trading centers, professional scribes were employed to keep records of many kinds. These writings were principally made on *amatl* paper screenfold manuscripts, using hieroglyphics in combination with representational figures, date-signs, and numbers. The knowledge of scribes was also applied in designing commemorative monuments. The Stone of Motecuhzoma I, the Stone of Tizoc, and the Teocalli Stone (Pyramid of Sacred War) all feature proper names, titles, place-signs, and date-signs in the context of human figures and objects, and in reference to the three-dimensional shapes of the sculptural monuments (ills. 121, 122).

There is every reason to believe that the character and outward appearance of Nahuatl hieroglyphic writing had very old roots in Central Highland

Mexico. We have seen on the sculptural reliefs of the Plumed Serpent Platform at Xochicalco, that there are glyphs of title, places, and signs of speech that are readily readable in Nahuatl. Most writing systems are very conservative, and the Nahuatl system was certainly so, providing a powerful vehicle for cultural continuity between the Aztecs and their predecessors.

In earlier chapters we have referred to pictorial manuscripts such as the divinatory Codex Borbonicus, illustrating the *veintena* months and days of the calendar with corresponding deities of good or bad influence. There are tribute lists such as the pre-Hispanic *Matrícula de Tributos* and part of the Codex

121, 122 The Teocalli (sacred house) Stone – probably a royal throne – was modeled in the likeness of a pyramid temple. The façade is shown as a flight of stairs flanked by hieroglyphic dates and offering bowls. A sun-disk was sculpted above the "altar," representing the sun as a source of heat and life, and also the present era, or "sun" in the Aztec sequence of mythical world-creations. The disk is flanked on the left by a figure wearing the hummingbird headdress of the deified hero, Huitzilopochtli, his left foot in the form of a fire serpent; the *tlatoani* Motecuhzoma II stands to the right.

Mendoza. Historical records are also shown in the latter, with the list of Tenochtitlan rulers and conquests, and a third section illustrating daily life and various professions. Our historical narrative has also drawn on the Codex Xolotl, the Codex Aubin, and the Codex en Cruz; and the Mapa Quinatzin illustrates aspects of Tetzcocan social organization and tribute obligations, as well as the Legal Code of Netzahualcoyotl. A great wealth of additional documents could be cited, for the indigenous scribal tradition continued to flourish from the 1520s to the early 17th century. The colonial period saw an outpouring of documents from different communities throughout the Nahuatl-speaking highlands, before the tradition dwindled and finally disappeared as the cultural context in which it was meaningful disintegrated. A succinct history of the decipherment of Nahuatl hieroglyphs written by Marc Zender begins by describing the early pioneering work of Joseph Marius Alexis Aubin.[4] In the 1840s Aubin took up the study of the Mapa Tlohtzin, the Mapa Quinatzin, and the Codex Vergara, all from the Tetzcoco region. His interest was to understand the logic of how this system of writing functioned. In 1849 he published an index of over 100 hieroglyphic signs, in which he recognized alternating phonetic and logographic spellings of the same names, plus a series of hieroglyphic compounds. A logogram is a word-sign that carries both sound and meaning. Logograms pertain to the *vocabulary* of the language, as opposed to grammar and syntax. Phonetic signs convey sound only; phonetic signs appear as groups to (1) spell words, or (2) to complement logograms by making their meaning clear or reinforcing their reading. For example, Aubin illustrated the logogram of Itzcoatl, "Obsidian Serpent." The hieroglyph consists of obsidian arrowheads corresponding to the Nahuatl word *itz(li)*, obsidian, and a serpent, corresponding to *coa(tl)*. The hieroglyph is logographic. Aubin also illustrated the equally acceptable logographic and phonetic spelling of this proper name. Below, we find the logographic sign for *itz*, represented by an obsidian-bladed weapon; above this we see a pottery jar, *com(itl)*, represented for the value of the phonetic value of *co*; a sign for water, *a(tl)*, is included above the jar for the phonetic value of *a(tl)*, thus spelling out Itz•co•a(tl) (ill. 123). Aubin published a list that included four phonetic signs, *chi*, *ka* (1), *ka* (2), and *ko*, which continue to stand today, plus the sign *cha*, which now has been discounted.

123 Name–hieroglyphs *Itzcoatl* illustrated by Aubin. As a logographic sign (a) the name consists of obsidian arrowheads representing *itz(li)*, "obsidian" and a serpent, *coatl*. In combined hieroglyphic form (b), the logograph *itz(li)* is represented by an obsidian-bladed weapon, a jar *com(itl)* for the phonetic value of co, plus the sign *a(tl)*, water, for the phonetic value of *a(tl)*.

124 LEFT The place-hieroglyph Acolhuacan, composed of the water sign *a(tl)* for the phonetic value of *a*, added to the logographic sign for shoulder, *ahkol*, to reinforce the reading of Acolhuacan. RIGHT Hieroglyph for the month *Atemoztli*, "descending water," with the logographic sign for water, *a(tl)*, reinforced by the sign for stone *te(tl)*, for the phonetic value of *te*, as in the word *tema*, "descend." The down-leading footprints reinforce the phonetic element *te*, by indicating descent.

The historian Maurice Pope has called attention to three conditions necessary for successful decipherment of any hieroglyphic system. First, there must be sufficient knowledge of the language transmitted in the texts. Second, there must be a large body of writings. Third, there must exist bi-lingual or bi-script texts containing known proper names, place-names, and titles. These conditions all existed when Aubin began his work. However, as other scholars entered the field of Nahuatl hieroglyphic decipherment in the second half of the 19th century, attention focused on manuscripts from Tenochtitlan-Tlatelolco. Little evidence was found of phonetic components in this body of texts. As a result, in the 1880s Phillip Valentini argued forcefully that colonial-era hieroglyphs containing phonetic components in both Maya and Nahuatl systems were purely Spanish inventions. This opinion came to be widely held, and in the case of Nahuatl, the work of decipherment was thereby delayed for more than 100 years. To be sure, Edward Taylor and Daniel Brinton did express the observation that phonetic elements might well be of native Mexican origin instead of Spanish influence, and that a more fully developed study of the many sources was necessary. Yet Valentini's assessment continued to influence the field deeply.

Although Zelia Nuttall accepted Valentini's outlook, in 1888 she did recognize that certain phonetic signs could complement or help to clearly define the readings of logograms. For example, the sign for water *a(tl)*, used for the phonetic value of *a*, was added to the logographic sign for shoulder, *ahkol*, to reinforce the reading of the place-glyph Acolhuacan (ill. 124, left). Similarly, she noted that the hieroglyph for the month *Atemoztli* was composed of the logographic water sign *a(tl)*, reinforced by the sign for stone, *te(tl)*, with the phonetic value of *te*, as in the word *temo*, "descend," complemented by feet signs indicating descent (ill. 124, right). Although Nuttall acknowledged the existence of a Nahuatl system of writing, she regarded it as not fully developed in terms of having a phonetic aspect.

Thus, as scholars continued to characterize the Nahuatl hieroglyphs throughout the 20th century, it came to be widely held that the Tetzcocan texts with their notable phonetic elements originally recognized by Aubin, were the result of Spanish influences, whose Latinate script is entirely phonetic. Nahuatl writing was characterized as "pictographic," or "imperfect" and, scholarly work became largely focused on compilations and cataloguing activities. Still, in 1970 the Aztec scholar Henry Nicholson expressed reservations about this view of Tetzcocan sources as compromised by Spanish influences. Although he believed that Nahuatl writing was indeed basically logographic, he reflected that phoneticism was perhaps not so restricted in pre-Hispanic times, and that the Tetzcocan documents might after all reflect traditional Nahuatl writing. His observations remained unheeded, and until the present it has continued to be widely assumed that the Tenochtitlan-Tlatelolco documents are most representative of the pre-Hispanic writing system, and that documents showing greater phoneticism such as those of the Tetzcocan region are influenced by Spanish alphabetic writing.[5]

Then, in 2003, Alfonso Lacadena began to reconsider the Tetzcocan manuscripts. Lacadena had a background in Maya hieroglyphic writing and was also familiar with decipherment in other ancient writing systems. Since the early 1960s when a crucial breakthrough in Maya hieroglyphic decipherment was made by Tatiana Proskouriakoff, it became amply evident that this system of writing made extensive use of phonetic elements. It was entirely reasonable to believe that Nahuatl-speaking scribes would have knowledge of Maya writing over the centuries. Lacadena argued that the Spanish authorities were not the addressees of Nahuatl hieroglyphic writing, for very few read the glyphs and relied instead on Spanish commentaries on the documents. Therefore, there was no motive for Indian scribes to modify the hieroglyphic system. Their phonetic rendering of Spanish names and hieroglyphic translations of Catholic religious texts reflected methods entirely consistent with their own traditional system. Furthermore, Lacadena and his associates have shown that the Tenochtitlan-Tlatelolco sources and the Tetzcocan documents exhibit the

a   b   c

same orthography and structure. It therefore began to appear increasingly that the Tetzcocan school was a *variant scribal tradition* with more extensive use of phonetic elements stemming from pre-Hispanic times. The phonetic components must be native.

Expanding on Aubin's original findings of 1849, Lacadena has now established a method for deciphering logograms and phonetic symbols, pointing out the necessity of cross-checking specific hieroglyphic elements and the need to take stock of the whole body of Nahuatl texts.[6] For example, in the case of the Codex Mendoza, the syllable *me* is represented by the sign of an upright drum, *huehuetl* (ill. 125a). The corresponding compound hieroglyph consists of a drum with stone markings, identified by the Spanish gloss as *tehuehuec*, "place of the drum (*huehuetl*) of stone." The *te* component derives from the word *tetl*, "stone." The conclusion is that the drum sign is a logogram with the value of *mewe*, as in *te/huehue/c*, the *c* corresponding to the suffix *co*, "place." The same drum sign appears again in the Tetzcocan Codex Xolotl, the Mapa Tlohtzin, the Codex en Cruz, and the Codex Santa María Asunción. It appears directly or indirectly identified with Tlacahuepan, Huetzin, Nochuetl, Tlahuel, or Tohuexiuh (ills. 125b–f). However, in these cases the value of the drum sign as *mewe* does not work, because the names would have to appear as tlaca*huehue*pan, *Huehue*tzin, etc. As a logogram the drum sign cannot be split apart; it must maintain its integral reading value. Thus the drum sign may *also* have a phonetic value, as *me*. This phonetic function of *me* is confirmed by two other examples, from the *Matrícula de Tributos* and the Codex Mendoza. In these instances the drum sign is united with the sign of a tree, corresponding to the name of the town Ahuehuepan (ill. 125g). Lacadena considers it possible that the tree sign has the value *awewe*, as in *Ahuehuetl*, "cypress." In this case the drum sign with the value *me*, corresponds to a phonetic complement, reinforcing the reading of the logogram as *awewe-we*, Awewepan (Ahuehuepan).

125 LEFT TO RIGHT (a) The compound hieroglyph Tehuehuec, "Place of the Drum of Stone," in the Codex Mendoza; drum signs in the Tetzcocan manuscripts Codex en Cruz (b), Codex Xolotl (c), and Codex Santa María Asunción (d, e, f) directly or indirectly identified with (b) Tlacahuepan, (c) Huetzin, (d) Nochhuetl, (e) Tlahuel, or (f) Tohuexiuh; another example of a drum sign from the *Matrícula de Tributos* and the Codex Mendoza (g).

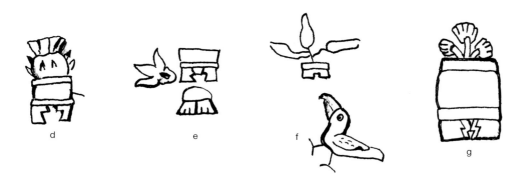

Apparently the scribe of the Codex Mendoza felt it necessary phonetically to complement or reinforce the logogram *aweme*, because the hieroglyphic image of the tree is generic and needed to be clearly identified as a cypress, *ahuehuetl*.

The long-delayed work of Nahuatl decipherment is now opened as a new area of inquiry; the hieroglyphs can no longer be considered a predominantly pictographic mode of communication, but a logophonetic or logosyllabic system as identified by Alfonso Lacadena.

The warriors

The structure of the Aztec military hierarchy has been outlined by the historian Ross Hassig.[7] A supreme council of four noblemen governed the army, fulfilling a function roughly analogous to that of a general staff. We have previously noted these high officials, the *tlacochcalcatl*, *tlaccatecatl*, *etzhuanhuanco*, and *tillancalqui*. There is evidence suggesting that the *tlaccatecatl* and *tlacochcalcatl* were titles in use long before the Aztecs and that, like the titles of the two chief priests, they reflect an older system of social organization. At Tenochtitlan the members of the council of four were all brothers or close relatives of the *tlatoani*. One would be heir apparent, usually the *tlaccatecatl*. The Codex Mendoza depicts these officials in regalia of state. The next levels of office were held by warriors either from the nobility or commoners, for although sons of the nobles tended to be more successful in the military by virtue of their education and general privileges, men from the lowest classes could attain all but the highest positions for their valor and battlefield leadership.

The two highest military societies or orders were the *otontin*, "otomies," and the *cuauhchique*, "shorn ones." Only the most daring battlefield veterans could be admitted, for it was required to have taken many captives and to have performed at least 20 deeds of exceptional bravery. The highest military commanders such as the *tlaccatecatl* and *tlacochcalcatl* were members of these two orders. All the warriors belonging to the eagle and jaguar societies were entitled to wear attire appropriate to their rank. Headgear, jewelry, cloaks, and other accessories and emblems were strictly prescribed, and were personally handed to the warriors during special ceremonies held for that purpose, sometimes by the *tlatoani* himself. The war suits given to commoners were of animal skins, while those of the nobility were woven with feathers. The Codex Mendoza depicts warriors capturing one, two, three, and four enemies, and the special attire awarded in each case (ill. 126). Even commoners achieving these feats were given special privileges, such as the right to wear cotton and sandals in the royal palaces, to drink *pulque* in public, to keep concubines, and to dine in the palace. Most of the common warriors wore body paint for identification and maguey cloth mantles, a breechcloth, and no sandals.

Military training for young boys began during schooling. Martial exercises were actually conducted on the premises of the eagle and jaguar warriors' meeting-houses, where youths assembled for instruction on the handling of arms, basic drill and maneuvers, and on discipline, military hierarchy, history, and battlefield lore. Although early Spanish colonial histories speak of military

126 Warriors were graded according to the number of captives they took, and each new rank entitled the warrior to wear a more elaborate costume; the highest ranking officers are at the bottom. From the Codex Mendoza.

houses in the royal palace, archaeological evidence indicates that the *cuauhcalli*, "Eagle House," was located in the main ceremonial center of Tenochtitlan. Platform bases with eagle sculptures on the moldings gave access to rooms surrounding two inner patios. Impressive life-size ceramic sculptures of eagle warriors were recovered from this setting, and a low bench running around the wall of one of the inner patios was found to be sculptured in low relief with processions of warriors converging on a sacrificial implement (ills. 127–131). The motif and style of this processional scene was quoted directly from Toltec art. Students gradually became adept in handling the obsidian-bladed clubs, stabbing javelins, and round shields with protective leather coverings. Throwing javelins using an *atlatl* also demanded practice: this ancient implement was grooved to hold a long dart; held as an extension of the arm, the *atlatl* gave additional power and accuracy to the throw. While training in the patios of the warriors' meetinghouses, the youths had ample opportunity to see the colorful and impressive regalia of their seniors, and to hear stories of their battle exploits. The novices' first experience of campaigning was to carry loads for the warriors, and there was much vying by the youths' families to find a warrior of the best possible qualifications for their boy to serve.

OPPOSITE: 127–130 TOP LEFT The stone head of an eagle warrior wearing a helmet. TOP RIGHT Aztec sculpture of a warrior carved in an archaic "Toltec" style. Compare with the figure of a warrior from the temple at Tula (ill. 26). CENTER LEFT Detail of the banquette frieze in the Eagle House patio at the Great Pyramid. Its style is distinctively Toltec and reflects the Aztecs' concern to match the military prowess of their predecessors. BOTTOM Patio of the Eagle House, showing the banquette which functioned as a seat of rank and authority.

131 ABOVE This life-sized ceramic sculpture of an eagle warrior was recovered in the excavation of the Eagle House at the Great Pyramid.

There was no standing army as exists in the modern world. Rather, warriors were called up for specific campaigns. The organization of the army was in units from local *calpulli*. In Tenochtitlan, each *calpulli* was required to contribute 400 men. Each unit marched under its own standards and was commanded by its own community leaders. There were probably several subdivisions of 100–200 men, much like platoons or squads. The large basic unit of the Aztec army consisted of 8,000 men, roughly like a battalion. Long-distance expeditions involved many units plus porters for supplies and equipment. The various divisions were identified by banners or standards strapped on the back of a bearer, who was usually positioned in the middle of a unit. As in modern armies, standards were objects of pride to the group, and were as strongly defended as they were aggressively sought by the enemy as trophies.

When the *tlatoani* and the supreme council decided to carry out a campaign, orders were given to collect supplies. Tribute-towns were obliged to send maize

War games

132, 133 LEFT and ABOVE A wooden drum (*panhuehuetl*) from Malinalco, carved with eagles and jaguars dancing and uttering the cry for war. The iconography of these anthropomorphic figures echoes that of the rock-cut temple at Malinalco and is related to Aztec military imagery.

cakes, maize meal, toasted maize, beans, chile, pumpkin seeds, and salt. Individual warriors also carried as much food as they could to supplement the basic rations. When all was prepared and the conch shells were sounded, the first units set out. Trails in ancient Mexico were maintained by local towns, but they were barely wide enough for two people to pass. First to depart were the scouts, followed by warrior-priests carrying sacred effigies, who marched a day ahead of the force. Then came the veteran warriors and members of prestigious military orders, including the *tlacochcalcatl* and *tlaccatecatl*, and the *tlatoani* himself if he was to direct the campaign in the field. The third great contingent of warriors from Tenochtitlan followed, with units spaced out at regular intervals. Then came contingents from Tlatelolco, Tetzcoco, Tlacopan, and other allied cities, also formed in long columns stretching for miles. Hassig has calculated that a basic unit of 8,000 men would stretch as far as 15 miles (24 km), or even 20 miles (32 km) along winding trails. The final units of warriors in the

134, 135 RIGHT This scene from the Codex Magliabechiano shows a two-man ballcourt. The popular ballgame – dating back to the beginnings of civilization in Mesoamerica – was played for sport and gambling, for resolving disputes, and as a form of divination. The skull markers indicate the game could be played "to the death." BELOW RIGHT The hips and shoulders were used to hit a solid rubber ball.

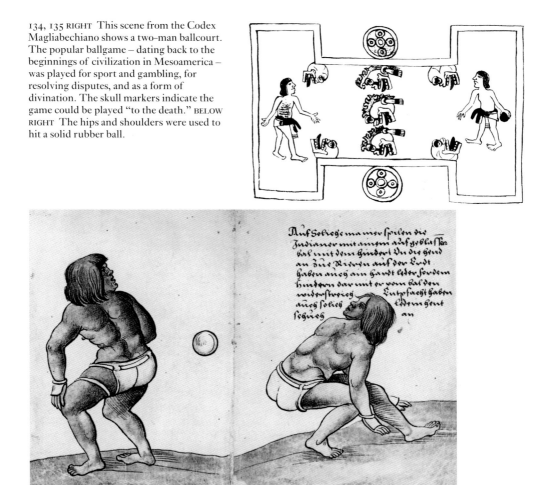

march came from subject towns as a form of tribute-payment. Camp was set up with reed mats for shelter, or tents for the high nobility, while the ordinary warriors slept in the open wrapped in their mantles.

Battlefield practices have been outlined in discussing Aztec imperial expansion, but no discussion of Aztec warriors can fail to mention the military ritual known as *xochiyaotl*, "flower war" (referring to the battlefield where finely attired warriors would fall like a rain of flowers). Flower wars were staged by previous mutual agreement between opposing communities for the sole purpose of capturing prisoners for sacrifice. These formal ritualistic encounters may be another custom transmitted from antiquity, but precedent has yet to be firmly traced. An early reference says that the conflict between the Tepanec-Mexica and the Chalca began as a *xochiyaotl* in 1376. By the 15th century flower wars were regularly held between the members of the Triple Alliance and Huexotzingo, Atlixco, and other towns in the Valley of Puebla. A generation ago, scholars assumed that they were a unique Mesoamerican phenomenon, but parallels have now been drawn with head-hunting tribal societies elsewhere in the world. Warfare among these peoples was not primarily waged for booty or land. Even among the Aztecs, who conducted regular campaigns to acquire tribute, ritual sacrifice invested their enterprise with a strongly religious character.

Among the Toltecs and the late Maya, ballgames involving human sacrifice were played as a form of jousting and a substitute for armed conflict (ills. 134, 135). The popularity of such games persisted under the Aztecs. Divination may also have been strongly featured in the outcome of such games, as it was in Classic Maya centers where ballgames were held during rites of passage. Waged with limiting game-like rules between equals or antagonists with equal rights, warfare in many early societies was conducted according to a way of thought that was deeply concerned with fate, chance, judgment, and contest as different expressions of the sacred. Flower wars may be seen as a type of mock-war with a still unknown past in Mesoamerica, that continued to be practiced intermittently within the larger pattern of Aztec warfare.

PART SIX
The Conquest
of Mexico

10 · The Arrival of the Strangers

The expedition of Hernán Cortés

There was no rival empire to threaten the dynamic expansion of Tenochtitlan, Tetzcoco, and Tlacopan. During the reigns of Ahuitzotl and Motecuhzoma II, old conquest domains were consolidated and new tributary territories taken. The advance seemed inexorable, the way was open. Only Tlaxcala in the east and the Tarascan realms to the west were successfully resisting the Aztec onslaught. Perhaps the Yucatan Peninsula would have been the next target, as it was in the time of the Toltecs. If the idea of such a project was ever conjectured by the allied city-states, it was destined never to take place. Far away, in a land unimagined beyond the sea, another idea long in discussion was being tested by a merchant-sailor from Genoa with support from the court of Spain. If the world was not flat, nor a disk, but a globe as leading cosmographers believed, it would be possible to establish a trade-route by sailing across the Western Ocean to the lands of the Khan by the China Sea. Columbus' landfall in 1492 on Samana Cay in the Bahamas led to three more voyages during which he found islands and coastlines he continued to perceive as outlying lands of Asia. It was only on the third voyage, when Columbus saw the immense volume of water flowing from the mouth of the Orinoco River in Venezuela, that he speculated that what had been found was "a very great continent, which until today has been unknown." Yet when he died in 1503 Columbus still had no clear conception of what he had achieved.

By the early 1500s permanent Spanish colonies were established on the islands of Hispaniola (Haiti and the Dominican Republic) and Cuba, and other explorers were beginning to chart the eastern contour of the hemisphere. Amerigo Vespucci, Vasco Nuñez de Balboa, and others traveled along the Venezuelan, Colombian, and Caribbean coastlines.

In 1517 Hernández de Córdoba was the first to sail west from Cuba, reaching the Yucatan Peninsula. At Catoche, Campeche, and Chanpotón, the Spanish expedition found impressive towns with many buildings of stone, a material not used by the West Indian natives or on the coasts to the south. They also met fierce resistance from Maya formations, and at Chanpotón, where the Spaniards landed for water, a desperate battle developed in which the intruders lost some 50 men. The Spanish contingent was barely able to regain its ships with a mortally wounded commander. Undaunted by this disaster, and fired by the accounts of masonry towns, the prospect of gold, and new lands to conquer, Diego Velásquez, the Governor of Cuba, authorized a new expedition. This force was commanded by Juan de Grijalva, who weighed anchor in early 1518. Following de Córdoba's route, the ships sailed farther west along the forested coast of Tabasco to a major river which they named Grijalva. The Spaniards established good relations with the Indians, bartering glass beads and other prized items for gold objects and provisions. At this place they first heard the Nahuatl words *Culhua* and *Mexica*, but they did not yet know who these people might be. At another river to the north on the coast, Grijalva's soldiers and sailors were beckoned ashore by a group of men waving banners. Upon investigation the Spaniards found a delegation of finely dressed chieftains wearing cotton capes, brilliant feathers, and gold jewelry, who courteously received the strangers with an excellent feast of fowl, fruit, and tortillas. Again the Spaniards exchanged glass beads for gold and supplies but, lacking an interpreter, Grijalva was never able to ascertain who his hosts were, or why he had been welcomed. A year later Hernán Cortés was to learn that these men had been representatives of Motecuhzoma II, who had heard stories of strange sailing ships since de Córdoba's expedition. Despite difficulties of communication it was clear to Grijalva that prizes much richer than those of the West Indies lay beyond the mountains towards the interior. The expedition returned to Cuba with this remarkable news and the gold obtained in barter. The promise of wealth was clearly perceived, and Diego Velásquez issued a call for another venture. In early 1519 he named Hernán Cortés the commander. Still unknown to Motecuhzoma, another empire was beginning the quest for a kingdom to conquer.

Rumors of outlandish people seen on the Gulf Coast began to be heard in Tenochtitlan and elsewhere in the Valley of Mexico sometime in 1517. Vague at first, there were stories of vessels larger than houses, of men with fair complexions and some very dark, and others riding deer with shining metal arms and garments. There had been a battle on the Yucatan coast. Then a credible eyewitness report from reliable officials was brought to Motecuhzoma's attention, together with glass bead necklaces as physical evidence: the gifts from Juan de Grijalva. Motecuhzoma ordered that this intelligence should remain confidential and that the coastline should be carefully watched:

> Motecuhzoma thereupon commanded [Pinotl] of Cuetlaxtlan and the others, and said unto them: "Ye shall order that a guard be kept everywhere on the shores [at the places] thus named: Nauhtlan, Toztlan, and Mictlanquauhtla – wheresoever the strangers would come to land." Then the stewards departed. They gave the command that watch be kept.[1]

The year 13-rabbit made its round and was about to meet the year 1-reed, 1519 in the Christian calendar. Suddenly the strangers were seen again.

The 500 soldiers and 100 sailors who set sail with Cortés were men of many kinds: sons with no inheritance, bored or failed planters, ex-gold miners, and men who liked soldiering, including numerous veterans of earlier voyages to South America and the Caribbean. Many had also sailed on the expeditions of de Córdoba and Grijalva to the Gulf of Mexico. Several soldiers of African descent were included in the expedition, as testified in the accounts of Indian witnesses. Everyone sought a new start, adventure, and the chance to win wealth fighting for Cortés. These individualistic, turbulent, and adventurous men had come to make their fortunes on the remote Caribbean frontier, yet they felt themselves bound both emotionally and legally to the Spanish Crown. They were also intensely religious, with an outlook still strongly influenced by the crusading spirit of the Middle Ages.

It was only in 1492, the year of Columbus' voyage, that the Moorish Caliphate of Granada had surrendered to the besieging army of the Catholic kings, Ferdinand and Isabella. During the centuries-long battle to reclaim Spain from Islamic domination, Christianity had taken a militant guise, and war automatically assumed the nature of a *jihad*. Following the recapture of Granada, the Spanish royal court discussed the prospect of extending the conquest across the Straits of Gibraltar; but as reports filtered through from the discovery voyages, it began to seem as if there might be unclaimed realms far greater than Europe, or even Roman antiquity, across the western ocean.

The example of ancient Rome was a theme that deeply affected educated men such as Cortés, for interest in the ideas and values of the Classical world had been diffusing from Renaissance Italy. Cortés grew up in Medellín in Extremadura, near the ancient city of Mérida where notable ruins were reminders of the greatness of the Roman era. Impressions of these early sights were reinforced by his studies at the University of Salamanca, where Cortés would have read translations of the Roman classics during his two years preparing for a career in law. In later life he could still debate in Latin, and his letters and public speeches show that he held the achievements of the Romans as an ever-present model. There is some evidence suggesting that Cortés first attempted to reach Italy to seek his fortune. Instead, at the age of 19, he embarked for the Caribbean colonies. He became a moderately successful planter on the island of Hispaniola, and eventually came to the attention of the governor Velásquez for his able assistance in the conquest and settling of Cuba. In 1519, now in his mid-30s, he was appointed commander of the new expedition and set sail for the mainland to the west, following the course of Grijalva.

Avoiding confrontations with the Maya towns in Yucatan, Cortés' ships proceeded to the Tabasco coast and anchored at Potonchán. A battle ensued in which Spanish horsemen, firearms, and tactics quickly won the day. Afterwards, in sign of submission, the defeated chieftains offered food, clothing, and gold ornaments, as well as a group of young women. Among these women was one named Malintzin, called "Marina" or "Malinche" by the Spaniards. She was destined to play a pivotal role in the events to come, for she knew the Nahuatl language of Central Mexico as well as the Chontal Maya tongue spoken on the coast. Working with Gerónimo de Aguilar, who had learned the Maya language when shipwrecked years before in Yucatan, Malintzin became Cortés' invaluable translator and confidante. Accompanying Cortés throughout the entire campaign to come, she also became his consort and was to bear him a son, Don Martín.

At Potonchán on the Tabasco coast the Spaniards again heard the words *Culhua* and *Mexica*, referring to a powerful people beyond the mountains to the north; but it was not until a few weeks later that the Spaniards fully grasped who these people were. The ships weighed anchor and headed northward up the coast. A range of forested mountains appeared beyond the palm-fringed beaches, and the snow-white cone of a great volcano rose inland in the distance. The expedition reached a protected channel by the island of San Juan de Ulúa where, on the dunes of the mainland shore, camp was laid out for Cortés' contingent. It was here and in the nearby town of Cempoala that Cortés first made direct contact with subjects of the Aztec empire, and came across a pair of haughty tax-gatherers from Tenochtitlan.

Motecuhzoma's embassy

When messengers arrived in Tenochtitlan with reports of new ships and an armed camp laid out in the dunes near Cempoala, it began to seem as if the earlier voyages had prepared the way for this much larger force. The strangers showed themselves to be troublesome, brashly mishandling the tax-gatherers and fomenting discord among the tribute-paying towns of the coast. Who were these people? Where had they come from? What was their objective? These questions, first posed after the earlier sightings, suddenly assumed much greater importance on Motecuhzoma's agenda. As fresh news arrived reporting Cortés' desire to meet Motecuhzoma in Tenochtitlan, the *tlatoani* called his council to decide a course of action.

From the beginning, Cortés and Motecuhzoma hid their mutually hostile intentions behind diplomatic overtones. Cortés' strong religious convictions and his moral commitment to convert the Indians to Christianity were tied to his worldly ambition to acquire riches and honor. Motecuhzoma too had important religious responsibilities and was no less an accomplished warrior with a successful record of conquests. Moreover, since his coronation in 1503 he had succeeded in creating a powerful, despotic central administration. Yet in the historical accounts, Motecuhzoma appears to have exhibited a curious, wavering uncertainty in dealing with Cortés. Much less powerful chieftains among the Maya and at Potonchán had readily displayed an aggressive fighting spirit. So how was it that the most feared ruler in Mesoamerica failed to take immediate and decisive action to repel the strangers? What occurrences led him to allow the Spaniards into Tenochtitlan, precipitating the disastrous events that led to his capture, death, and within a period of only two years, the ruin and fall of the empire?

These questions have been discussed in innumerable accounts from early colonial times to the present.[2] Since the 16th century, scholars have emphasized Motecuhzoma's perception of Cortés as the incarnation of the legendary Toltec ruler, Quetzalcoatl, who was said to have prophesied in ancient times that he would return to regain his lost throne in a year 1-reed (1519). According to this interpretation of the Quetzalcoatl legend, Motecuhzoma was unnerved by the prospect of the return of Quetzalcoatl to reclaim his title. However, as ethnohistorian Nigel Davies points out, native versions of the myth do not mention any *prophesy* about the return of Quetzalcoatl in the year 1-reed, or in any other year.[3] Davis concludes that after the Spanish Conquest, the original legend was transformed with the story of a prophetic return. More recently, anthropologist Susan Gillespie has argued convincingly that the whole story of

Cortés as Quetzalcoatl was created after the Conquest by Indian historians in an attempt to make sense of the Spaniards' arrival and victory, interpreting it as the outcome of a pattern of events set in motion in the remote Toltec past.[4] Given that the Aztecs viewed history in terms of cyclical events, it is plausible that their historians would have sought to explain the Aztec defeat in terms of inevitable, pre-ordained destiny.

It can no longer be said with any assurance that Motecuhzoma "trembled on his throne in the mountains" at the thought of meeting Cortés as a supernatural being. Nevertheless there can be no doubt that the Spanish landing sounded a dire warning in the Aztec capital. A council convened to consider the strangers and the time and place of their arrival from various points of view. The visitors were certainly unlike any other people known within or without the empire. Uncouth in physical appearance and also unbathed, they also showed open disregard for established norms of behavior. Consultation of the pictorial manuscripts and calendrical records by Aztec historians and divination specialists revealed that there were several important historical and cosmological associations surrounding the strangers' arrival. The Spaniards' presence evoked a curious parallel with the Aztecs' own history. The Aztecs had originally traveled from an unknown place far to the north on their long migration to the Valley of Mexico. As strangers they had fought and eventually risen to create a powerful empire. Similarly, the strangers had arrived from a distant location, a place veiled in mystery; they were intruders in ordered lands; and they might well have warlike designs on the center of power. The arrival of the visitors also carried geographical associations. They came from the primordial waters, traveling from the east, traditionally held as the direction of authority among Mesoamerican peoples. Finally, the date of the Spanish landing in the year 1-reed was significant, associated not only with the year of Quetzalcoatl's banishment from Tula, but also with the plumed serpent's influence as a cosmological sign.

Thus, several historical and cosmological themes were associated with Cortés and his armed force camping near Cempoala. From a European point of view these themes might hardly seem significant. But the Indian imagination placed special importance on the coincidence of events in time and space, and mythological happenings and legendary history were always compared with recent events to legitimize, justify, or otherwise explain them. From the Aztec point of view, occurrences were not unique or sequential, but were seen as episodes in an essentially cyclical concept of time and history, as has been pointed out by art historian Emily Umberger.[5] At the very least, the circumstances surrounding Cortés' arrival would have been seen in terms of an ominous pattern.

Motecuhzoma's council recommended that it would be diplomatic to honor the visitors as royal emissaries and to acknowledge their obvious importance. The *tlatoani* decided to send an embassy with gifts appropriate to the status of the strangers, which would simultaneously affirm his own supremacy. Descriptions of Motecuhzoma's gifts by Cortés, Bernal Diaz, and Bernardino de Sahagún differ as to the exact contents and place of the presentation. Nevertheless it is clear that two objects were especially important. The first

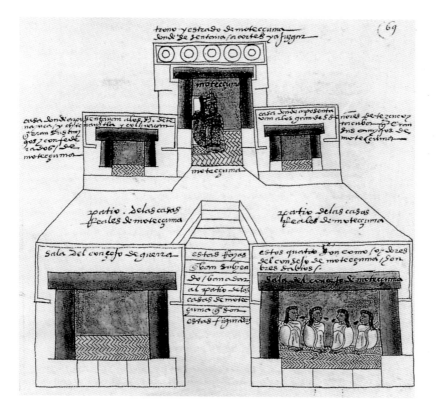

136 Motecuhzoma's palace in Tenochtitlan. Painted by an Aztec artist soon after the city's conquest, this page from the Codex Mendoza depicts the ruler seated within his throne-room (top), while a council of judges convenes in the chamber below.

was a golden disc "as large as a cartwheel," valued by the Spaniards at 20,000 ducats. The disk was fashioned to represent the sun and was covered with other figures and symbols. The second object was a silver disk larger in size, said to represent the moon. While the Spaniards admired these objects for their craftsmanship and intrinsic value, they had no way of understanding their significance. We shall never know exactly what the disks looked like, as they were eventually melted for the value of the metal. Similar works of art and associated mythological texts indicate that images of the sun and moon, as sources of light and markers of time, also carried symbolic associations with rulership, the creation of the world, the place of the Aztecs in cosmic history, and the divine authority of the emperor of Tenochtitlan. The Stone of Tizoc, the Calendar Stone, and the Pyramid of Sacred War are monuments suggesting the possible imagery of the large gold and silver disks sent by Motecuhzoma to communicate his authority.

A second group of objects presented to Cortés is mentioned only in Sahagún's account. The gift consisted of four elaborate ritual costumes of the

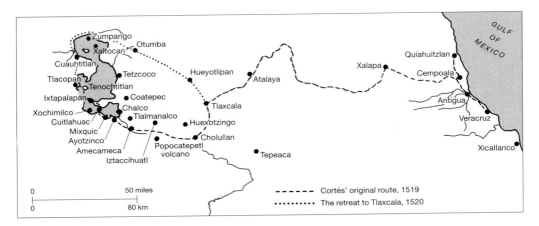

137 Cortés' route from Veracruz on the coastal plain to the Valley of Mexico, and the retreat to Tlaxcala after the Spaniards and their Indian allies were defeated in the battle of the Noche Triste.

kind worn by performers who impersonated the deities in the festivals of Tenochtitlan. It was an old and widespread Mesoamerican custom for lords and chieftains to wear, or to sponsor others to wear, the attire of deities on festival occasions. Finally, Motecuhzoma sent a present of food, consisting of tortillas, maize, eggs, turkeys, and many kinds of fruit including zapotes, hog plums, guavas, nopal cactus fruit, and various kinds of pitayas, as well as avocados and possibly sweet potatoes and manioc. According to Sahagún's account, part of this feast was set aside as a ritual offering; and as was the custom in the temples of Tenochtitlan, this food was sprinkled and spattered with the blood of a sacrificed human being. The Spaniards shook their heads at this appalling display, and turned to the rest of the feast presented by Motecuhzoma's emissaries.

Soon after this meeting with Motecuhzoma's ambassadors, Cortés received instructions from governor Velásquez to return to Cuba. But, now knowing of the kingdom beyond the mountains, Cortés decided to disregard the governor. A garrison town was founded at Veracruz, and bypassing Velásquez, Cortés sent a ship bearing the exotic gifts from Motecuhzoma directly to Charles V of Spain. Then he burned all the remaining ships to forestall thoughts of return among his men and the Velásquez supporters. With an inspiring speech to his tiny army, Cortés and his men set out on 16 August 1519 for Tenochtitlan.

Tenochtitlan

The despatches of Cortés and the straightforward prose of Bernal Diaz del Castillo describe the crossing of the mountain ranges and the first stretches of the plateau (ill. 137). As the Spanish expedition approached the borders of Tlaxcala, the nation that had fiercely resisted the armies of Motecuhzoma for many years, a host of warriors determined to stop the invaders:

And when they came to reach [the region of] Tecoac on land of the people of Tlaxcala, there dwelt their [subject] Otomi. And the Otomi met them in battle; with shields they moved against them. And the Otomi, the men of Tecocac, [the Spaniards] completely overwhelmed. Verily, they destroyed them. They speared them; they were pierced with spears. They turned their guns against them; they shot them with iron bolts; they shot them with crossbows. Not just few but great numbers of them they destroyed.

And when [the region of] Tecoac had perished, those of Tlaxcala – when they heard and knew of it, when they had been told – could not control their alarm; they swooned with fear. Great was the dread which overcame them. Terror seized them. Then they gathered themselves together and took counsel. There was a lord's council; there was a ruler's council. They considered the news.[6]

In Tlaxcala the military competence of the Spaniards was decisively demonstrated. The defeat of the Otomi-Tlaxcalan force was one of the turning points in the Conquest, for it made a profound impression in Tenochtitlan when spies reported the action. A plan for containing the enemy force began to take shape in the Aztec councils. The critical element in their calculations was the Spaniards' proficiency in battle drill as well as their arms and armor. Their disciplined maneuvers and weaponry had never been seen before in Mexico, and their deadly effect on Indian formations cannot be overemphasized. The basic units of the Spanish forces were infantry and cavalry to which were added separate units of arquebusiers (musketeers) and crossbowmen, as well as crews that manned the small Lombard cannons. The principal use of firearms was to break down the enemy charges before the warriors could effectively launch their darts, slingstones, and arrows. Cavalry was used to break the enemy lines by charging and following up with swords, after which the infantry moved in, wielding swords and long pikes tipped with steel blades. These weapons were more effective than the obsidian-bladed clubs carried by the Indians, for not only was more time required to lift and swing a club than to thrust and jab with a sword, but more space was also needed, requiring the Indians to advance in loose formations. By contrast the Spanish pikemen advanced shoulder to shoulder in deep file formations, with the projecting line of pikes offering an almost impregnable barrier. By raising the pikes vertically, about-facing and lowering them again, a new threat to the rear could be repelled. Marching in tight columns, the Spanish infantry could quickly form pointed wedges to move into enemy crowds, or form squares for defense, or open out and wheel around in serried ranks to envelop or push their opponents into vulnerable positions. The troops were also protected by metal helmets and armor, although some preferred layers of leather, and many adopted the quilted cotton jackets worn by Indian warriors.

The Spaniards were always vastly outnumbered by their opponents, but their battlefield superiority was proven as the fiercely spirited but more lightly armed Indian squadrons in open formations sought in vain to swamp the Spaniards after volleys of projectiles. Only when hampered by very broken terrain or confined by buildings in urban zones might the Spaniards be disadvantaged. The Spanish concept of battle, in which every man protected his neighbor and aimed to kill the enemy, was also highly effective against the Indians who placed higher value on individual duels and heroism rather than close teamwork. It was an Indian warrior's priority to capture an enemy alive when possible, either to sacrifice the prisoner on the battlefield, or to bring him home for sacrifice on the pyramid temples. A captor was awarded the highest battlefield honors, like the Plains Indians of North America, who sought to "count coup" by touching the enemy in the heat of the battle.

The Spanish success in approaching Tlaxcala gained powerful new allies for Cortés, who persuaded the Tlaxcalans to join his expedition on the march to Tenochtitlan. The support of thousands of tough and resilient warriors, and a logistical base in Tlaxcala, would prove indispensable in the campaign to come. Cortés marched with his new allies to the city of Cholollan (modern Cholula). The Cholollans were allied to the Aztecs, who now decided to use them in a bold stratagem to trap and destroy the Spaniards. The lesson of Tlaxcala was not lost on Motecuhzoma and his counselors, who planned this next course of action. Having noted the superiority of the Spanish in the open field, they were unwilling to risk an army in a major confrontation. Instead, the Cholollans were pressured to invite the Spaniards into the city as honored guests, where they might be contained and killed from the rooftops and in narrow streets where maneuver was impossible. Invitations were sent out and the Spaniards entered, while ditch traps with stakes were secretly dug and rocks were piled on the flat roofs of houses in the center of the city. Meanwhile, a considerable force of Aztec warriors took up hidden positions in nearby ravines, waiting to join the assault when the attack was underway. But, the plot was disclosed by an informer and the Spanish immediately took secret measures for reprisal. Early one morning the Spaniards trapped the Cholollan chiefs and warriors who were assembling for a ceremonial event in the central plaza. At Cortés' order his troops closed in and put many to death without quarter. Motecuhzoma heard the discouraging news with consternation, and suffered a crisis of confidence that found expression in the fateful decision to welcome the Spaniards into Tenochtitlan. Nevertheless, this decision may also be seen in terms of pragmatic military expediency: unwilling to risk his army in the open field against the menacing strangers, the next best thing would be to try a variant of the stratagem that had almost worked at Cholollan. To allow the force of some 500 men plus 2,000–3,000 Tlaxcalans into Tenochtitlan, an island city of about 250,000 inhabitants, would be the best way of ensuring control until another action could be effectively taken.

Within a few days of their victory at Cholollan, Cortés and the allies were camped on the cold pass between Popocatepetl and Iztaccíhuatl (ill. 138). From the height they looked down on the spacious Valley of Mexico with Tenochtitlan on the glittering lake in the distance. At the pass they were met by a delegation of nobles, bearing presents from Motecuhzoma in the form of gold necklaces, gold streamers, and long quetzal feathers; one purported to be Motecuhzoma himself, only to be identified as an impostor by the Tlaxcalans and others, and contemptuously dismissed. The expedition marched down from the mountain pass to a fork in the road where the Mexica had planted maguey agaves to hide the correct route, in the hope that the Spaniards and their allies would take the route to Tetzcoco. Kicking these obstacles aside, the column moved along to sleep that night in Amecameca. Next day the route led across the plain and through towns on the shore of Lake Chalco. Cortés and his men were visibly impressed by the ordered landscape with its grid-plan towns and temple pyramids, and the regular pattern of raised *chinampa* fields bordered by lines of willows. The expedition camped that night at Cuitlahuac. Next morning, crowds of people drew close to the road in increasing numbers, reminding the Spaniards that they were only a few miles from the capital. It was only a short march to Ixtapalapan at the head of the southern causeway, where camp was again made and plans were prepared for the formal entry to Tenochtitlan. All were up before dawn. The sun rose over the dark blue ridge of Mt Tlaloc, sending a flood of light across the water of Lake Tetzcoco and throwing the long straight causeway into bold relief. Thousands of onlookers were swarming in fleets of dugout canoes. The sight of the strangers' march along the causeway was remembered by Sahagún's Indian informants as if it were yesterday:

> And the four horse[men] who came guiding, preceding, and moving ahead of the others and occupying the vanguard, were the leaders. They kept turning; they moved back and forth repeatedly; they went on, facing people. They looked hither and thither; they went on to scan every aside and to look everywhere, peering among groups of houses.... Likewise the dogs – their dogs –

138 The Spanish expedition crosses the pass between Iztaccíhuatl and Popocatepetl, on the way into the Valley of Mexico. An Aztec delegation from Motecuhzoma awaits on the road below. From an illustration in Bernardino de Sahagún's *True History of the Things of New Spain* (Florentine Codex, Vol. III).

ran ahead, quickly smelling and sniffing at things and ever panting. By himself came as a guide, going as a leader....one who bore the standard upon his shoulders. He proceeded, waving it back and forth, making it circle, and tossing it from side to side....Following him passed the bearers of iron swords. Bared were their iron swords, which flashed brightly. They each bore and carried upon their shoulders their shields – wooden and leather shields. The second group, the second file to come, was of horses carrying upon their backs many [soldiers] in their cotton armor cuirasses, each with a leather shield and iron lance; and all with their iron swords hanging down the flanks of the horses. All had rattles; they had clatterers; they galloped along jingling, and the rattles clacked and resounded. The horses – the deer – neighed and whinnied.... And as they advanced great was the clangor and pounding of their hooves.... The third group was of those who bore the crossbows. They came wielding and repeatedly testing them, sighting along them.... And their quivers went hung at their sides or passed under their arms; [these] went filled, crammed, with arrows – with iron bolts...The fourth group was likewise of horse[men], similar in array to what hath been told. The fifth group were those bearing arquebuses on their shoulders.... And when they had come unto the great palace, the residence of the rulers, they fired them – they repeatedly shot the arquebuses.... And at the very last came, directing from the rear, the greatest warrior, who was like the commanding general, experienced as war ruler and commander of warriors. Surrounding him... went his brave warriors, his standard bearers, those who served him – those who were like his shaven ones, his [Otomi warriors], his brave and intrepid ones; the mainstay and support of city – its soul and foundation.

Then all the dwellers in cities beyond the mountains – those of Tlaxcala, of Tiliuhquitepetl, of Uexotzinco – sped along at the rear. They came girt for war, with their cotton armor, their shields, their bows; their quivers crammed with feathered arrows.... They came crouching, and as they went, loosed cries and shrieks while striking their mouths with their hands; they screeched and whistled, and shook their heads. And some bore burdens on their backs; they carried rations on their backs.... some dragged the great Lombard guns, which rested on wooden wheels. And they moved along shouting.[7]

Some 4 miles (6 km) ahead on the causeway, gleaming pyramids rose from the thin haze of cooking fires on the island city. At the entrance to Tenochtitlan, Motecuhzoma came out to meet Cortés borne by four nobles on a palanquin. His iridescent green plumes, turquoise diadem, and golden jewelry signaled his royal status. Descending, Motecuhzoma approached the Spaniard supported on the arms of two chiefs, the ceremonial manner of walking to express highest respect. Motecuhzoma reached out and bestowed on Cortés a necklace of golden crabs. He received in return a prized necklace of Venetian glass beads, strung on a golden filament and scented with musk. With an elegant speech he welcomed Cortés into the city (ill. 139).

After Cortés' return address, the army was quartered in the old palace of Axayacatl, to the east of the ritual enclosure. In the days that followed the

Tenochtitlan.

139 Motecuhzoma II and Cortés hold discussions in the palace, with Malintzin interpreting. The bound deer, quail and maize at their feet represent supplies given to Cortés and his Indian allies by their Aztec hosts; from the Lienzo de Tlaxcala.

Spaniards were shown the sights of the capital. Bernal Diaz, who accompanied Cortés on one of these memorable outings, described the visit to the Tlatelolco pyramid and market. Cortés and his party were led up the pyramid stairs to be received by Motecuhzoma on the upper platform. Taking Cortés by the hand, the emperor walked to the edge and invited him to view the city. The Great Pyramid of Tenochtitlan could be seen across the residential zones 2 miles (3 km) to the south. Rising in tiers with twin temples on its summit, its white lime-plastered surfaces and brightly painted temples stood against the background of the lake and the mountains in the distance. Elsewhere the urban skyline was lined by other pyramids rising above lesser ritual centers in the four wards of the city. The greatest marketplace in Mexico lay below and to the south of the Tlatelolco pyramid. From their vantage point Cortés and Motecuhzoma could hear the hubbub of voices and see the colorful crowds. Thousands of people were attracted on that day in larger numbers than usual because of the strangers' presence. From their vantage point, the Spaniards saw a splendid city larger than any in Spain, that would seem to be invulnerable. Yet on the long march to the capital they had already begun to understand some of its inner tensions and instabilities – in Tlaxcala, in the streets of Cholollan, and even now while standing next to Motecuhzoma. In his person all power and decisions were concentrated, and it would be in the Spaniards' dealings with him that the future would be decided.

11 · The Fall of the Aztec Empire

The death of Motecuhzoma

The epic events following the Spanish entry into Tenochtitlan are vividly recounted in the narratives of Cortés, Bernal Diaz, and the Conquistador Anónimo, and by Sahagún's Indian informants. In the latter account, certain episodes are especially significant for what they tell about Aztec perspectives on the final catastrophe.

The Spaniards and Tlaxcalans had been in Tenochtitlan about two weeks when Cortés and his captains began to think of how to advance their purpose. They were guests of the Mexica state, but they were well aware that the Cholollan trap might be tried again. They knew themselves to be hostages in the center of a vast city from which there would be no easy escape across the causeways and bridges. However, they might ensure their safety and proceed with the plan of conquest if they could capture Motecuhzoma. Under the pretext that an Indian attack on the garrison at Veracruz had been secretly ordered by the *tlatoani*, Cortés and his most steadfast captains asked for an imperial audience. Once admitted to the royal apartments they swiftly seized Motecuhzoma. From the Aztec point of view this move was unimaginable, for the authority of Motecuhzoma was paramount and he was to some extent a sacred person. Such a danger within the palace was therefore overlooked. Taken by surprise, Motecuhzoma had no choice but to submit or possibly lose his life. This calculating and ruthless monarch, counted among the most successful in Aztec history, had failed to assess the unswerving purpose of Cortés. In the shock of surprise, he allowed himself to be conducted across the plaza to Axayacatl's palace where the Spaniards and Tlaxcalans were quartered. To cover the humiliation of his capture he gave out that he was going willingly as a guest of Cortés. But Motecuhzoma had lost the initiative. Those whom he thought to be hostages in Tenochtitlan now held *him* hostage in the heart of his city.

Even so, Motecuhzoma continued to conduct affairs of state with his advisers and commanders from guarded apartments. Outside, the population of the city remained submissive beneath a growing sense of disquiet. In the months that followed, Spanish contingents traveled to different parts of the empire on official missions to see and record the location of mines and other sources of tribute. By early 1520 Motecuhzoma formally declared his vassalage to Charles V of Spain, and gave a hoard of treasure stored within the palace to the soldiers of Cortés. Another extraordinary concession was then demanded by Cortés, who asked for a place of Christian worship on the Great Pyramid. A crucifix was installed there with an image of the Virgin, and the Spanish leaders ascended the stairs to kneel for mass at the summit. This act of worship, conducted in full view of the city, was surely seen as an act of symbolic appropriation by the population. The dramatic sight precipitated suppressed anger among the Indians, and a faction of Motecuhzoma's chieftains began to take concrete steps to rid Tenochtitlan of the visitors. Demands for action were made. Prodded by these restive and warlike men, Motecuhzoma informed Cortés that the mood of the city was such that he could no longer guarantee safety. He suggested that they should depart or face an armed uprising.

At this critical point Cortés was unexpectedly called away to the base at Veracruz, taking a contingent of troops. Pedro de Alvarado was left in charge in the capital. A new Spanish force had landed on the coast under Pánfilo Narvaez, charged by the governor of Cuba to arrest Cortés and take control of the expedition. Governor Velásquez had long since learned that Cortés had broken from his control and was writing directly to Charles V. Cortés crossed the mountains, surprised Narvaez, and captured him in a skirmish. He then persuaded Narvaez' troops to join his own forces in Tenochtitlan. Upon returning to the city they found the streets strangely deserted and silent. Alvarado had committed a grave blunder by attacking and killing a large contingent of Aztec lords assembled for one of the most important dances of the ritual calendar. This was done, he said, to destroy a threatening conspiracy. The city now waited in shock and silence as their leaders conferred. Motecuhzoma, failing to put his life on the line, had broken his warrior's code; his appeasement policy had proved disastrous; and now Cortés returned with reinforcements, placing the city in peril.

Smothered resentment burst forth in a furious cry for vengeance as squadrons of Aztec warriors assaulted the Spaniards and Tlaxcalans in the palace. The 16th-century Lienzo de Tlaxcala depicts this episode, when the Aztecs propelled stones and darts into the patio and the Spanish retaliated using cannons to clear the gate of charging enemy formations (ill. 140). The first attack was no sooner repelled than another was mounted. Motecuhzoma was persuaded by the Spaniards to address his people from the rooftop parapet. The warriors dispersed, submitting to the imperial command even in these extreme circumstances. But it was Motecuhzoma's last effective act, for all could see that he no longer embodied the Aztec ideal of kingship.

Motecuhzoma's brother, Prince Cuitlahuac, was elected as the new *tlatoani* and the attack was renewed with conviction. The humiliated Motecuhzoma was again persuaded to stand on the flat rooftop and calm the besieging warriors. His words were received in incredulous silence; then amid whistles, taunts, and jeers, a hail of stones and arrows was flung. Motecuhzoma fell with concussion and was taken to his rooms where he lingered and died – the result of the stoning said the Spaniards; the result of a secret strangling according to later Indian accounts.

Storming the Great Pyramid and the escape from the city

The Great Pyramid overlooked Axayacatl's palace, where the Spanish were housed. From closer platforms the Aztec warriors continually launched missiles towards the flat roof and courtyard below. Cortés was determined to

140 This scene from the Lienzo de Tlaxcala portrays the Spaniards and their allies besieged in the palace by Aztec warriors. The defenders group in the courtyard and a cannon is fired against an Aztec formation charging the principal entrance.

capture the pyramid and he personally led the attack, supported by fire from muskets and crossbows. Missiles, beams, and burning logs were hurled down the stairway by the defenders, who massed at the landings to contest the passage of the determined Spanish force. The assailants pressed on, pushing the Aztec warriors to the upper platform. At the top the opponents faced each other in full view of the city. No quarter was asked or given as the Spaniards drove in the attack (ill. 141). Struggling men fell or were pitched over the edges of the pyramid. Superior weapons and battle practice gained the upper hand and as the last group of Aztec warriors defended themselves, the Spaniards rushed to the temples. Seizing the idols, the troops cast them down the stairways and set fire to the shrines before the eyes of the horrified city. A column of smoke rose behind the victorious troops as they descended the steps of the pyramid.

Despite this tactical success, Cortés knew that his position was untenable and resolved to escape from the city by night. The Spanish realized that four of the eight bridges in the causeway to Tlacopan were missing, and to secure passage over the gaps a portable bridge was constructed. Hidden by darkness, and taking every care not to make noise, the allied forces opened the gates of the palace and made their way toward the Tlacopan causeway. War was not traditionally waged at night by the Aztecs, and no sentries had been posted. The alarm was given by a group of women at a watering place. Hurrying on, the army was strung along the causeway when the first gap was reached.

ycqtla ti tetzavitl yn mal ques.

141 The Spaniards attack the Great Pyramid, supported by cavalry and Tlaxcalan warriors in the plaza below. From the Lienzo de Tlaxcala.

The portable bridge was fitted and the crossing began, but the vanguard soon reached the second gap before everyone had crossed the first. The portable bridge had jammed and panic ensued as thousands of Aztec warriors began appearing in canoes along the sides of the causeway. In the darkness, the Spaniards and Tlaxcalans pushed forward amid an unceasing hail of stones, darts, and arrows. The gap began to fill with baggage and bodies as the troops pressed on pell mell. Many fell victims to greed as they were borne under the water by the weight of booty taken from the palace. Dawn approached, and in the grey twilight the wild carnage continued the length of the causeway. Spanish captains who reached relative safety on the shore spurred back to the aid of their comrades. It is said that Alvarado saved himself by shoving his lance into the debris and vaulting across one of the gaps. At last the main body of the army made the crossing and regrouped to continue their escape as the Aztecs turned their attention to booty and captives. Why the Spaniards were allowed to escape from this battle (referred to as the Noche Triste) can only be attributed to the fact that the Indians had little concept of fighting to annihilate the enemy. Their goal to gain booty, sacrificial victims, and status were more important and immediate objectives.

The badly wounded but still fighting Spanish expedition made its way to Tlaxcalan territory after defeating yet another Aztec force on the open plains near Otumba. That the Spaniards were able to find sanctuary in Tlaxcala speaks of the rancorous divisions among Indian nations who could have made

common cause against the foreign invaders. Deep-seated feelings of humiliation and enmity, the result of decades of military, economic and political
aggression from Tenochtitlan, had already gained invaluable Tlaxcalan
assistance for Cortés, and now led to other alliances. As the army recuperated,
Cortés made diplomatic overtures to the nearby town of Tepeaca. The Cholollans also saw the chance to secure their own independence from Aztec
domination and decided to join the allies. By April 1521 the army departed
again for the Valley of Mexico. This time their objective was to lay siege and to
capture Tenochtitlan.

The siege and surrender of Tenochtitlan

A critical part of Cortés' strategy was to gain a landing place from which a fleet
of armed sailing brigantines, built on the lakeshore, could blockade the island
city. No harbor was more suitable than that of Tetzcoco. The leaders of this
most important ally of Tenochtitlan had in fact long resented the high-
handedness of its neighbor and the arrogance of Motecuhzoma, who had precipitated a decline in the power and prestige of the Tetzcocan court. With
Motecuhzoma gone, the impetus toward centralization and authoritarian
control lost its most forceful figure. The bonds of the old alliance, already
strained, were now questioned by the Tetzcocan chieftains. As the Spaniards
and their allies approached, a pro-Tenochtitlan ruler fled by canoe and a new
ruler was appointed by the dissident faction. This man shortly died of disease,
and Prince Ixtlilxóchitl was elected with the approval of Cortés. Ixtlilxóchitl
was an ebullient youth who had won high honors as a warrior. Hating Motecuhzoma, he lent his full support to Cortés and was to prove an invaluable ally.
The empire of the Aztecs was beginning to unravel with this Tetzcocan
defection. Collaboration among the city-states was at best uneasy in a land
where the political independence of each community was jealously maintained.
Before the rise of Tenochtitlan, Tetzcoco, and Tlacopan as paramount powers,
small-scale raids and seasonal wars were a normal state of affairs between rival
neighboring cities. These local conflicts seldom resulted in total defeat or
victory, because their primary purpose was to obtain tribute and sacrificial
victims. As the authoritarian, centralizing structure personified by Motecuhzoma began to collapse, the old, underlying tendency toward fragmentation
reappeared.

Step by step Tenochtitlan became isolated. Cortés led an expedition south
to Chalco and neighboring *chinampa* towns, while another column circled
north to Zumpango and Xaltocan, and on around the western side of the lake to
reach Tlacopan. Later, Cortés marched across the Ajusco mountains into the
rich Tlahuica territories on the road to Cuauhnahuac. Meanwhile the fleet of
armed brigantines built and based in Tetzcoco kept up a blockade along the
lakeside landing places of Tenochtitlan. By early summer 1521 the Spaniards
and their allies, divided into three forces, were in position at the head of the
causeways – Gonzalo de Sandovál stationed to the north, Pedro de Alvarado to
the west, and Cortés and Cristóbal de Olid to the south. The three-pronged
attack met fierce resistance, and the Aztecs caused considerable damage as the

fighting see-sawed back and forth. The besieging army of about 900 Spaniards plus several thousand Indian allies was small compared with the huge population of the city, and the gains made on one day were often lost on the next as the defenders returned by circuitous routes and regained the rooftops. The Spaniards began systematic demolition: as bridges were captured and advances were made, all buildings were razed, clearing the ground to give the troops wider space to maneuver.

These slow but effective tactics gave the attackers the upper hand. The siege was tightened, while the city's population was gradually decimated by starvation, disease, and lack of fresh water, and by frightful massacres perpetrated by the Tlaxcalans. The ferocity of the Indian allies against their former oppressors could not be restrained by the Spaniards, who were shocked by the thousands of women and children who perished in wholesale slaughter. By then the inhabitants were severely suffering from the deadly effects of a raging smallpox epidemic, an appalling contagion brought by a member of Cortés' forces upon landing in Veracruz. Unknown in the Americas, smallpox swept through the Indian populations and was destined to kill millions in the course of the 16th century. The advance continued day by day amid piles of bodies and the rubble of buildings. The new *tlatoani* Cuitlahuac died of disease. The Great Pyramid and the royal palaces were captured as the Mexica were hemmed into the district of Tlatelolco. Cortés sent messages to Prince Cuauhtemoc, the new *tlatoani*, inviting him to surrender. These communications were steadfastly refused. Determination to resist had changed into a will to perish. After 93 days of siege, on 13 August 1521, Cuauhtemoc was captured with his wife and chieftains as he tried to escape by canoe, seeking to continue the war from some other sanctuary. Cuauhtemoc was taken to a rooftop where Cortés received his brave surrender with honor and respect. The scene is depicted in the Lienzo de Tlaxcala with the Nahuatl inscription: "This is where came the end of the Mexica."

Many factors played a part in the fall of Tenochtitlan: calendrical coincidences surrounding the Spaniards' arrival; the brilliance of Cortés as a commander-in-chief, and the superior Spanish arms and tactics; Motecuhzoma's unsuccessful strategy of entrapment and the inflexibility of a strongly centralized chain of command that depended ultimately on decisions by the *tlatoani* himself; the Aztec way of waging war, tied to religious practice; and the fearful toll of smallpox and other diseases for which the native populations had no natural resistance. Also significant was the inherent instability of an empire where coercion and fear had exacted tribute from cities that otherwise tended to maintain a strong sense of independence. Despite decades of effort by the Aztecs to build political and military alliances, kinship connections, a legalist system, religious obligations and systems of patronage, a structure of government that might have successfully resisted the invaders had not yet been achieved.

Cuauhtemoc's surrender marked more than the demise of Tenochtitlan. It also signaled the political end of all the great Indian nations and the beginnings of a profound transformation in the civilization that had flourished in Mesoamerica for millennia.

Epilog

When the Tepanecs, Chichimecs, Acolhua, and Mexica migrated into the Valley of Mexico they were determined to win a place for themselves in that fertile, luminous setting. A long adaptive experience began as these incoming tribes grafted themselves on the land and assimilated cultural ways from the older town-dwelling agricultural peoples. In due time this process gave rise to social and economic forms and symbolic expressions that voiced the tribes' own adaptation and adjustment to the ancient patterns of Mesoamerican civilization.

By November 1519, when Cortés and his Spaniards and their Tlaxcalan allies crossed the causeway to meet Motecuhzoma II in Tenochtitlan, the Aztec city-states had successfully built the largest empire in Mesoamerican history. For almost a century the advance of their power was virtually relentless, as successive warlords engaged in campaigns of conquest and in developing dominant relations with neighboring peoples. The aggressive expansion belongs to one of those exceptional moments in history when military, political, and economic and cultural opportunities are grasped by imaginative and forceful leaders and a vigorously creative people.

Scholars have researched and debated a variety of motivations and causes that propelled this dynamic process. It is apparent today that no single, dominant "prime mover" cause can be found; rather, explanations lie in tracing the interaction of diverse factors. There was the favorable geography of the valley, with its volcanoes and lesser peaks where the summer rainstorms take form. An abundant and varied flora and fauna flourished in the mountains, the piedmont, and waters of the valley and in neighboring highland basins. Elaborate methods of cultivation had a long history in the region. Since before the florescence of Teotihuacan, *chinampas* and farming terraces as well as farming in open fields were fundamental to the economy.

Other considerations affecting the rise of the Aztecs include the location of Tenochtitlan on its island in Lake Tetzcoco. The original unclaimed outcrops and reedbeds proved to be a safe haven and a strategic site between powerful neighboring cities. The Mexica were able to establish a "neutral zone" for their market in a place favoring trade and easy transportation of goods by canoe. The city grew in comparative safety. Although Tenochtitlan first paid tribute to Atzcapotzalco, it was never besieged or invaded before the Spanish arrived.

The role of individuals shaped the course of historical events during the 15th and early 16th centuries. The idea and methods of building a tributary empire, first learned in service to the Tepanec *tlatoani* Tezozomoc, were applied and improved by leaders of the Triple Alliance. They built elaborate tributary networks through force of arms; promoted alliances and marriage connections; and developed an elaborate system of ritual obligations. Laws were proclaimed that strongly favored the centralized authority of the *tlatoanis* and the harsh rule of the state. Even Ahuitzotl, who most ruthlessly employed force and terror, could not forget that Aztec hegemony also needed to be maintained by extended family bonds and favorable client-state relationships. Archaeological evidence and the ethnohistoric texts also speak of colonization by the Aztecs in Oztoman, Malinalco, Calixtlahuaca, and Tepoztlán. Monuments at these places asserted an imperial presence and territorial claims. The empire ultimately rested on armed force, and although rebellion remained an ever-present threat, it is evident that the rulers were taking a variety of steps to broaden and strengthen their hold within regions already conquered.

The quest for wealth was undoubtedly a driving motive for Aztec expansion. The desire to obtain enormous riches is clearly seen on tribute lists illustrated in the Codex Mendoza and the *Matrícula de Tributos*. However, for the Aztecs the lure of great wealth lay not in being able to store it away in the form of bankable capitalist riches; for beyond the immediate needs of extended families, lineages and their dependants, foods and sumptuary goods were accumulated in large measure for purposes of display and redistribution during festivals. As a result of the incoming flow of tribute, the lords of Tenochtitlan, Tetzcoco, and Tlacopan were obliged to assert their rank and authority with ever more lavish patronage. At the highest level, coronations, royal funerals, and triumphs were celebrated with unequaled splendor, attended by thousands of guests who had to be housed, fed, and supplied with gifts, just as they were obligated to present gifts in return. Through the expenditure of huge resources on ritual occasions, the Aztec magnates affirmed greater power and prestige. To a very significant degree, the demands of the festival system formed a major part of the Aztec economy. The pageantry, communal dances, and dramatic theatrical presentations powerfully affected the Aztec imagination and formed a fundamental mechanism for achieving social integration and cohesion. Curiously, we are reminded of Plato's observation that the ancient Greeks regarded their cities and political institutions as works of art, thinking more in terms of aesthetic qualities than economic or moral ones.

Did the Aztecs have a sense of historical destiny? Their civilization has been characterized as a renascence of the metropolitan legacy transmitted since the centuries of Teotihuacan.[1] The Aztecs cultivated a cultural and historical affinity with the "Toltecs," whom they identified with an idealized past. The adoption of the ways of agricultural peoples long settled in the Valley of Mexico, learning the Nahuatl language, the quoting of symbolic forms stemming from antiquity, notions of cyclical time and the repetition of past events are all evidence of cultural continuity.

In *The Aztecs: People of the Sun*, Alfonso Caso viewed Aztec warfare as an eternal quest for sacrificial victims to feed the gods in repayment for having offered their own blood in the original creation of humankind. Undeniably, human sacrifice was an integral part of Mesoamerican religion, but the scale and spectacle of human sacrifice practiced in Tenochtitlan must also be seen as a calculated political strategy. Warriors were required to capture enemies on the battlefield as a means of recognition and promotion, contributing to the rise of a military aristocracy. Were the Aztec armies motivated by a religious need to convert conquered peoples? There is no evidence to suggest so. The cult of Huitzilopochtli was not widely found beyond Tenochtitlan, and was acknowledged in Tetzcoco as an expression of political and economic alliance. Yet the Mexica-Aztecs of Tenochtitlan surely drew inspiration from the violent myth of their ancestor-hero. The fundamental religious practice of conducting all important aspects of human life in step with the seasonal rhythm undoubtedly gave them a sense of rightness and conviction when the dry season time for war was proclaimed, or when the time of rain and cultivation began. All the great commemorative monuments legitimize conquests, showing the state as an integral part of the cosmic order by a charter established since the time of beginnings.

The fact remains that for all the integrating features of their social, religious, and economic life, the Aztecs never outgrew the predatory instinct of their Tepanec and Toltec predecessors. They enriched themselves principally by capturing wealth and securing tribute with the menace of violent retribution. Their expansive dynamic was based on subjecting new towns and regions as the primary path to economic growth and social advancement. Although the great majority of conquered towns were allowed to retain their native rulers, these local potentates remained humiliated, their estates diminished, and their people reduced; hatred and bitterness spread with the loss of power, place, and property, and hosts of enemies were everywhere created as the process of empire aggressively advanced. There were no significant benefits for those communities living in constant apprehension, in a state of vigilance and anxiety under the threat of destruction. Fierce emotions were ready to be unleashed, the memory of injuries was keen and vivid, and new conquests helped to recall old ones to mind. So in 1519 the mood and temper which prevailed beyond the Aztec strongholds were those of subjected or threatened peoples who had wrongs to remember and were chafing at having to endure Aztec rapacity. Within the growing structure of empire there existed a great and constant mass of disaffection and antagonism. The Aztecs had mastered the arts of war but not yet those of government. As the Spaniards and Tlaxcalans gathered new forces and set out in April 1521 on their second march to Tenochtitlan, a pivotal change began to be perceived by many who deeply resented Aztec supremacy. Tepeaca and Cholollan were persuaded to join as allies; sedition spread as others joined in, and soon even Tetzcoco's new *tlatoani* declared for Cortés. The expansive dynamic of the Aztec empire was lost, and its final collapse was as much an Indian revolt as it was a Spanish conquest.

As the empire of the Aztecs collapsed, the process of Spanish colonization immediately began in Central Mexico. In Mexico City the most visible changes took place with the razing of the ceremonial precinct and royal palaces to make way for the colonial seat of government, the first cathedral, and the Plaza de la Constitución. Smaller ward temples were also cleared and the sites made ready for Christian churches. These changes in the urban setting were matched in towns around the Valley and soon throughout central and southern Mexico the great system of monastic missions began to be built by Franciscan, Augustinian, and Dominican orders. Yet these missions with their mixture of

Renaissance, Gothic, and Mudéjar features were also designed with great spreading atriums and open chapels suited to the conversion of Indian communities accustomed to religious events in open-air settings. Many aspects of indigenous life continued and eventually became fused with Hispanic cultural and economic features. The Nahuatl language remained widely spoken, and still is spoken by well over a million people, especially in mountain towns and villages throughout the Central Highlands. Not surprisingly, Mexican Spanish has a recorded vocabulary of some 3,000 "Nahuatlisms," including the names of plants, animals, towns, geographic features, and a variety of manufactures, instruments, and activities.

Other impressions of the Aztec heritage can be seen as one travels through the countryside: fields bordered by rows of blue-green maguey, village yards fenced with columnar cactus, and nopal orchards standing nearby. Between the towns of Chalco and Xochimilco, *chinampa* gardens still supply a range of vegetables and ornamental plants to the markets in Mexico City; and in rural settings the weekly markets are well attended, offering all the old staples. In these markets there will also be the native herbalists, the *curanderos*, whose selections of medicinal plants, minerals, and animal products are recommended with knowledge transmitted from antiquity. Even today at Tetzcotzingo, *curanderos* will come from the high mountain towns with patients bringing offerings of flowers to Netzahualcoyotl's ruined shrines. Their recitations may come from reading books about Aztec history and poetry, yet the sense of the hill as a therapeutic place has surely been kept for centuries. Pilgrimages are also annually made by people from the Tetzcoco region to the Vale of Tlalocto, where an aqueduct begins its long descent to the piedmont settlements and terraces. And in the Plaza de la Constitución of Mexico City, the tricolor flag of the republic waves with the eagle and cactus where the palace of Motecuhzoma I once stood. In the National Museum of Anthropology, the Mexica Hall is where national pride in the Indian heritage is most dramatically expressed. The huge Calendar Stone, on axis with the museum courtyard, stands as a central altarpiece.

Beyond such sights and impressions there is another less immediately tangible theme, transmitted for hundreds, even thousands of years before its Aztec manifestation – a theme still awaiting wide recognition. The Poet Laureate Octavio Paz has noted that the national project might be defined as an effort to build a nation from a conglomerate of peoples whose customs, languages, and rivalries reach back many centuries, long before the Spanish viceroyalty. In Mexico as elsewhere in the post-colonial world among countries of old and diverse cultural heritage, the past may hold an ambiguous position – at once to be valued and salvaged, yet also to be overcome on the path to modernity. From this point of view modernity also carries an extended critique of the past.[2] Among the many cultural features of Aztec inheritance and that of their predecessors, there is the fundamental idea that humankind was obliged to play a pivotal role in a relationship of reciprocity with the structures and workings of nature. This ancient principle is of universal significance and is salvageable and ever perfectable in new and different cultural contexts as a contribution from the indigenous past.

Annual Ceremonies of the Aztecs

AZTEC "MONTH"	CEREMONY NAME	ENGLISH TRANSLATION	CHRISTIAN CORRELATION	MAIN DEITIES	RITES AND CUSTOMS
I	Atlcaualo[1] Cuauhitleua	Ceasing of Water Raising of Trees	14 Feb–5 March	TLALOC CHALCHIUHTLICUE CHICOMECOATL XILONEN QUETZALCOATL	Poles erected and decorated with ritual banners in temples and homes. Offerings to maize deities. Children sacrificed on mountains, dances
II	Tlacaxipe-hualizlti	Flaying of Men	6 March–25 March	XIPE TOTEC	Dances, mock skirmishes, young warriors present sacrificial captives at initiation. Gladiatorial sacrifice. Priests wear skins of victims 20 days. Ruler participates in military ceremonies and agricultural dance
III	Tozoztontli Xochimanaloya	Small Vigil Offering of Flowers	26 March–14 April	TLALOC CHALCHIUHTLICUE CENTEOTL COATLICUE	First ritual in fields, ceremonial planting (probably in *chinampa* zone). Flowers offered. XIPE TOTEC skins worn by priests from previous festival deposited in Yopico temple "cave"
IV	Huey Tozoztli	Great Vigil	15 April–4 May	TLALOC CHALCHIUHTLICUE CENTEOTL CHICOMECOATL COATLICUE XILONEN	Procession of maidens to maize goddess, carrying seed corn to be blessed. Feast offering and child sacrifice on Mt Tlaloc and at Pantitlan in Lake Tetzcoco. Participation by the rulers of four cities
V	Toxcatl Tepopochtli	Dry Thing (?) Incensing	5 May–22 May	TEZCATLIPOCA HUITZILOPOCHTLI MIXCOATL CAMAXTLI YACATECUHTLI	Major renewal festival, sacrifice of youth impersonator of TEZCATLIPOCA during previous year. Similar sacrifice for HUITZILOPOCHTLI, and related ancestral hero-deities in Tlaxcala and Valley of Puebla
VI	Etzalcualiztli	Eating of Etzalli (Maize and Beans Porridge)	23 May–13 June	TLALOC CHALCHIUHTLICUE QUETZALCOATL	End of the dry season and beginning of rains. Priests fast for rain, the lords dance with maize stalks (from the *chinampas*) and carry pots with maize and beans. Offerings made to agricultural implements. Reeds brought from lake for new mats, seats, and to adorn temples
VII	Tecuilhuitontli	Small Feast of the Lords	14 June–3 July	XOCHIPILLI HUIXTOCIHUATL	Sacrifice to the deity of feasting and vegetation. Salt goddess sacrifices. The lords host commoners at feasts. The ruler dances and distributes gifts

AZTEC "MONTH"	CEREMONY NAME	ENGLISH TRANSLATION	CHRISTIAN CORRELATION	MAIN DEITIES	RITES AND CUSTOMS
VIII	Huey Tecuilhuitl	Small Feast of the Lords	4 July–23 July	XILONEN CIHUACOATL	First tender maize festival. Lords again host commoners. The ruler dances, distributes gifts. Young warriors and women dance. Sacrifices made
IX	Miccailhuitontli Tlaxochimaco	Little Feast of the Dead Giving of Flowers	24 July–12 Aug	TEZCATLIPOCA HUITZILOPOCHTLI ANCESTORS	Feasts, dances, and offerings of flowers in honor of the dead. Sacrifice to HUITZILOPOCHTLI and TEZCATLIPOCA
X	Huey Miccailhuitl Xocotlhuetzi	Great Feast of the Dead Fall of Xocotl Fruit	13 Aug–1 Sept	HUEHUETEOTL XIUHTECUHTLI YACATECUHTLI ANCESTORS	Sacrifices to fire. Pole-climbing ceremony (xocotl tree) competition by boys. Commemoration of ancestors
XI	Ochpaniztli	Sweeping	2 Sept–21 Sept	TOCI TLAZOLTEOTL TETEOINNAN COATLICUE CINETEOTL CHICOMECOATL	Major harvest season begins. Ceremonies honoring earth goddesses. General cleaning, sweeping, repairing. Ripe corn deity honored, seed corn cast to populace. In preparation for the coming war season, the ruler gives insignia to warriors. Ruler participates in dances. Military ceremonies at borders of traditional enemies in Valley of Puebla. Priests begin 80-day fasts to culminate in Panquetzaliztli festivals, Nov.–Dec.
XII	Teotleco	Arrival of the Deities	22 Sept–11 Oct	ALL DEITIES HONOURED	Return of deities to participate in grand harvest festival. Their advent signaled by appearance at midnight of footprint in a maize-flour bowl in temple. Youngest deity (TLAMAZINCATL) arrives first; oldest (HUEHUETEOTL) last. Fire sacrifice to XIUHTECUHTLI and YACATECUHTLI. Feasting, rejoicing, dancing, offering of food
XIII	Tepeilhuitl	Mountain Feast Day	12 Oct–31 Oct	TLALOC TLALOQUE TEPICTOTON OCTLI (Pulque deities) XOCHIQUETZAL MAJOR RAIN MOUNTAINS: POPOCATEPETL IZTACCÍHUATL MT TLALOC MATLALCUEYE	Offerings of thanks at shrines on major rain mountains. Amaranth-dough effigies and serpent-like branches covered with amaranth paste in rituals and sacrifices. Mat-makers honor NAPPATECUHTLI; fishermen OPOCHTLI; turpentine-makers, ZAPOTLANTENAN; weavers, embroiderers, and painters, XOCHIQUETZAL

continued overleaf

AZTEC "MONTH"	CEREMONY NAME	ENGLISH TRANSLATION	CHRISTIAN CORRELATION	MAIN DEITIES	RITES AND CUSTOMS
XIV	Quecholli	Precious Feather (Roseate spoonbill)	1 Nov–20 Nov	MIXCOATL CAMAXTLI TLAMATZINCATL	Feasting of warriors. Manufacture of weapons for hunt and war. Commemoration of dead warriors. Ancient tribal hunting rites, communal hunts and prizes to best hunter. Prisoners bound like deer and sacrificed
XV	Panquetzaliztli	Raising of Banners	21 Nov–10 Dec	HUITZILOPOCHTLI TEZCATLIPOCA	Major military rites celebrating birth of HUITZILOPOCHTLI and his victory over COYOLXAUHQUI, enacted at Great Pyramid of Tenochtitlan. Large sacrifice of prisoners. Major procession led by PAYNAL from Great Pyramid to Tlatelolco, Chapultepec, Coyoacan, and back to Great Pyramid. Paper flags on fruit trees and houses
XVI	Atemoztli	Water Descent	11 Dec–30 Dec	TLALOQUE MOUNTAINS	This period may bring light rains, mountains are again honored
XVII	Tititl	Stretching (?)	31 Dec–19 Jan	CIHUACOATL ILAMATECUHTLI TONANTZIN YACATECUHTLI	Great dance of priests dressed as deities, feast with lords and priests. Ritual dances in which the ruler participates. Merchants sacrifice slaves in traders' initiation rites. Weavers honor ILAMATECUHTLI (old mother goddess)
XVIII	Izcalli Huauhquil-tamalcualiztli	"Growth," "Resucitation" Eating of Tamales Stuffed with Huauhquihuitl Greens	20 Jan–8 Feb	XIUHTECUHTLI TLALOC CHALCHIUHTLICUE	Amaranth-dough effigy of XIUHTECUHTLI (fire god) honored. Sacrifice of animals to fire, toasting of corn. Rulers participate in ceremonies as this deity is their patron. Tamales with greens eaten. Children pulled by neck to "make them grow." Every four years, special lordly dance, children have ears pierced and are assigned "godparents"
	Nemontemi	Useless Days (considered unlucky), "full/complete in vain," "worthless"	9 Feb–13 Feb		No rituals, general abstinence, no business conducted

Two Special Non-Annual Ceremonies

CEREMONY NAME	ENGLISH TRANSLATION	CHRISTIAN CORRELATION	RITES AND CUSTOMS
Toxiuhmolpilia	Binding of the Years (New Fire Rites)	Every 52 years in 2 *Acatl*	All fires extinguished, all activities cease. Quietness observed. New Fire Rites at Huixachtlán Hill, torches taken by runners to light temple fires in all cities. Renewal of clothing and utensils, old clothing and utensils discarded
Atamalcualiztli	Eating of Water Tamales	Every 8 years in *Tecpatl*	Seven-day initial fast. Only water-soaked tamales eaten, no condiments, "to give the maize a rest." Dances, ceremonial swallowing of water-snakes and frogs

Notes to the Text

Chapter 1
1 Maudslay 1909.
2 Sahagún 1951–69, Book 6,
   Rhetoric and Moral Philosophy.
3 Durán 1967.

Chapter 2
1 Sahagún 1951–69, Book 1, *The Gods.*
2 *Ibid.*, Book 6, *Rhetoric and Moral Philosophy.*
3 *Ibid.*, Book 6, *Rhetoric and Moral Philosophy.*
4 *Ibid.*, Book 3, *The Origin of the Gods.*
5 Chimalpahín 1965.
6 Dibble 1980, plate I.
7 Ixtlilxóchitl 1895.
8 Gillespie 1989, pp xvii–xli.
9 Durán 1967, p. 217–18.
10 Tezozomoc 1949, p. 23.
11 Kirchhoff 1961.
12 Gillespie 1989, pp. 56–95.
13 Durán 1964, p. 44

Chapter 3
1 Durán, 1967, pp. 79–80. This well-known passage has been questioned as apocryphal by Nigel Davies (Davies 1987, p. 40), who points out that it suggests the elite might abdicate power to the proletariat – a pattern unknown in Mesoamerican culture. However it may well be a metaphorical expression, perhaps misconstrued from the original Nahuatl in the Cronica X as a formalized expression of communal solidarity.
2 Ixtlilxóchitl 1895, vol I, p. 316.
3 Davies 1982, p. 78.

Chapter 4
1 Parsons 1976, pp. 233–57.
2 Hassig 1988.
3 Offner 1988, pp. 88–95.
4 *Ibid.*, p. 95.
5 *Ibid.*, pp. 106–9.
6 *Ibid.*, p. 104.
7 De Vega Nova 1991.
8 Smith 1992.
9 Berdan et al. 1996.
10 Zorita 1942, pp. 200–3.
11 Townsend 1982b, pp. 111–40.
12 Offner 1982, pp. 153–55.

Chapter 5
1 Hassig 1988.
2 Spores 1967 and 1984; Flannery and Marcus 1983.
3 Hassig 1988, pp. 157–75.
4 *Ibid.*, pp. 176–188.

5 Davies 1982.
6 Nicholson 1971, Table 3
7 Payón 1936.
8 Stanislawski 1947, pp. 45–55.
9 Hassig 1988, pp. 208–213.
10 Moedano 1948.
11 Davies 1982, p. 201.

Chapter 6
1 Nicholson 1971.
2 Sahagún 1951–69, Book 1, *The Gods.*
3 Tedlock 1985.
4 Nicholson 1971, pp. 397–408
5 Caso 1958.
6 Sahagún 1951–69, Book 7, *The Sun, The Moon, and the Binding of the Years*, p. 4.
7 *Ibid.*, p. 6.
8 *Ibid.*, p. 7.
9 Nicholson 1971, pp. 400–401.
10 Durán 1971, p. 396.
11 Durán 1971; Sahagún 1951–69.
12 Wilhelm 1950.
13 Tedlock 1985.
14 Sahagún 1951–69, Book 7, p. 27
15 Aguilera 1988.
16 Aguilera 1988, 1994.
17 Iwaniszewski 1994, pp. 158–176
18 Durán 1971, pp. 154–171.
19 Durán 1971, pp. 161–166.
20 Townsend 1982a, pp. 37–62
21 Sahagún 1951–69, Book 1, *The Ceremonies*, pp. 59–61
22 Matos Moctezuma 1987, pp. 186–209; Matos Moctezuma 1988, pp. 109–145.
23 Read 1991, pp. 260–300.

Chapter 7
68 Sahagún 1951–69, Book 6, *Rhetoric and Moral Philosophy*, p. 175.
69 Townsend 1979, pp. 23–34.
70 Martínez 1972, pp. 125–135; León-Portilla 1963.
71 Durán 1971, pp. 154–171.
72 Mendieta 1945.
73 Martinez 1972, p. 101 (translated by Richard Townsend).

Chapter 8
1 Parsons, J. "Environment and Rural Economy" in The Aztec World, ed. Brumfield & Feinman, pp. 23–52.
2 Sanders, Parsons and Santley 1979.
3 Calnek 1972; Parsons 1971.
4 Palerm and Wolf 1971; Palerm 1955.
5 Nuttall 1925, pp. 453–464.
6 *Ibid.*

7 Quoted in Nuttall 1925.
8 Coe, S. 1994, p.30.
9 Sahagún 1951–69, Book 10, p. 93.
10 Diaz 1970, pp. 215–217.
11 Charlton et al. 1991, pp. 98–114.
12 Townsend 1970; Berdan 1978, pp. 187–198; Berdan 1980, pp. 37–41; Berdan 1986.
13 Zorita 1942.
14 Sahagún 1951–69, Book 9, *The Merchants*, p. 22.
15 *Ibid.*, Book 2, *The Ceremonies*, pp. 130–138.
16 *Ibid.*, Book 1, *The Gods*, pp. 1–2.
17 Smith 1996

Chapter 9
1 Diaz 1956, pp. 104–105.
2 Acosta Saignes 1946, pp. 147–205.
3 Sahagún 1951–69, Book 10, *The People*, p. 29.
4 Aubin 1849.
5 Zender 2008, pp. 24–37.
6 Lacadena 2008, pp. 1–22.
7 Hassig 1988, pp. 17–47.

Chapter 10
1 Sahagún 1951–69, Book 12, *The Conquest of Mexico*, p. 9.
2 *Ibid.*, Book 12, *The Conquest of Mexico*; Prescott 1931; Collis 1954; White 1971.
3 Davies 1982, pp. 257–260.
4 Gillespie 1989, pp. 173–207.
5 Umberger 1981, pp. 10–17.
6 Sahagún 1951–69, Book 12, *The Conquest of Mexico*, p. 27.
7 *Ibid.*, Book 12, *The Conquest of Mexico*, pp. 37–39

Epilog
1 Davies 1982, p. 204.
2 Paz 1990.

Annual Ceremonies Table
1 English translations after Nicholson 1971.

Further Reading

There is a vast number of books about the Aztecs, and a selection is listed here. For an introduction to Aztec history, the general reader is referred to Nigel Davies, *The Aztecs: A History*. Michael Smith's *The Aztecs* presents a synthesis of ethnohistory and anthropology with an archaeological emphasis, portraying the development of the empire and patterns of Aztec economy, religion, and daily life in the capitols and provincial locations. Michael Coe's *Mexico* provides a general summary of the development of early civilizations in Mexico. For readers interested in the art of this period, see Esther Pasztory's well-illustrated *Aztec Art* and Mary Miller's *Art of Mesoamerica*. A valuable work on Aztec kingship is Susan Gillespie's *The Aztec Kings*, and on warfare Ross Hassig's *Aztec Warfare*. Older classics include Alfred Maudslay's excellent translation of Bernal Diaz del Castillo's vivid eyewitness description of the Spanish conquest of Tenochtitlan, *The Discovery and Conquest of Mexico*. William H. Prescott's *History of the Conquest of Mexico*, first published in 1843, remains a luminous account, while Hugh Thomas's *Conquest: Montezuma, Cortés, and the Fall of Old Mexico* brings many new insights from archival research, widening our understanding of the Spanish expansion. In recent years, major Aztec exhibitions have been launched, with comprehensive catalogues written from an interdisciplinary perspective. "Aztecs," curated by Eduardo Matos Moctezuma and Felipe Solís Olguín, was presented by the Royal Academy of Arts, London, in 2002; and "The Aztec Empire," curated by Felipe Solís Olguín, went to the Guggenheim Museum in New York in 2004; and "The Aztec World," curated by Elizabeth M. Brumfiel and Gary M. Feinman, opened at the Field Museum, Chicago, in 2008. These projects have not only featured major works of art, but have also offered new insights into such traditional subjects as Aztec antecedents, religion, political history, and economy, while also portraying the environment, urbanism, the role and status of women, the effect of the Spanish conquest on Aztec society, and the Aztec inheritance in the formation of modern Mexico. A new exhibition, "Moctezuma," opens in 2009 at the British Museum, as part of a series on emperors of ancient civilizations in China, Iran, Rome, and Mexico. The Aztec achievement has emerged from its Pre-Columbian context and the history of conquest and nationalist concerns in the 20th century, to be understood in a comparative global context of early civilizations worldwide.

Abbreviations

INAH = Instituto Nacional de Antropología e Historia
UNAM = Universidad Nacional Autónoma de México
SEP = Secretaría de Educacíon Pública

ACOSTA SAIGNES, MIGUEL. "Los Teopixque," in *Revista Mexicana de Estudios Antropológicos* 8, 1946.

AGUILERA, CARMEN. "The Temple Mayor as a Dual Symbol of the Passing of Time," in *Estructuras Bipartitas en Mesoamerica*, ed. Rudolph van Zantwijk. International Congress of Americanists, ISOR, Amsterdam, 1988.

—— "The New Fire Ceremony, Its Meaning and Calendrics," in *Time and Astronomy at the Meeting of Two Worlds*, ed. Stanislaw Iwaniszewski et al. Center for Latin American Studies, Warsaw University, 1994.

—— "Of Royal Mantles and Blue Turquoise: The Meaning of the Mexica Emperor's Mantle," in *Latin American Antiquity* 8 (1), 1997.

ANAWALT, PATRICIA R. *Indian Clothing before Cortés*. Foreword by Henry Nicholson. University of Oklahoma Press, Norman, 1981.

AUBIN, JOSEPH M. A. *Mémoirs sur la peinture didactique et l'écriture figurative des anciens Mexicaines*. Paris, 1849 [Reprinted in 1885, Mission Scientifique au Mexique et dans l'Amerique Centrale, Recherches Historiques et Archéologiques. Première partie: Histoire. Paris.]

AUSTIN, ALFREDO LOPEZ and LEONARDO LOPEZ LUJÁN. "Aztec Human Sacrifice," in *The Aztec World*, ed. Elizabeth M. Brumfiel and Gary M. Feinman. Abrams, New York, in association with the Field Museum, Chicago, 2008.

AVENI, ANTHONY. *Empires of Time: Calendars, Clocks, and Cultures*. I. B. Tauris & Co., London, 1990.

—— "Mapping the Ritual Landscape: Debt Payment to Tlaloc During the Month of Atlcahualco," in *To Change Place: Aztec Ceremonial Landscapes*, ed. David Carrasco. University Press of Colorado, Niwot, Colorado, 1992.

—— "Moctezuma's Sky: Aztec Astronomy and Ritual," in *Moctezuma's Mexico: Visions of the Aztec World*, ed. David Carrasco and Eduardo Matos Moctezuma. University Press of Colorado, Niwot, Colorado, 1992.

AVENI, ANTHONY, EDWARD E. CALNEK, and HORST HARTUNG. "Myth, Environment and the Orientation of the Templo Mayor of Tenochtitlan," in *American Antiquity* 53, 1988.

AVENI, ANTHONY and SHARON GIBBS. "On the Orientation of Pre-Columbian Buildings in Central Mexico," *American Antiquity* 41, 1976.

BAIRD, ELLEN T. *The Drawings of Sahagún's Primeros Memoriales: Structure and Style*. University of Oklahoma Press, Norman, 1993.

BARLOW, ROBERT H. "The Titles of Tetzcotzingo" in *Tlalocan* II (2). Mexico City, 1946.

BECKER, MARSHALL. "Moieties in Ancient Mesoamerica," in *American Indian Quarterly* 2 (3), 1975.

BELLEREZA, JUAN ALBERTO ROMÁN. "Health and Disease Among the Aztecs," in *The Aztec World*, ed. Elizabeth M. Brumfiel ad Gary M. Feinman. Abrams, New York, in association with the Field Museum, Chicago, 2008.

BERDAN, FRANCES. "Ports of Trade in Mesoamerica: A Reappraisal," in *Cultural Continuity in Mesoamerica*, ed. D. Browman. Mouton Publishers, The Hague, 1978.

—— "Markets in the Economy of Aztec Mexico," in *Markets and Marketing*, ed. Stuart Plattner. University Press of America, Lanham, MD, 1985.

—— "The Economics of Aztec Luxury Trade and Tribute," in *The Aztec Templo Mayor*, ed. Elizabeth Boone. Dumberton Oaks, Washington, D.C., 1987.

BERDAN, FRANCES F. and PATRICIA R. ANAWALT (eds.). *The Codex Mendoza*, 4 vols. University of California Press, Berkeley, 1993.

BERDAN, FRANCES F., RICHARD E. BLANTON, ELIZABETH
H. BOONE, MARY G. HODGE, MICHAEL E. SMITH, and
EMILY UMBERGER. *Aztec Imperial Strategies*. Dumbarton Oaks, Washington D.C., 1996.

BERLO, JANET C. "Early Writing in Central Mexico: *In
Tlilli, In Tlapalli*, before A.D. 1000," in *Mesoamerica
after the Decline of Teotihuacan, A.D. 700–900*, ed.
Richard A. Diehl and Janet C. Berlo. Dumbarton Oaks
Research Library and Collection, Washington, D.C.,
1989.

BIERHORST, JOHN (trans.). *History and Mythology of the
Aztecs: The Codex Chimalpopoca*. University of
Arizona Press, Tucson, 1992.

BOONE, ELIZABETH. "Migration Histories and Ritual
Performance," in *To Change Place: Aztec Ceremonial
Landscapes*, ed. David Carrasco. University Press of
Colorado, Niwot, Colorado, 1991.

—— "In Tlamantinime: The Wise Men and Women of
Aztec Mexico," in *Painted Books and Indigenous Knowledge in Mesoamerica: Manuscript Studies in Honor of
Mary Elizabeth Smith*, ed. Elizabeth Hill Boone.
Middle American Research Institute, Tulane University, New Orleans, 2005.

—— *Cycles of Time and Meaning in the Mexican Books of
Fate*. University of Texas Press, Austin, 2007.

—— "Aztec Writing and History," in *The Aztec World*,
ed. Elizabeth M. Brumfiel and Gary M. Feinman.
Abrams, New York, in association with the Field
Museum, Chicago, 2008.

BORAH, WOODROW and SHERBURNE F. COOK. "The Aboriginal Population of Central Mexico on the Eve of the
Spanish Conquest," in *Ibero Americana*, no. 45. University of California Press, Berkeley, 1963.

BRETON, ADELA. "Some Notes on Xochicalco," in *Transactions of the Department of Archaeology, Free Museum
of Science and Art*. University of Pennsylvania, 1906.

BRODA, JOHANNA. "The Provenance of the Offerings:
Tribute and Cosmovision," in *The Aztec Templo
Mayor*, ed. Elizabeth Boone. Dumbarton Oaks, Washington D.C., 1987.

—— "The Sacred Landscape of Aztec Calendar Festivals: Myth, Nature and Society," in *To Change Place:
Aztec Ceremonial Landscapes*, ed. David Carrasco. University Press of Colorado, Niwot, Colorado, 1991.

BRUMFIEL, ELIZABETH M. "Specialization, Market
Exchange, and the Aztec State: A View from Huexotla," in *Current Anthropology* 21, 1980.

—— "Aztec Women: Capable Partners and Cosmic
Enemies," in *The Aztec World*, ed. Elizabeth M. Brumfiel and Gary M. Feinman. Abrams, New York, in
association with the Field Museum, Chicago, 2008.

BRUMFIEL, ELIZABETH M. and GARY M. FEINMAN. *The
Aztec World*. Abrams, New York, in association with
the Field Museum, Chicago, 2008.

CALNEK, EDWARD E. "Settlement Patterns and Chinampa Agriculture in Tenochtitlan," in *American
Antiquity* 37 (1), 1972.

—— "The Internal Structure of Tenochtitlan," in *The
Valley of Mexico: Studies in Pre-Hispanic Ecology and
Society*, ed. Eric R. Wolf. University of New Mexico
Press, Albuquerque, 1976.

—— "Tenochtitlan-Tlatelolco: The Natural History of a
City," in *Urbanism in Mesoamerica*, vol. 1, ed. William
T. Sanders, A. C. Mastache, and R. H. Cobean. INAH
and Pennsylvania State University, 2003.

CARBALLAL STAEDTLER, MARGARITA, and MARÍA
FLORES HERNÁNDEZ, "Hydraulic Features of the
Mexico-Texcoco Lakes during the Postclassic Period,"
in *Precolumbian Water Management*, ed. Lisa J. Lucero
and Barbara W. Fash, University of Arizona Press,
Tucson, 2006.

CARRASCO, DAVID (ed.). *To Change Place: Aztec Ceremonial Landscapes*. University Press of Colorado, Niwot,
Colorado, 1991.

—— *Quetzalcoatl and the Irony of Empire. Myths and
Prophecies in the Aztec Tradition*. Revised edition. University Press of Colorado, Boulder, 2000.

CARRASCO, PEDRO. "Social Organization of Ancient
Mexico," in *Archaeology of Northern Mesoamerica*, ed.
Ignacio Bernal and Gordon F. Ekholm, *Handbook of
Middle American Indians*, vol. 10. University of Texas
Press, Austin, 1971.

—— "The Extent of the Tepanec Empire," in *The
Native Sources and the History of the Valley of Mexico*,
ed. J. de Durand-Forest, pp. 73–92. Proceedings of the
44th International Congress of Americanists, BAR
International Series, 204, Oxford, 1984.

—— *The Tenochca Empire of Ancient Mexico: The Triple
Alliance of Tenochtitlan, Tetzcoco, and Tlacopan*. University of Oklahoma Press, Norman, 1999.

CASO, ALFONSO. *The Aztecs: People of the Sun*. Translated by Lowell Dunham. University of Oklahoma
Press, Norman, 1958.

CHARLTON, THOMAS H., DEBORAH L. NICHOLS, and
CYNTHIA OTIS CHARLTON. "Aztec Craft Production
and Specialization: Archaeological Evidence from the
City-State of Otumba, Mexico," in *World Archaeology*
25, 1991.

CHIMALPAHÍN, DOMINGO FRANCISCO DE SAN ANTON
MUÑON. *Relaciones originales de Chalco Amequemecan*.
Edited by S. Rendón. UNAM, Mexico City, 1965.

CLENDINNEN, INGA. *Aztecs: An Interpretation*. Cambridge University Press, Cambridge and New York,
1991.

CODEX BORBONICUS. Edited by Karl Nowotny.
Akademische Druck-u. Verlagsanstalt, Graz, 1974.

CODEX BORGIA (Cod. Gorg. Messicano 1). Edited by Karl
Nowotny. Akademische Druck-u. Verlagsanstalt,
Graz,, 1976.

CODEX BORGIA. *The Codex Borgia: a Full-Color Restoration of the Ancient Mexican Manuscript*, ed. Gisele Diaz
and Alan Rodgers with a commentary by Bruce E.
Byland. Dover Publications, New York, 1993.

CODEX MAGLIABECHIANO. *Codex Magliabechiano and the
Lost Prototype of the Magliabechiano Group*, 2 vols., ed.
with a commentary by Elizabeth H. Boone. University
of California Press, Berkeley, 1983.

CODEX MENDOZA. Edited and translated by James
Cooper Clark. Waterlow & Sons, London, 1938.

CODEX MENDOZA. *The Codex Mendoza*, 4 vols., ed.
Frances F. Berdan and Patricia R. Anawalt. University
of California Press, Berkeley, 1993.

CODEX TELLERIANO-REMENSIS. *Codex Telleriano-Remensis: Ritual, Divination and History in a Pictorial Aztec
Manuscript*. University of Texas Press, Austin, 1995.

CÓDICE AUBIN. *Historia de la nacion Mexicana: reproduccion a todo color del códice de 1576*, ed. Charles E.
Dibble. José Porrua Turanzas, Madrid 1963.

COE, MICHAEL D. "Religion and the Rise of Mesoamerican States," in *The Transition to Statehood in the New
World*, ed. Grant D. Jones and Robert R. Kautz. Cambridge University Press, Cambridge, 1981.

—— *Mexico*. Thames & Hudson, London and New
York, 1994; 6th edn 2008.

COE, SOPHIE. *America's First Cuisines*. University of Texas Press, Austin, 1994.

CORTÉS, HERNÁN. *Letters from Mexico*. Translated by A. R. Pagden. Orion Press, New York, 1971.

DAVIES, NIGEL. *The Toltecs until the Fall of Tula*. University of Oklahoma Press, Norman, 1971.

—— *The Toltec Heritage from the Fall of Tula to the Rise of Tenochtitlan*. University of Oklahoma Press, Norman, 1982.

—— *The Aztecs: A History*. University of Oklahoma Press, Norman, 1982.

—— *The Aztec Empire: The Toltec Resurgence*. University of Oklahoma Press, Norman, 1987.

DE LA FUENTE, BEATRIZ, et al. *La Acrópolis de Xochicalco*. Instituto de Cultura de Morelos, México, 1995.

DE VEGA NOVA, HORTENSIA, and PABLO MAYER GUALA, "Proyecto Yautepec," in *Boletín del Consijo de Arqueología*, 1991.

DIAZ DEL CASTILLO, BERNAL. *The Discovery and Conquest of Mexico*. Translated by A. P. Maudslay. Farrar, Straus, and Cudahy, New York, 1956.

DIBBLE, CHARLES E. (ed.). *Códice Xolotl*, 2nd edition, vol. 2. UNAM, Mexico City, 1980.

—— *Codex En Cruz*, 2 vols. University of Utah Press, Salt Lake City, 1981.

DIEHL, RICHARD and JANET BERLO. *Mesoamerica after the Decline of Teotihuacan AD 700–900*. Dumbarton Oaks, Washington D.C., 1989.

DURÁN, DIEGO. *The Aztecs: The History of the Indies of New Spain (1581)*. Translated by Doris Heyden. University of Oklahoma Press, 1991.

—— *Book of the Gods and Rites and the Ancient Calendar*. Translated by Doris Heyden and Fernando Horcasitas. University of Oklahoma Press, Norman, 1971.

ELLWOOD, ROBERT. *The Feast of Kingship*. Sophia University Press, Tokyo, 1978.

ELSON, CHRISTINA M. and MICHAEL E. SMITH. "Archaeological Deposits from the Aztec New Fire Ceremony," in *Ancient Mesoamerica* 12, 2001.

EVANS, SUSAN T. *Excavations at Cihuatecpan, an Aztec Village in the Teotihuacan Valley*. Vanderbilt University Publications in Anthropology, no. 36, Department of Anthropology, Vanderbilt University, Nashville, 1988.

—— "The Productivity of Maguey Terrace Agriculture in Central Mexico During the Aztec Period," in *Latin American Antiquity* 1 (2), 1990.

—— "Architecture and Authority in an Aztec Village: Form and Function of the Tecpan," in *Land and Politics in the Valley of Mexico*, ed. Herbert R. Harvey. University of New Mexico Press, Albuquerque, 1991.

—— *Ancient Mexico and Central America: Archaeology and Culture History*. Thames & Hudson, London and New York, 2004; 2nd edn 2008.

FRANKFORT, HENRI. *Kingship and the Gods*. University of Chicago Press, Chicago, 1948.

GENNEP, ARNOLD VAN. *The Rites of Passage*. University of Chicago Press, Chicago, 1960.

GIBSON, CHARLES. "Structure of the Aztec Empire," in *Archaeology of Northern Mesoamerica*, ed. Ignacio Bernal and Gordon F. Ekholm, *Handbook of Middle American Indians*, vol. 10. University of Texas Press, Austin, 1971.

GILLESPIE, SUSAN. *The Aztec Kings*. University of Arizona Press, Tucson, 1989.

GRAULICH, MICHAEL. *Montezuma ou l'apogée et la chute de l'Empire azteque*. Fayard, Paris, 1994.

HASSIG, ROSS. *Aztec Warfare*. University of Oklahoma Press, Norman, 1988.

HEYDEN, DORIS. "Los ritos de paso en las cuevas," *Boletín INAH* II, vol. 19, 1976.

—— "Caves, Gods and Myths: World-View and Planning in Teotihuacan," in *Mesoamerican Sites and World Views*, ed. Elizabeth P. Benson. Dumbarton Oaks, Washington D.C., 1981.

HICKS, FREDERIC. "Tetzcoco in the Early 16th Century: The State, the City and the Calpolli," in *American Ethnologist* 9, 1982.

—— "Rotational Labor and Urban Development in Prehispanic Tetzcoco," in *Explorations in Ethnohistory: Indians of Central Mexico in the Sixteenth Century*, ed. Herbert R. Harvey and Hanns J. Prem. University of New Mexico Press, Albuquerque, 1984.

—— "Prehispanic Background of Colonial Political and Economic Organization in Central Mexico," in *Ethnohistory*, ed. Ronald Spores. *Handbook of Middle American Indians*, supplement no. 4, University of Texas Press, Austin, 1986.

—— "Subject States and Tributary Provinces: The Aztec Empire in the Northern Valley of Mexico," in *Ancient Mesoamerica* 3, 1992.

—— "Cloth in the Political Economy of the Aztec State," in *Economies and Polities in the Aztec Realm*, ed. Mary G. Hodge and Michael E. Smith. Institute for Mesoamerican Studies, Albany, 1994.

—— "Class and State in Official Aztec Ideology," in *Ideology and the Formation of Early States*, ed. Henri J. M. Claessen and Jarich G. Oosten, pp. 256–77. E. J. Brill, Leiden, 1996.

HIRTH, KENNETH G. and ANN CYPHERS GUILLÉN. *Tiempo y asentamiento en Xochicalco*. UNAM, Mexico City, 1988.

HOCART, A. M. *Kingship*. Oxford University Press, London, 1927.

HODGE, MARY G. "Politics Composing the Aztec Empire's Core," in *Economies and Polities in the Aztec Realm*, ed. Mary G. Hodge and Michael E. Smith. Institute for Mesoamerican Studies, Albany, 1994.

—— *Chimalpahin and the Kingdom of Chalco*. University of Arizona Press, Tucson, 1991.

HODGE, MARY G. AND LEAH D. MINC. "The Spatial Patterning of Aztec Ceramics: Implications for Prehispanic Exchange Systems in the Valley of Mexico," in *Journal of Field Archaeology* 17, 1990.

HODGE, MARY G. AND MICHAEL E. SMITH (eds.) *Economies and Polities in the Aztec Realm*. Institute for Mesoamerican Studies, Albany, 1994.

HVIDTFELDT, ARILD. *Teotl and Ixiptlatli: Some Central Conceptions in Ancient Mexican Religion, with a General Introduction on Cult and Myth*. Munksgaard, Copenhagen, 1958.

IWANISZEWSKI, STANISLAW. "Archaeology and Archaeoastronomy of Mount Tlaloc, Mexico: A Reconsideration," in *Latin American Antiquity* 5 (1), 1994.

IWANISZEWSKI, STANISLAW and IVAN SPRAJC. "Field Reconnaissance and Mapping of the Archaeological Site at Mt Tlaloc." Unpublished manuscript and map, 1987.

IXTLILXÓCHITL, FERNANDO DE ALVA. *Obras Históricas*, Editorial Chavero, Mexico City, 1985.

KARTTUNEN. FRANCES. *An Analytical Dictionary of Nahuatl*. University of Oklahoma Press, Norman, 1983.

KIRCHHOFF, PAUL. "Land Tenure in Ancient Mexico," *Revista Mexicana de Estudios Antropológicos*, vol. 14, pt. 1, 1954–55.

—— "Se puede localizar Aztlán?" in *Anuario de Historia, año 1*. UNAM, Facultad de Filosofía y Letras, Mexico City, 1961.

KIRCHHOFF, PAUL, LINA ODENA GUEMAS, and LUIS REYES GARCIA. *Historia Tolteca-Chichimeca*. CISINAH, Mexico City, 1976.

KLEIN, CECELIA F. "Who was Tlaloc?" *Journal of Latin American Lore* 6 (2). University of California Press, Los Angeles, 1980.

KUBLER, GEORGE. *The Art and Architecture of Ancient America*. Penguin Books, Harmondsworth and Baltimore, 1962.

LACADENA, ALFONSO. "Regional Scribal Traditions: Methodological Implications for the Decipherment of Nahuatl Writing," in *The PARI Journal* 8 (4), pp. 1–22. Pre-Columbian Research Institute, 2008.

—— "The *Wa1* and *Wa2* Phonetic Signs and the Logogram for *Wa* in Nahuatl Writing," in *The PARI Journal* 8 (4), pp. 38–45. Pre-Columbian Research Institute, 2008.

LEÓN Y GAMA, ANTONIO. *Descripción histórica y cronológica de las dos piedras ...* Mexico, 1832. (Reprinted INAH, Mexico City, 1990).

LEÓN-PORTILLA, MIGUEL. *Aztec Thought and Culture*. Translated by Jack Emory Davis. University of Oklahoma Press, Norman, 1963.

LOPEZ AUSTIN, ALFREDO. *Human Body and Ideology*, 2 vols., trans. Thelma Ortiz de Montellano and Bernard R. Ortiz de Montellano. University of Utah Press, Salt Lake City, 1988.

LOPEZ LUJÁN, LEONARDO. *The Offerings of the Templo Mayor of Tenochtitlan*. Revised edition. University of New Mexico Press, Albuquerque, 2005.

LOPEZ LUJÁN, LEONARDO, ROBERT COBEAN and ALBA GUADALUPE MASTACHE. *Xochicalco y Tula*. Consejo Nacional para la Cultura y las Artes, Editoriale Jaca Book, Milan, 1995.

MAPA QUINATZIN. Edited by J. M. A. Aubin. Published in *Anales del Museo Nacional de México*, pt. 1, vol. 3, 1886.

MAPA TLOTZIN. Edited by J. M. A. Aubin. Published in *Anales del Museo Nacional de México*, pt. 1, vol. 3, 1886.

MARTÍNEZ, JOSÉ LUIS. *Nezahualcoyotl: vida y obra*. Mexico City, Fondo de Cultura Económica, 1972.

MATOS MOCTEZUMA, EDUARDO. "Symbolism of the Templo Mayor," in *The Aztec Templo Mayor*, ed. Elizabeth Boone. Dumbarton Oaks, Washington, D.C., 1987.

—— *The Great Temple of the Aztecs*. Thames & Hudson, London and New York, 1988.

—— *Caxaxtla*. Citicorp, México D. F., n.d.

MATOS MOCTEZUMA, EDUARDO, FELIPE SOLÍS OLGUÍN, et al. *Aztecs*. Royal Academy of Arts, London, 2002 [exhibition catalogue].

MAUDSLAY, ALFRED P. "Plano hecho en papel de maguey que se conserva en el Museo Nacional de México," in *Anales del Museo Nacional de México*, 1909.

MENDIETA, GERÓNIMO DE. *Historia eclesiástica Indiana*. Editorial Chavez Hayhoe, Mexico City, 1945.

MILLER, MARY ELLEN. *The Art of Mesoamerica: From Olmec to Aztec*. Thames & Hudson, London and New York, 1986; 3rd edn 2001.

MILLER, MARY ELLEN and KARL TAUBE. *The Gods and Symbols of Ancient Mexico and the Maya: An Illustrated Dictionary of Mesoamerican Religion*. Thames & Hudson, London and New York, 1993.

MOEDANO, H. "Oztotitlan," in *El occidente de México*. Sociedad Mexicana de Antropología, 4. Mexico City, 1948.

NICHOLS, DEBORAH L. "Artisans, Markets, and Merchants," in *The Aztec World*, ed. Elizabeth M. Brumfiel and Gary M. Feinman. Abrams, New York, in association with the Field Museum, Chicago, 2008.

NICHOLSON, H. B. "Religion in Pre-Hispanic Central Mexico," in *Archaeology of Northern Mesoamerica*, Part 1, ed. Ignacio Bernal and Gordon F. Ekholm, *Handbook of Middle American Indians*, vol. 10. University of Texas Press, Austin, 1971.

—— "The Annual Royal Ceremony on Mt Tlaloc: Mountain, Fertility, Ritualism in the late Pre-Hispanic Basin in Mexico," in *Mesas and Cosmologies in Mesoamerica*. ed. Douglas Sharon, pp. 33–49. San Diego Museum Papers no. 43, 2003.

NUTTALL, ZELIA. "The Gardens of Ancient Mexico," in *Annual Report of the Smithsonian Institution 1923*. U.S. Government Printing Office, Washington D.C., 1925.

—— "On the Complementary Signs of the Mexican Graphic System," republished in *The PARI Journal* 8 (4), pp. 46–48. Pre-Columbian Research Institute, 2008.

OFFNER, JEROME. "Aztec Legal Process: The Case of Texcoco," in *The Art and Iconography of Late Post-Classic Central Mexico*, ed. Elizabeth Boone. Dumbarton Oaks, Washington D.C., 1982

—— *Law and Politics in Aztec Texcoco*. Cambridge University Press, Cambridge, 1988.

OLGUÍN SOLÍS, FELIPE, et al. *The Aztec Empire*. Guggenheim Museum, New York, 2004 [exhibition catalogue].

OLGUÍN, FELIPE SOLÍS, RICHARD F. TOWNSEND, and ALEJANDRO PASTRANA. "Monte Tláloc: un proyecto de investigación de etnohistoria y arqueología," in *Los arqueólogos frente a las fuentes*, ed. Rosa Brambila Paz and Jesús Monjarás-Ruiz, INAH, Serie Etnohistoria. Mexico City, 1996.

OLIVIER, GUILHEM. *Mockeries and Metamorphoses of an Aztec God: Tezcatlipoca, "Lord of the Smoking Mirror."* University Press of Colorado, Boulder, 2003.

OTIS CHARLTON, CYNTHIA. "Obsidian as Jewelry: Lapidary Production in Aztec Otumba, Mexico," in *Ancient Mesoamerica* 4, 1993.

—— "Plebians and Patricians: Contrasting Patterns of Production and Distribution in the Aztec Figurine and Lapidary Industries," in *Economies and Polities in the Aztec Realm*, ed. Mary G. Hodge and Michael E. Smith. Institute for Mesoamerican Studies, Albany, 1994.

PALERM, ANGEL. "La base agrícola de la civilización urbana de Mesoamerica," in *Las civilizaciones antiguas del viejo mundo y de América*. Unión Panamericana, Washington, D.C., 1955.

PALERM, ANGEL and ERIC R. WOLFE. "El desarrollo del area calve de imperio Texcocano," in *Agricultura y Civilización en Mesoamérica* 32. SEP, Mexico City, 1971.

PARSONS, JEFFREY. *Prehistoric Settlement Patterns in the Texcoco Region, Mexico*. Memoirs of the Museum of Anthropology, no. 3. University of Michigan, Ann Arbor, 1971.

—— "The Role of Chinampa Agriculture in the Food Supply of Tenochtitlan," in *Cultural Change and Continuity*, ed. Charles E. Cleland. Academic Press, Albuquerque, 1976.

—— "Environmental and Rural Economy," in *The Aztec World*, ed. Elizabeth M. Brumfiel and Gary M. Feinman. Abrams, New York, in association with the Field Museum of Chicago, 2008.

PARSONS, JEFFREY R., MARY H. PARSONS, DAVID J. WILSON, and ELIZABETH M. BRUMFIEL. *Prehispanic Settlement Patterns in the SouthernValley of Mexico: The Chalco-Xochimilco Region*. University of Michigan Museum of Anthropology, Memoirs no. 14, Ann Arbor, 1982.

PASZTORY, ESTHER. *Aztec Art*. Harry Abrams, New York, 1983.

PAYÓN, JOSÉ GARCIA. *La zona arqueológica de Tecaxic-Calixtlahuaca y los Matlazinca*. Talleres Gráficos de la Nación, Mexico City, 1936.

—— *Los monumentos arqueológicos de Malinalco*. Talleres Gráficos de la Nación, Mexico City, 1947.

PAZ, OCTAVIO. *In Search of the Present: Nobel Lecture*. Trans. Anthony Stanton. Harcourt Brace Jovanovich, New York, 1990.

POMAR, JUAN BAUTISTA. "Relación de Texcoco," in *Nueva colección de documentos para la historia de México*, vol. 3, ed. Joaquín García Icazbalceta. Editorial Porrúa, Mexico City, 1891.

PRESCOTT, WILLIAM H. *History of the Conquest of Mexico*, Random House, New York, 1931.

RANDS, R. "Artistic Connections between the Chichén Itzá Toltec and the Classic Maya," *American Antiquity*, vol. 19, 1954.

READ, KAY D. *Time and Sacrifice in the Aztec Cosmos*. Indiana University Press, Bloomington and Indianapolis, 1998.

—— "More than Earth: Cihuacoatl as Female Warrior, Male Matron, and Inside Ruler," in *Goddesses and Sovereignty*, ed. Elizabeth Bernard and Beverly Moon, Oxford University Press, Oxford and New York, 1999.

ROBERTSON, DONALD. *Mexican Manuscript Painting of the Early Colonial Period*. Yale University Press, New Haven, 1959.

SAHAGÚN, BERNARDINO DE. *Florentine Codex: General History of the Things of New Spain*, 12 vols. Translated by Arthur J. O. Anderson and Charles Dibble. The School of American Research, Santa Fe, 1951–69.

SANDERS, WILLIAM T. "Tenochtitlan in 1519: A Pre-Industrial Megalopolis," in *The Aztec World*, ed. Elizabeth M. Brumfiel and Gary M. Feinman. Abrams, New York, in association with the Field Museum, Chicago, 2008.

SANDERS, WILLIAM T., JEFFREY R. PARSONS, and ROBERT S. SANTLEY. *The Basin of Mexico: Ecological Processes in the Evolution of a Civilization*. Academic Press, New York, 1979.

SAVILLE, MARSHALL H. *The Goldsmith's Art in Ancient Mexico*. Museum of the American Indian, Heye Foundation, Indian Notes and Monographs, no. 7, New York, 1920.

—— *Turquoise Mosaic Art in Ancient Mexico*. Museum of the American Indian, Heye Foundation, Indian Notes and Monographs, no. 8, New York, 1922.

—— *The Wood Carver's Art in Ancient Mexico*. Museum of the American Indian, Heye Foundation, Indian Notes and Monographs, no. 9, New York, 1925.

SELER, EDUARD. *The Temple of Tepoxtlan*. Bureau of American Ethnology, 28. U.S. Government Printing Office, Washington, D.C., 1960–61.

SMITH, MICHAEL E. *Excavations and Architecture*. Archaeological Research at Aztec-Period Burial Sites in Morelos, Mexico, vol. 1. University of Pittsburgh, Monographs in Latin American Archaeology, no. 4, Pittsburgh, 1992.

—— "Economies and Polities in Aztec-Period Morelos: Ethnohistoric Overview," in *Economies and Polities in the Aztec Realm*, ed. Mary G. Hodge and Michael E. Smith. Institute for Mesoamerican Studies, Albany, 1994.

—— "Rural Economy in Late Postclassic Morelos: An Archaeological Study," in *Economies and Polities in the Aztec Realm*, ed. Mary G. Hodge and Michael E. Smith. Institute for Mesoamerican Studies, Albany, 1994.

—— *The Aztecs*. Blackwell, Oxford and Malden, Mass., 1996; 2nd edn 2003.

—— *Aztec City-State Capitals*. Ancient Cities of the New World. University of Florida Press, Gainsville, 2008.

SMITH, MICHAEL E. and T. JEFFREY PRICE. "Aztec Period Agricultural Terraces in Morelos, Mexico: Evidence for Household-Level Agricultural Intensification," in *Journal of Field Archaeology* 21, 1994.

SMITH, MICHAEL E., CYNTHIA HEATH SMITH, RONALD KOHLER, JOAN ODESS, SHARON SPANOGLE, and TIMOTHY SULLIVAN. "The Size of the Aztec City of Yautepec: Urban Survey in Central Mexico," in *Ancient Mesoamerica* 5, 1994.

SPORES, RONALD. *The Mixtec Kings and their People*. University of Oklahoma Press, Norman, 1967.

—— *The Mixtecs in Ancient and Colonial Times*. University of Oklahoma Press, Norman, 1984.

STANISLAWSKI, DAN. "Tarascan Political Geography," *American Anthropologist* 49, 1947.

SULLIVAN, THELMA. "Tlaloc: A New Etymological Interpretation of His Name and What it Reveals of His Essence and Nature," *Proceedings of the 40th International Congress of Americanists*, vol. 2. Rome, 1974.

SULLIVAN, THELMA and TIMOTHY J. KNAB. *A Scattering of Tales*. University of Arizona Press, Tucson, 2005.

TEDLOCK, DENNIS (trans.). *Popol Vuh*. Simon and Schuster, New York, 1985.

TEZOZOMOC, HERNANDO ALVARADO. *Crónica Mexicáyotl*. Paleography and Spanish version by Adrián León. Imprenta Universitaria, Mexico City, 1949.

THOMAS, HUGH. *Conquest: Montezuma, Cortés, and the Fall of Old Mexico*. Simon and Schuster, New York, 1995.

TOWNSEND, RICHARD F. *State and Cosmos in the Art of Tenochtitlan*. Dumbarton Oaks, Washington, D.C., 1979.

—— "Pyramid and Sacred Mountain," in *Archaeoastronomy and Ethnoastronomy in the American Tropics*, ed. Anthony Aveni and Gary Urton. New York Academy of Sciences, vol. 385. New York, 1982a.

—— "Malinalco and the Lords of Tenochtitlan," in *The Art and Iconography of Late Post-Classic Central Mexico*, ed. Elizabeth Boone. Dumbarton Oaks, Washington, D.C., 1982b.

—— "Coronation at Tenochtitlan" in *The Aztec Templo Mayor*, ed. Elizabeth Boone. Dumbarton Oaks, Washington, D.C., 1987.

—— "The Renewal of Nature at the Temple of Tlaloc," in *The Ancient Americas: Art from Sacred Landscapes*. ed. Richard F. Townsend. Art Institute of Chicago, 1992.

TURNER, VICTOR. *The Forest of Symbols*. Cornell University Press, Ithaca, New York and London, 1967.

UMBERGER, EMILY. "The Structure of Aztec History," *Archaeoastronomy* 4 (4), 1981.
—— "Antiques, Revivals, and References to the Past in Aztec Art," *Res* 13, 1987.
—— "Aztec Art and Imperial Expansion," in *Latin American Horizons*, ed. Don Rice. Dumbarton Oaks, Washington, D.C., 1993.
—— "Art and Imperial Strategy in Tenochtitlan," in *Aztec Imperial Strategies*, ed. Frances Berdan, et al. Dumbarton Oaks, Washington, D.C., 1996.
VEGA SOSA, CONSTANZA (ed.). *El recinto sagrado de Mexico-Tenochtitlan: Excavaciones 1968–76*. INAH, Mexico City, 1979.
WHITE, JON MANCHIP. *Cortés and the Downfall of the Aztec Empire*. Carroll and Graf, New York, 1971.
WICKE, C. *Once More Around the Tizoc Stone: A Reconsideration*. Paper presented at the 41st International Congress of Americanists, Mexico City, 1976.

WILHELM, RICHARD (trans.). *I Ching or Book of Changes*. Rendered into English by Cary F. Baynes. Bollingen Series XIX, Princeton, 1950.
ZANTWIJK, RUDOLF VAN. "Aztec Hymns as the Expression of the Mexican Philosophy of Life," *Internationales Archiv für Etnographie* 48 (1), 1957.
—— "Principios organizadores de los Mexicas: una introducción al estudio del sistema interno del régimen Azteca," in *Estudios de Cultura Náhuatl*, vol. 4, 1963.
—— *The Aztec Arrangement: The Social History of Pre-Spanish Mexico*. University of Oklahoma Press, Norman, 1985.
ZENDER, MARC. "One Hundred and Fifty Years of Nahuatl Decipherment," in *The PARI Journal* 8 (4), pp. 46–48, Pre-Columbian Research Institute, 2008.
ZORITA, ALONSO DE. *Breve y sumaria relación de los señores de la Nueva España*. UNAM, Mexico City, 1942.

Sources of Illustrations

Abbreviations
MNA = Museo Nacional de Antropolgía, Mexico
INAH = Instituto Nacional de Antropología e Historia, Mexico

I Bridgeman Art Library, London. II Painting by Scott Gentling. III From *Historia Tolteca-Chichimeca*, Bibliothèue Nationale, Paris. IV, V, VI From *Codex Mendoza*, Bodleian Library, Oxford. VII Museum für Völkerkunde, Vienna. VIII Cleveland Museum of Art, Leonard C. Hanna, Jr. Fund, 1984.37. IX From *Codex Ixtlilxochitl*, Bibliothèque Nationale, Paris. X Museo del Templo Mayor, Mexico City. XI From *Codex Ixtlilxochitl*, Bibliothèque Nationale, Paris. XII, XIII INAH. XIV Photo © Michel Zabé/AZA. XV, XVI From *Codex Borbonicus*, Bibliothèque Nationale, Paris. XVII, XVIII, XIX Photos © Michel Zabé/AZA. XX Photo Jorge Pérez de Lara. XXI, XXII British Museum, London.

Frontispiece MNA. Photo Irmgard Groth Kimball. 1 Photo Gabriel Figueroa Flores. 2, 3 Drawn by Annick Petersen. 4 MNA. Photo Richard Townsend. 5 Drawing by ML Design. 6 Reconstruction model by Marquina. 7 From *Codex Matritense*. Courtesy E. Matos Moctezuma, from *The Great Temple of the Aztecs*, Thames & Hudson, 1988. 8 Drawn by Annick Petersen. 9 From *La Preclara Narratione di Fernando Cortese*, 1524. 10 Museo del Templo Mayor, Mexico City. Photo Michel Zabé. 11 Biblioteca Apostolica Vaticana, Vatican City. 12, 13 Photo courtesy Art Institute of Chicago. 14 Drawing after R. Millon, '*Teotihuacan*', *Scientific American* (1967). 15 Photo Gabriel Figueroa Flores. 16 Pyramid of the Feathered Serpent, Teotihuacan. 17, 18 Courtesy Great Temple Project. Photo Salvador Guilliem Arroyo. 19 Photo Richard Townsend. 20 Photo Michael D. Coe. 21 Richard Townsend. 22 Drawing by David Kiphuth, after a photo by Michael D. Coe. 23 Chichén Itzá chacmool. 24 Photo Michael D. Coe. 25 MNA. 26, 27 Photos Michael D. Coe. 28, 29 Photos Charles Townsend. 30 From *Mapa Quinatzin*. 31 From *Codex Xolotl*, Bibliothèque Nationale, Paris. 32 After *Codex Boturini*. Courtesy E. Matos Moctezuma, from *The Great Temple of the Aztecs*,

Thames & Hudson, 1988. 33 The arrival at Coatepec, *Codex Tovar*. 34 After Palacios, 1929, fig.2. 35 Photo courtesy DETENAL, Mexico City. 36 From Plano en Papel de Maguey. 37 Photo Richard Townsend. 38 From *Codex Mendoza*, Bodleian Library, Oxford. 39 From *Mapa Quinatzin*. 40 From Pasztory, *Aztec Art*, 1983, plate 152. 41 From Pasztory, *Aztec Art*, 1983; redrawn after Barlow 1950, pls. 1 and 2. 42 Drawn by Annick Petersen. 43, 44 From *Codex Mendoza*, Bodleian Library, Oxford. 45 MNA. 46, 47 After Orozco y Berra 1877. 48 Richard Townsend. 49 From *Codex Magliabechiano*, Biblioteca Nazionale Centrale, Florence. 50 Photo Michael D. Coe. 51 MNA. Photo Irmgard Groth-Kimball. 52 From Durán. 53, 54, 55 Photos Richard Townsend. 56 After Marquina, 1964. 57 Photo Richard Townsend. 58 From *Codex Borgia*. 59, 60 Photos Richard Townsend. 61 From *Codex Borbonicus*, Bibliothèque de l'Assemblée Nationale, Paris. 62 Courtesy Great Temple Project. Photo Salvador Guilliem Arroyo. 63 MNA. 64 Photo Richard Townsend. 65 From *Codex Florentine*, Templo Mayor Library, Mexico/Art Archive, London. 66, 67 From *Codex Borbonicus*, Bibliothèque de l'Assemblée Nationale, Paris. 68 Photo courtesy Art Institute of Chicago. 69 From *Codex Borbonicus*, Bibliothèque de l'Assemblée Nationale, Paris. 70 Adapted from Michael D. Coe in A. Aveni (ed.), *Archaeoastronomy in Pre-Columbian America*, University of Texas Press, 1975. 71 MNA. 72 From Michael D. Coe 1984; drawing Dr Patrick Gallagher. 73 From *Codex Fejervary-Mayer*. 74 From *Codex Telleriano-Remensis*. 75, 76 Photos Richard Townsend. 77 From *Codex Borgia*. 78 From *Codex Borbonicus*, Bibliothèque de l'Assemblée Nationale, Paris. 79 From *Codex Florentine*, Biblioteca Medicea Laurenziana, Florence. 80, 81 Photos Richard Townsend. 82 Drawn by Annick Petersen, after Matthew Pietryka. 83 Photo Richard Townsend. 84 From *Codex Borbonicus*, Bibliothèque de l'Assemblée Nationale, Paris. 85, 86, 87, 88 Photos Richard Townsend. 89 From E. Matos Moctezuma, from *The Great Temple of the Aztecs*, Thames & Hudson, 1988. 90 After Matos Moctezuma and Rangel, *El Templo Mayor de Tenochtitlan: Planos, Cortesy Perspectivas* (INAH, 1982). 91, 92 Courtesy Great Temple Project. Photo Salvador Guilliem Arroyo. 93

Photo Richard Townsend. **94** From *Codex Ixtilxóchitl*, Bibliothèque Nationale, Paris. **95** MNA. **96, 97** Courtesy Great Temple Project. Photos Salvador Guilliem Arroyo. **98** After Michael D. Coe 1984; drawing by David Kiphuth. **99, 100** Courtesy Great Temple Project. Photos Salvador Guilliem Arroyo. **101** MNA. **102** From *Codex Telleriano-Remensis*, Bibliothèque Nationale de France, Paris. **103** From *Codex Mendoza*, Bodleian Library, Oxford. **104** From *Codex Mendoza*, Bodleian Library, Oxford. **105** INAH. **106** MNA. **107** From *Codex Mendoza*, Bodleian Library, Oxford. **108** From Sahagún, Biblioteca Mediceo-Laurenziana, Florence. **109** After Michael D. Coe; Drawing ML Design. **110** From Sahagún, Biblioteca Mediceo-Laurenziana, Florence. **111** British Museum, London. **112, 113** Courtesy Great Temple Project. Photos Salvador Guilliem Arroyo. **114** From *Codex Mendoza*, Bodleian Library, Oxford. **115** Courtesy Museum für Völkerkunde, Vienna. **116** From Sahagún, Biblioteca Mediceo-Laurenziana, Florence. **117** Metropolitan Museum of Art, New York. **118** Cour-

tesy Great Temple Project. Photo Salvador Guilliem Arroyo. **119** From *Codex Mendoza*, Bodleian Library, Oxford. **120** Photo Richard Townsend. **121** After Palacios, 1929, fig 1. **122** INAH. **123** Richard Townsend after Aubin, 1849. **124 above** Richard Townsend after Nuttal, 1888. **124 below** Richard Townsend after the *Codex Mendoza*. **125** Richard Townsend after Aubin, 1849. **126** From *Codex Mendoza*, Bodleian Library, Oxford. **127** INAH. **128** Photo Richard Townsend. **129** MNA, INAH. **130** Photo Richard Townsend. **131** INAH. **132** INAH. **133** From *Codex Magliabechiano*, Biblioteca Nazionale Centrale, Florence. **135** Sketch by Karl Weiditz, 1528. **136** From *Codex Mendoza*, Bodleian Library, Oxford. **137** Drawn by Annick Petersen. **138** From *Codex Florentine*, Biblioteca Medicea Laurenziana, Florence. **139** From Lienzo de Tlaxcala, American Museum of Natural History, New York. **140, 141** After Lienzo de Tlaxcala; Courtesy E. Matos Moctezuma, from *The Great Temple of the Aztecs*, Thames & Hudson, 1988.

Index